Dealing with Disaffection
Young people, mentoring and social inclusion

D0223558

Tim Newburn and Michael Shiner
with Tara Young

WILLAN
PUBLISHING

Published by

Willan Publishing
Culmcott House
Mill Street, Uffculme
Cullompton, Devon
EX15 3AT, UK
Tel: +44(0)1884 840337
Fax: +44(0)1884 840251
e-mail: info@willanpublishing.co.uk
website: www.willanpublishing.co.uk

Published simultaneously in the USA and Canada by

Willan Publishing
c/o ISBS, 920 NE 58th Ave, Suite 300,
Portland, Oregon 97213-3786, USA
Tel: +001(0)503 287 3093
Fax: +001(0)503 280 8832
e-mail: info@isbs.com
website: www.isbs.com

ISBN 1-84392-065-4 Paperback

British Library Cataloguing-in-Publication Data

A catalogue record for this book is available from the British Library

Project managed by Deer Park Productions, Tavistock, Devon
Typeset by GCS, Leighton Buzzard, Bedfordshire, LU7 1AR
Printed and bound by T.J. International Ltd, Trecerus Industrial Estate, Padstow, Cornwall

Contents

List of figures and tables

Figures

Tables

Appendices

Acknowledgements

As with all lengthy and complicated research studies we have accrued a large number of debts. At the heart of the study are the views and experiences of the young people themselves and we would like to thank all of them for their time and their help in completing our questionnaires and talking to us about their lives. We are also very grateful to the mentors who shared their hopes and fears with us and to the project workers and the staff of the referral agencies who spoke to us about the programme. The project workers who staffed and ran the mentoring programmes gave us enormous help and without their co-operation and support the work would never have been completed.

The core of the study was funded by the Joseph Rowntree Foundation and Breaking Barriers/Crime Concern and our initial forays into the literatures on 'youth disaffection' were supported by the government's Social Exclusion Unit. We are very grateful to our funders for supporting the research and for showing faith in what was a difficult study. We owe a particular debt to Charlie Lloyd at the Joseph Rowntree Foundation for support over many years, for trusting us to get this work done and for improving the final products. A similar debt is owed to Claire Reindorp of Crime Concern who was the initial driving force behind the study and to Sarah Benioff who provided significant support at the outset. We are also very grateful for the support of the staff of Breaking Barriers and Mentoring Plus/Crime Concern – particularly Amanda Howells, Lucy

Matthews and Jan Smith – and to the other members of the research advisory group – Alan Clarke, Jane Hury, Helen Powell and Mike Stein.

Though there are two primary authors of this book the research team consisted of four people. Tara Young and Sylvie Groben displayed enormous skills and tenacity as field researchers, working with a diverse range of professionals, practitioners and, most of all, young people. That they were able to gain and retain the trust of all those they worked with is a reflection of their own professionalism. Both contributed substantially to the writing of the research report that preceded this book, and Tara Young made a number of important contributions to this publication too. We thank them both.

Brian, Jim and Emma at Willan Publishing have as ever been superb publishers and a true pleasure to work with. Similarly, our copy-editor, David Kershaw, and the production team at Deer Park Productions provided their customary friendly, quick and efficient service. Our thanks to them all. Of course our biggest debt is to our families and we would like to record our gratitude to them for their love, patience and support. Tim would like to thank Mary, Gavin, Robin, Lewis and Owen. Mike would like to thank Nicoline, Linda and John.

Tim Newburn
Michael Shiner

London, February 2005

Chapter 1

Introduction

As transitions towards employment have been extended in recent decades, so too has the period of youthful semi-dependence on adults. While many young people manage successfully to navigate this increasingly complicated course, a large number experience significant difficulties along the way. There is considerable concern that, either as a consequence of these difficulties, or for other reasons, many young people are deciding against, or being prevented from, participating fully in civil society. It is these young people – who encounter significant problems in the worlds of education, training and employment, are often in trouble with the criminal justice system, or exhibit other forms of problematic behaviour – that are often referred to as 'disaffected'. Responding to, and seeking to prevent or mitigate such difficulties, has become a major focus for public policy. Under New Labour, one of the most talked about (and talked up) forms of intervention with disaffected youth has been 'mentoring'.

Mentoring generally involves establishing a relationship between two people with the aim of providing role models who will offer advice and guidance in a way that will empower both parties. Mentoring is believed to hold much promise in reducing youth crime and drug and alcohol misuse while promoting social inclusion and attachment to mainstream social values. Indeed, so heavily has it been promoted in recent years that it has become the latest in a long line of 'silver bullets'. Yet, as is so often the case, there has hitherto been remarkably little empirical evidence on which the efficacy of this approach may be assessed. Early mentoring programmes in this area first developed in the USA. 'Big Brothers, Big Sisters of America' has become something of a prototype for mentoring schemes and has been influential in the rapid expansion of mentoring on both sides of the Atlantic. Yet, the most thorough review of the research evidence conducted by Sherman and colleagues (1999) for the National Institute of Justice in Washington, DC found that community-based mentoring programmes could, at best, only be described as 'promising'. Having reviewed all the evidence, they concluded:

> Even with the encouraging findings from the most recent controlled test of community mentoring, there is too little information for adequate policymaking. The priority is for more research, not more unevaluated programs. The danger of doing harm is far too great to promote and fund mentoring on a broad scale without carefully controlled evaluations.

In this book we provide a critical examination of both the idea and the practice of mentoring, and report the results of the first major UK study of mentoring based on the largest and most rigorous research conducted to date. Using a self-report study, with a longitudinal design, the research follows a group of over 300 highly disaffected young people during and after their involvement in mentoring programmes. Together with a large number of in-depth interviews with the young people themselves, with their mentors and with the staff responsible for running the programmes, the study gives a vivid insight into the nature of such disaffection, the realities of contemporary social exclusion among young people and the experience and outcome of mentoring. We begin in Chapters 2 and 3 by reviewing the existing literature on youthful disaffection, how it is to be understood and what the 'causes' of such disaffection appear to be. In Chapter 4 we consider briefly the history of mentoring and the research evidence, limited though it is, on the impact of such interventions. Chapters 5–9 then explore the nature and impact of mentoring, looking at mentors' and young people's experiences of the programme and assessing its effect on the young people's engagement with education, training and work, and on their offending and drug and alcohol use. What is the promise of mentoring and how realistic is it to believe that it can have a significant impact on youthful offending and disaffection more generally? Are there particular young people who are likely to benefit from mentoring and particular ways that this intervention can be most successfully delivered? These and related questions are explored in the concluding chapter and recommendations are made for future policy and practice in this area.

Chapter 2

Youth disaffection

Introduction

There is a vast literature, across a range of disciplines, concerned with the 'problems' of youth.[1] Popular discussion frequently, and academic discussion on occasion, treats concerns about youth as if they were almost entirely without precedent – in nature or extent, or sometimes both. It is important to recognize, however, that complaint and concern about young people are far from new (Pearson 1983). While recognizing the considerable historical continuities which underpin much discussion of youth, it is also clear that there have been profound changes affecting young people in Britain over the past two decades. In particular, a considerable quantity of social science research has charted changing education and labour market experiences during this period.

Where once the majority of young people left full-time education at the end of compulsory schooling, now the majority stay on. Thus, for example, whereas in the early 1970s the vast majority of the two thirds of young people who left school at 15 (the then school leaving age) moved straight into employment, by the early 1990s the proportion moving into full-time employment was less than one fifth (Courtenay and McAleese 1993). At the heart of such changes was the rapid contraction of the youth labour market. In the 1980s youth unemployment increased rapidly and successive governments introduced a series of strategies intended to increase skills and qualification levels among young people (expanding further education and introducing training schemes) and to discourage non-participation (via, for example, the removal of state benefits for 16–17-year-olds in 1988).

Predictably enough, therefore, the transitions experienced by young people in Britain at the beginning of the twenty-first century have become considerably more complex. Where once the 'transition from school to work' was a primary focus, the emphasis is increasingly on the differentiation and elongation of multiple transitions. In particular, there has been a significant expansion of 'traditional' routes through academic education, the creation of new routes via vocational education, and the growth of a relatively new 'destination': temporary or permanent unemployment. Crucially, for many young people, the length of time taken to complete transitions to employment is now considerably extended.

It is not only the way young people experience the transition to work which has been affected by the restructuring of the adult labour market and the decline in the youth labour market. Additionally, the other key transitions faced by young people – the transition from family of origin to family of destination, and the transition from the parental home into independent living – have also been transformed (Coles 1995). The extension and differentiation of the transition into employment have complicated the domestic and housing transitions faced by young people. At its most positive this may be presented as an increased series of choices confronting contemporary youth – sometimes seen as characteristic of a process of 'individualization'. It has also been characterized in the literature as an increase in the range of 'risks' faced by young people (Furlong and Cartmel 1997). Roberts (1995: 118) summarizes such an idea in the following way:

> It is as if people nowadays embark on their life journeys without reliable maps, all in private motor cars rather than the trains and buses in which entire classes once travelled together …The 'cars' in which individuals now travel do not all have equally powerful engines. Some young people have already accumulated advantages in terms of economic assets and socio-cultural capital. Some have to travel by bicycle or on foot. But everyone has to take risks. No one can be certain where the roads that they can take will lead.

The outcome of all this, it is argued, is that young people are faced with a more uncertain world. Transitions towards employment, and by implication youthful (semi) dependence on adults, have been extended. For many young people such transitions are successfully negotiated and managed; for others, though, there are considerable hurdles to be overcome. For these or other reasons many young people experience a sense of being outside the mainstream; or being prevented in some way from participating; they become what are often referred to as 'disaffected young people'. In this chapter we explore this idea of 'disaffection', what it is taken to mean, what research has to tell us about so-called disaffected young people, primarily, but not exclusively, between the ages of 13 and 19. We begin by considering the nature of school disaffection – including under-achievement, disruptive behaviour, truancy and exclusion – and then move on to consider young people not in education, employment or training (NEET) and other indications of disaffection such as drug (ab)use and youth crime. We examine the size of the particular populations concerned, look at recent trends, and at who truants, who is excluded from school and who is 'not in education, employment or training'. Part of our concern is with transitions and trajectories; we examine the outcomes for young people who truant, are excluded from school and who are outside education, training and employment for different periods of time. Given the nature of the social backgrounds of the young people involved in the mentoring programmes that form the core of this book we pay particular regard to what is known about the experiences and outcomes for young people living in particularly poor neighbourhoods.

The meaning of disaffection

As Williamson and Middlemiss (1999: 13) note, discussion of 'disaffected' youth 'is hampered by such a catch all phrase incorporating those who are temporarily sidetracked, the essentially confused and the deeply alienated'. It is hard not to agree with such a sentiment, particularly given the tricky nature of this and cognate terms such as 'the underclass'. The arrival of the 'New Labour' government in May 1997 saw a significant increase in the emphasis placed on tackling what is currently referred to as 'social exclusion' (see Levitas 1998; Byrne 1999). Such exclusion and its impact on British society have been described in various ways: as the 'thirty, thirty, forty society' (Hutton 1996), the 90/10 Society (see Le Grand 1998) and, perhaps best known of all, in references to the emergence of a so-called British 'underclass' (Murray 1990). Each of these descriptions differs and each of them can be, and has been, challenged. However, what links them all is the perception that British society is increasingly socially polarized. There is a concern that the gap between the majority and an 'excluded' minority is growing. Such concerns are longstanding and have traditionally coalesced around the issue of poverty (Townsend 1979). The term 'social exclusion' broadens the focus from poverty to other forms of 'participation' in civil society. Thus, in addition to the very clear evidence that differences in income between the bottom 10 per cent and the rest have been widening (Joseph Rowntree Foundation 1995; Oppenheim and Harker 1996), evidence of the differential impact of other 'harms', such as crime, has also been taken as an indicator of exclusion (Hope 1996).

In the bulk of the literature on youth disaffection, or non-participation, there is a split focus on two groups (see, for example, Pearce and Hillman 1998). The first is those of compulsory school age who, for whatever, reason are absent from education or, while remaining in education, are significantly under-achieving or exhibiting disruptive behaviour. The second group are those who have passed the age of compulsory education and have neither continued in education nor are to be found in training or employment. We use this general organizing approach to structure our discussion of youth disaffection in this chapter.

Educational under-achievement

There have been major changes within education in the past two decades. Significantly more young people are staying on in full-time education for longer. Participation in higher education has expanded massively. Copious new forms of vocational education and new educational credentials have developed (and yet more are mooted). Alongside the increased emphasis on, and participation in, education there continues to be a significant group of young people who, at least as measured by formal qualifications, achieve little in school or thereafter. Thus, for example, approximately 5 per cent of boys and 4 per cent of girls have no GCSE passes at any grade at the age of 16 and approximately one quarter of all children aged 16 achieve no GCSE passes at grade A–C (DfES 2002).

Despite the massive expansion in educational participation, research evidence points to the continued influence of social class differences in attainment. Analysis of the Youth Cohort Study (YCS) has found some narrowing of class differentials in high attainment, but has pointed to a solidifying of class differences among people with few or no qualifications (Payne 1995). Research would appear to indicate a significant school effect. However, even when this is particularly positive it may not be enough to overcome the combined effects of social disadvantage (Rutter *et al.* 1979). Gender differentials have changed in a similar way. Thus, although there has been a well publicized increase in relative achievement of girls over boys in relation to high grades and number of A–C GCSE passes, the proportions of girls and boys leaving education with few or no qualifications are not nearly so dissimilar. The association between poverty and deprivation in children's families and in their neighbourhood and their performance in school is perhaps best illustrated by the analysis in Table 2.1.

Data on ethnic differences in educational achievement are more difficult to come by. The first point to make, however, is that whatever pupils' ethnic origin, those from the higher social class backgrounds do better on average (Gilborn and Gipps 1996). Research by the Policy Studies Institute (Hagell and Shaw 1996) found that ethnic minority pupils tended to have lower attainment levels than whites (Courtenay and McAleese 1993). In the PSI study, however, 'Black other' and 'Black Caribbean' pupils had the lowest average attainment scores, whereas Indian and Chinese pupils had the highest. According to Gilborn and Gipps (1996) those at greatest 'risk' are Caribbean young men, for it is they who achieve the equivalent of a higher grade (A–C) pass less frequently than the other groups (the differences are very small for girls). Analysis of the Youth Cohort Survey (DfES 2001) suggests that there are significant differences in achievement at GCSEs by ethnic origin (see Table 2.2).

Focusing more directly on the most 'vulnerable' there are some very stark messages in the research. According to a study by Barnardos (1996), three quarters of children looked after by local authorities leave school without *any* formal qualifications (compared with 8 per cent of the population overall) and only 12 per cent continue in further education after the end of compulsory schooling (Barnardos 1996). Few gain qualifications thereafter. The Barnardos picture is supported by other studies. Two studies by Stein (1983 1986) found the majority of young

Table 2.1 Poverty and school performance

Pupils with free school meals (%)	Number of schools	GCSE (% of pupils attaining 5 grades A–C	GCSE (% of pupils attaining 5 grades A–G
0–10	987	58	95
11–20	894	42	90
21–30	453	31	84
31–40	231	25	79
41–50	169	22	76
51–60	98	20	73
over 60	74	18	70

Source: Glennerster (1998).

people leaving care to have no qualifications (the proportions without qualifications being 90 per cent and 54 per cent respectively). A further study of 16–19-year-old care leavers found that two thirds had no qualifications, that only 15 per cent had an A–C grade GCSE and, of a total sample of 183, only one respondent had an A level (Biehal *et al.* 1995). In 2000, the Department of Health published statistics on the educational qualifications of care leavers for the first time. These suggested that 70 per cent left care without any GCSE or GNVQ passes (DOH 2000).

Research on 'looked after' young people identifies a number of factors associated with the extremely poor levels of attainment among this population:

- Damaging pre-care experiences.
- Non-attendance at school.
- Emotional stress experienced prior to and during care.
- Inadequate liaison between carers and schools.
- Low expectations of carers and teachers.
- Prioritization of welfare above educational concerns.
- Disruption caused by placement moves and the low priority given to education when moves are being arranged (Stein and Carey 1986; Jackson 1988).

Table 2.2 Attainment at GCSE level at the end of Year 11 by ethnic background (2000) (per cent of each ethnic group)

Ethnic origin	5+ GCSEs A*–C	1–4 GCSEs A*–C	5+ GCSEs D–G	1–4 GCSEs D–G	None reported
Other Asian	72	15	8	–	4
Indian	60	23	13	–	–
White	50	25	17	3	4
Other	43	32	15	–	9
Black	39	30	20	7	5
Pakistani	29	32	31	3	4
Bangladeshi	29	41	19	–	5
Not stated	26	22	21	8	23
All	49	26	18	3	5

Source: DfES (2001).

There may also be other factors at work. A small-scale study of the results of statutory medical examinations of 194 children entering care or in care in southeast London found that almost three fifths (58 per cent) of school-age children had 'educational problems' and approximately one sixth (17 per cent) were statemented as having special educational need. For only one third (35 per cent) was educational progress 'said to be normal' (Mather *et al.* 1997). It is not just those children living in residential homes or in short-term placements that have low educational attainment (Colton and Jackson 1993). Research by Heath *et al.* (1994) focusing on young people in stable long-term foster care in middle-class environments found no appreciable increase in educational performance – i.e. they continued to perform well below national norms for their age group. Though drawing causal inferences is problematic given the data on which the study is based (the administration of tests to a small sample over a three-year period) the authors suggest that what they were witnessing was, at least in part, 'the lasting effects of early deprivation or maltreatment' (1994: 256).

An even more 'problematic' population would appear to be those young people who are or have been resident in secure treatment settings. Bullock *et al.*'s (1998) study of 204 former residents of two youth treatment centres found that 56 per cent had 'seriously failed to fulfil their academic potential'. Over a third (36 per cent) had attended school irregularly and nearly half (46 per cent) had been 'expelled' at some point, rising to over two thirds (62 per cent) of those who had been in state care. As if this weren't stark enough, they went on to conclude:

> Educational disadvantage for some was extreme; 12 (6 per cent) were said to have little knowledge of the outside world, 22 (11 per cent) had very limited ability to help themselves in terms of dress, washing and basic functioning and 23 (11 per cent) were seen as unlikely to survive outside an institution (1998: 41).

Disruptive behaviour in schools

Clearly, low attainment or under-achievement are not, and should not be seen as, straightforward proxies for 'disaffection'. More often, it is truancy and exclusion from school that are taken as more direct indicators of pupil disenchantment. Before moving on to discuss each of these, it is important to consider the (sometimes related) matter of disruptive behaviour. Disruption may cover a variety of forms of behaviour from the most serious forms of violence to much lower-level forms of misbehaviour. Reid

(1986: 35) reports research on teachers' views of behaviour that they regarded as 'unacceptably disruptive'. This included: 'blank defiance, rejection of reasoning, unacceptable noise levels, physical violence between pupils, threats to pupils or teachers, theft, extortion, graffiti and vandalism, verbal abuse, lack of concentration, boisterousness and lack of consideration to others.'

According to most sources, the frequency of the more serious forms of incident remains relatively rare (OFSTED 1996). Unfortunately, relatively few data on disruptive behaviour are available. A survey of 65 primary headteachers, conducted by Sanders and Hendry (1997), inquired into the most common types of disruption, the most difficult forms to cope with, and the most effective sanctions.

The survey suggests that 'fighting' is the most common form of disruption, followed 'by attention-seeking', 'not working' and 'dis-obedience'. Interestingly (although the methods for determining this are not entirely clear) the authors found that only the last of the categories – 'disobedience' – appeared to be affected by social class (as indicated by the nature of housing in the school's catchment area). Though most research focuses on truancy and exclusion, Reid reports work by HMIC in the late 1970s which examined 'indiscipline and disruptive behaviour' in secondary schools. Their survey found that disruptive behaviour 'emerged as a much greater problem in inner-city schools, particularly those located in deprived areas with older housing and a large number of pupils with learning difficulties' (1986: 40).

Truancy

Most reports on truancy note how difficult it is to get reliable data on its extent. The DfES collects data on unauthorized absences but acknowl-edges that these significantly underestimate the extent of truancy. O'Keefe's (1994) survey of young people provides a more realistic estimate, but the school-based nature of the survey also means that this is likely to be an underestimate and, more crucially for our purposes here, would not have 'caught' the most disaffected young people.[2] O'Keefe's survey covered both 'blanket truancy' and 'post-registration' truancy. The overall scale and frequency of truancy were as shown in Table 2.3.

According to this survey almost one third of pupils truant at some time, and over 8 per cent truant at least once a week (rising to one in ten pupils in Year 11). Whichever form of truancy is measured, truancy levels rise significantly from Year 10 to Year 11. A similar picture is painted by the YCS which suggests that 5 per cent of Year 11 pupils truant for 'days or

Table 2.3   Levels and frequency of truancy – any type (per cent)

	All	Year 10	Year 11
Every day	1.5	1.3	1.6
2–4 times a week	3.2	2.6	3.8
Once a week	3.5	2.5	4.5
2–3 times a month	5.4	4.0	6.8
Once a month	4.7	4.0	6.8
Less often	12.2	10.8	13.6
Never	69.5	74.8	64.2

Source: O'Keefe (1994).

weeks at a time', among which 2.5 per cent had truanted for 'weeks at a time' (Casey and Smith 1995). This is probably the closest estimate possible of the number of 'disaffected' pupils in the final year of compulsory education. With a total population in this school year in excess of half a million, it is probably safe to estimate the minimum size of the 'hardcore' of the truanting population at 11,000 pupils, though if those truanting 'for several days at a time' are included the figure increases to between 23,000 and 28,000.

The important questions in relation to 'disaffected youth' are, first, who truants and, secondly, what are the causes of truancy? The data from the YCS (Casey and Smith 1995) relating to the first question suggest the following:

- Rates of truancy reported by males and females are roughly similar.

- There are some regional differences, but these are generally small. The rate of reported truancy in London is significantly higher than elsewhere.

- Young black pupils report a higher rate of truancy than other ethnic groups.

- Parental socioeconomic group is significantly related to truancy. The highest rates of truancy are among children of low-skilled workers.

In relation to the 'causes' of truancy, the picture is fairly complicated. Thus, for example, rates of truancy are very strongly related to exam score in Year 11. However, unravelling the precise reasons for the close relationship between exam score and truancy is complex. Casey and Smith (1995: 11) conclude:

There are a number of underlying reasons for this strong relationship, and these cannot be disentangled from the present data.
Children with defiant attitudes towards school have rejected
academic success as a goal, so they do not want to succeed in those
terms. Because they are hostile to school, they are unlikely to learn.
Because they tend to be away from school, they do not have the
opportunity to learn. Finally, if they are not at school, they cannot
take the exams.

Research examining the attitudes of pupils who truant points to particular
focuses for disaffection within school, and also suggests that overall the
curriculum is accepted as worth while by most pupils. Approximately two
thirds of the respondents in O'Keefe's (1994) research said that they
truanted in order to avoid particular lessons. They did not express a
particular dislike for school. This was even more marked among frequent
truants (arguably more likely to be 'disaffected'). Four fifths of frequent
post-registration truants absented themselves in order to miss a particular
lesson. A similar proportion of frequent blanket truants gave the same
reason. O'Keefe (1994: 56) concludes that there is 'powerful evidence that
truancy is primarily a response to lessons seen as unsatisfactory'. This is
important because it suggests that there are factors underpinning truancy
(and therefore school disaffection) over which, in principle, schools have
some control. As we shall see when we come to consider the experiences
and attitudes of those on the mentoring programmes, truancy and other
possible illustrations of disaffection should not be read as a simple
indicator of a more general alienation; it is perfectly possible to absent
oneself from school and remain of the view that education is important.
    This is only part of the picture, however, for there are also structural
correlates of truancy. Thus, in addition to school-related factors there is
also strong evidence pointing to the importance of socioeconomic factors
in explaining levels of truancy. This is an area of 'youth disaffection' where
the influence of living in a 'poor neighbourhood' is fairly clear cut. We turn
again to the two main sources of data: the YCS and O'Keefe's survey. The
YCS found a marked relationship between parental socioeconomic group
and truancy, with the highest rates among children of low-skilled workers.
The odds of a young person from a low-skilled family engaging in a high
level of truancy are 80 per cent higher than for a person from a professional
or managerial family. The rate of truancy is also affected by parental
unemployment. The proportion who had truanted 'frequently or
habitually' was 24 per cent where neither parent was in work, compared
with 15 per cent where one or both parents was in work. Family structure
and housing tenure were also linked to truancy rates. Thus, the odds of a

young person living with neither parent engaging in a high level of truancy are 200 per cent higher than for someone living with both parents, and the rate of truancy has been found to be considerably higher among those living in housing rented from a local authority than among those in owner-occupied housing. The odds of a young person living in local authority housing engaging in a high level of truancy were 120 per cent higher than for a pupil in owner-occupied housing. A socioeconomic 'effect' is quite compatible with the research evidence which suggests that what happens within school has an important influence on levels of truancy. As O'Keefe (1994: 85) puts it:

> Many children in the poorer regions of the country, or from low income groups in affluent areas, may find, quite simply, that the margin of choice between the curriculum as a desirable good, and non-attendance, comes at a lower threshold than is the case with their better-off peers.

O'Keefe's survey found some evidence of a what he called an 'inner-city effect'. Thus, schools categorized as mainly inner-city, or inner-city and industrial, had a mean truancy level of 32.9 per cent against 30.5 per cent for all others. Moreover, in schools whose headteachers maintained that there were no pupils of an 'inner-city background' the mean absence levels were 13.6 per cent. In schools where 50 per cent or more pupils were from inner-city areas, the mean absence level was 26.3 per cent. Similarly, there was a significant though small relationship between the proportion of children in school eligible for free school meals and truancy levels. Finally in this regard, Bentley and Gurumurthy (1999: 57) report one study which 'found that in secondary schools serving "difficult to let" estates, one in four children gain no GCSEs compared to a national average of one in twenty and truancy rates are four times the national average'.

Exclusion from school

Exclusion from school may take two main forms: fixed term and permanent. Until recently, both types had been increasing for some time. It is only since 1993, however, that local education authorities have been required to keep accurate records. Godfrey and Parsons (1998) estimate that there was an increase well in excess of 450 per cent in permanent school exclusions between 1990 and 1997. In the late 1990s up to 13,000 young people were permanently excluded from school each year, since when the figure has dropped to somewhat less than 10,000 (see Table 2.4).

Table 2.4   Numbers of permanent exclusions from schools in England 1990–2002

Year	Primary	Secondary	Special	Total
1990/1	378	2,532	—	2,910
1991/2	537	3,296	—	3,833
1992/3	1,215	7,421	—	8,636
1993/4	1,291	9,433	457	11,181
1994/5	1,438	10,519	501	12,458
1995/6	1,872	11,159	550	13,581
1996/7	1,573	10,463	632	12,668
1997/8	1,539	10,187	572	12,298
1998/9	1,366	8,636	436	10,438
1999/00	1,226	6,713	384	8,323
2000/01	1,436	7,305	394	9,135
2001/02*	1,450	7,740	340	9,540

Source: 1990/1–1995/6, Parsons (1999); 1996/7–2001/2, DfES (2003).
*Provisional figures.

Generally speaking, the term permanent exclusion means what it says. Just under three quarters of primary school-age children who are permanently excluded are never successfully reintegrated into full-time education. Only 15 per cent of secondary pupils permanently excluded return to mainstream schooling. Even if these figures exaggerate the extent to which the excluded remain outside formal educational provision (and Parsons suggests they do), they still indicate that there are a very significant number of young people (between 6,000 and 7,000) whose education will be completed, if at all, within a Pupil Referral Unit (PRU) (approximately one half), through home tuition (approximately one third), or through other means.

Slightly over four fifths of exclusions are from secondary schools, and the rate of exclusions rises sharply up until Year 10 and then drops back slightly at Year 11. Fourteen and 15-year-olds account for approximately half of all permanent exclusions. There are some regional variations. Metropolitan and county education authorities differ little, but London boroughs have exclusion rates which are twice those of metropolitan authorities and counties. Exclusion rates vary between authorities by as much as a factor of ten, and these differences cannot be explained by socioeconomic differences alone (Parsons 1999).

Who, then, is excluded from school? Pearce and Hillman (1998) point to a number of groups that are disproportionately at risk of exclusion:

- Boys.
- African-Caribbean pupils.
- Young people with special educational needs.
- Young people from lower socioeconomic groups.
- Young people with disturbed or disrupted family circumstances.
- Looked-after young people.

Boys are approximately four times as likely as girls to be permanently excluded from school (Parsons 1996). At the primary level exclusion is almost entirely a problem associated with boys (excluded boys outnumbering girls by a ratio of over 13:1 – see Parsons, undated). African-Caribbean and other black pupils are significantly more likely to be permanently excluded from school than pupils of other ethnic origins. The overall ratio is approximately four to one (DfES 2003). Moreover, African Caribbean pupils are five times more likely to be excluded than white pupils (Parsons 1999).

A joint OFSTED/SSI report (1995) found that 12 per cent of school-age children in care were either excluded or did not attend school regularly. Over a quarter of 14–16-year-olds in care fell into this category. Sinclair and Gibbs' (1998) study of 223 young people resident in children's homes found at the time of interview that 17 per cent of the school-age children reported themselves to be excluded or suspended and a further 13 per cent were 'waiting for a new school'. Male residents (39 per cent) were twice as likely as female (18 per cent) to be absent from school. Although the number of exclusions from special schools is small, they represent a significant proportion of pupils. According to the DfEE (1997), exclusion of those with special education needs or emotional and behavioural difficulties is six times higher than that for other pupils. In addition, although recent years have seen a slight decline in the number of exclusions from primary and secondary schools, this has not been true of special schools. According to Parsons (1999: 24) 'it is not rare to hear of statemented children with emotional and behavioural difficulties (EBD) being excluded from residential EBD schools. They may then be placed part-time in PRUs which are less well resourced and staffed to deal with them'.

Work by OFSTED has shown a link between the socioeconomic context of schools and exclusion rates. Similarly, research by Hayden (1997) on exclusion from primary schools has indicated that young people from poorer families, and those with disturbed or disrupted family circumstances (which are linked with poverty), are at greater risk of exclusion. The only attempt to 'model' the factors which underpin school exclusion is the recent work by Parsons and Godfrey (1999). On the basis of the analyses conducted, Parsons and Godfrey (1999: 72) conclude that permanent exclusions of secondary pupils 'is most strongly associated with the proportion of black households in the LEA (as measured by the Census), followed by low home ownership rates, high proportions of poor home facilities. Then, with considerably lower correlations, come funding and unemployment'. Their conclusion, then, is remarkably similar to that reached above in relation to truancy. Social factors, particularly those indicative of deprivation and disadvantage, play a considerable role in the determination of exclusion in both schools and LEAs. They by no means account for all the variation, especially between schools. The latter, they suggest, may partly be explicable in terms of school effectiveness and, as with truancy, may be subject to a degree of influence by the school.

'Not in education, employment or training'

As we noted earlier, the 'youth labour market' has been radically restructured in the last decade or so – indeed some have described it as having 'collapsed' (Furlong and Cartmel 1997). The numbers staying on in education have increased markedly – as the numbers moving straight from school into full-time employment have been slashed. With youth unemployment an increasing problem, employment training schemes for young people have expanded. Various 'incentives', positive and negative, have been developed to encourage young people beyond compulsory school age without jobs to remain in education or training and yet it is clear that many do not do so.

In recent times increasing attention has been focused on that 'group' of young people who do not participate in further education, in training or in work. These have been variously referred to as 'Status 0' (Istance and Williamson 1996) or 'NEETs' ('not in education, employment or training'). The proportion of 16–19-year-olds falling into this category varies over time – partly as a result of changes in the economy (Pearce and Hillman 1998) – and it is difficult to provide accurate estimates. Estimates vary according to the source of data used (for example the YCS, Careers Service pupil destination surveys and the Labour Force Survey) and whether the data are collected nationally or locally. Until recently estimates of the size of this population were based on national statistics. However such statistics tend to underestimate the size of this group, largely as a result of changes to the benefits system introduced in the late 1980s (Education and Employment Select Committee 1998). Thus, for example, one of the most common 'proxies' for 'NEET' was traditionally the youth training 'guarantee group' (those registered with the Careers Service as available for training but waiting for a suitable place) which indicates that between 1.5 and 4.5 per cent of the age group are not in work, training or education (Williamson 1997a). Recent Youth Cohort Survey data (DfES 2000) suggest that approximately 8 per cent of 16 and 17-year-olds can be classified as NEET, the figure rising to 12 per cent of 18-year-olds.

By contrast, two studies from South Wales, and a broader study of inner-city school leavers, all show higher levels of non-participation. Research in South Glamorgan in the early 1990s (Istance *et al.* 1994) used Careers Service Destination Surveys, estimates of non-participation drawn from monthly totals of 16 and 17-year-olds looking for training or employment together and an analysis of records of early school leavers. The estimate of those in South Glamorgan who were 'NEET' was made up as follows. Of the school leaver cohort in 1991 between 5 and 12 per cent were registered with the Careers Service as seeking training or work (the estimates vary according to the month). To this were added what were called 'the missing' – those in the cohort not accounted for in the official records. This produced a final figure of between 16 and 23 per cent of all 16–18-year-olds not in education, training or employment.

This research was followed by a study in Mid Glamorgan two years later using largely the same methods.[3] In terms of immediate destinations, Istance and Williamson (1996) found 13.5 per cent of 16 and 17-year-olds to be NEET in 1994. The contrasts between this group and those continuing in education in terms of educational achievement are stark (see Table 2.5).

The overall picture of destinations 12 and 18 months later had, if anything, worsened. Approximately half the young people had stayed in, or returned to, education. Of the remainder, roughly one quarter were still in employment or training and the remainder were 'already on the fringes of learning and labour markets' (Istance and Williamson 1996: 18). This relatively large group which encompasses all those Istance and

Table 2.5 Proportions entering particular 'employment destinations' in Mid Glamorgan by qualifications (per cent of each group)

	4 or more GCSEs A–C	No graded results
Continue in school	85	10
Youth training	3	26
Unemployed or 'unknown'	2	43

Source: Istance and Williamson (1996: 16).

Williamson refer to as 'Status 0' may be divided into those who are 'registered' and those who are 'missing'. The 'registered' group includes those who are registered for both training and employment (the 'guarantee group') and those who are simply registered as looking for work (an indication of what is referred to as 'training refusal'). The Mid Glamorgan study found a very clear trend towards greater training refusal, concluding that this was evidence 'of a worrying disinclination to see training – or at least the training available through Youth Training – as an acceptable alternative' (Istance and Williamson 1996: 20). To the registered group Istance and Williamson added those who were 'unavailable' or 'unknown' from the Careers Service's client diary records. On this basis three estimates of possible measures of 'NEET' are derived. The authors suggest that the 'likely' estimate of 'NEET' is 18 per cent, with a 'conservative' estimate being 16 per cent, rising to a 'possible' high of 20 per cent. The lower figure, extrapolated for all England by the Education and Employment Select Committee (1998), produces an estimated 190,000 young people aged 16–18 in this group.

A slightly older population (18–20-year-olds) were studied by Aspire Consultants for the Department for Education and Employment (Aspire Consultants 1996). Using a definition which encompassed 18–20-year-olds recorded by the Labour Force Survey as 'inactive' (34,000) together with those designated 'unemployed' (188,000), Aspire estimate that up to approximately 250,000 young people may be considered to fall within the 'disaffected' category in England. More recent research, adopting a slightly different methodology again, has been conducted in Northern Ireland (Armstrong *et al.* 1997). The study was based primarily on existing official data sources (to present a 'snapshot' picture of NEET youth) together with a representative sample survey of young people aged 16 and 17 sampled from Careers Service records (in order to examine the 'dynamic' aspects of NEET). The official sources of data (the census, 5th form destinations survey, LFS and official household survey) all produced figures between 4 and 6 per cent in the NEET category (i.e. significantly below those produced in South Wales). In part, this almost certainly reflects the different methodologies used. Some of what Istance and Williamson (1996) referred to as the 'missing' were not captured in the official surveys used in Northern Ireland (Armstrong 1997).

Reanalysis of the Labour Force Survey (LFS) by Bentley and Gurumurthy (1999) suggests that approximately one in ten 16- and 17-year- olds are not in work, full-time education or training. Removing part-time students from this total, a figure of 8.2 per cent remains. This is lower than the estimates from local surveys and reasonably in line with recent DfES estimates. The authors suggest that as this estimate is derived from a household survey it is likely itself to be an underestimate – by how much they do not conclude. Finally in this regard, Hagell and Shaw (1996) conducted research into the post-16 destinations of a sample of 'inner city' youth (and therefore a sample of particular relevance for our concerns). The sample consisted of approximately 2,500 young people from Year 11 in 34 inner- city schools. Overall, in terms of initial destinations (at the September after the end of compulsory education), 6 per cent described themselves as unemployed, 2 per cent as waiting for a Youth Training place, 1 per cent waiting for employment and 2 per cent were doing a variety of other things. We may assume, therefore, that a minimum of 6 per cent of these 16-year-olds could be considered NEET rising to a maximum of 11 per cent.

What, then, are the characteristics of those young people likely to be outside education, employment and training for an extended period of time? Predictably, educational attainment is a key factor. As Table 2.5 indicates, those without any formal qualifications at the end of their compulsory education are significantly more likely to be NEET than those with four or more GCSE A–C passes. Such young people are highly likely to have truanted or have been excluded from school (Wilkinson 1995). Gender differences are not particularly marked. Thus although young women are more likely to stay on in education at the age of 16, rates converge at the age of 17. According to Istance and Williamson (1996) the proportions of young men and women found outside education, employment and training are not markedly different. However, there may be some differences according to the length of time spent in this position. In the Mid Glamorgan study there were more males than females (55 as opposed to 45 per cent) among the 'long-term NEET', but more females than males (again 55 as opposed to 45 per cent) among the 'very long-term NEET'. It is possible that these figures may partly reflect the number of young women who occupy domestic and caring responsibilities. The influence of this is, however, likely to be slight. The location of the only studies to have considered NEET in any detail – South Wales, Sunderland and Belfast – means that there are few useful data on ethnicity. The available evidence suggests that 'staying on' rates are generally higher for all ethnic minority groups than they are for whites. Of the 'persistently unemployed' group in the PSI study, for example, young whites were over-represented (Hagell and Shaw 1996).

There are also particular groups that appear especially 'vulnerable'. Thus, there is evidence to suggest that those with difficult and disturbed backgrounds feature disproportionately among 'non-participants'. Sinclair and Gibbs' (1998) study of young people in children's homes found that approximately 30 per cent of the sample of 223 young people in care were beyond the age of compulsory education (most still aged 17). Of these, approximately one half described themselves as 'unemployed'. It also appears that young people with learning difficulties and/or disabilities are over-represented among those who are 'status zero'. According to Istance and Williamson (1996) between a quarter and a third of those in various NEET categories are young people with particular special training needs. Of those young people in the study who had been NEET between 6 and 19 months, having returned temporarily to education after the end of compulsory schooling, nearly half had special needs.

Although, as with both truancy and school exclusion, the data that might link such non-participation to growing up in poor neighbourhoods are somewhat limited, there is nevertheless enough evidence to suggest that socioeconomic factors are an important influence. Thus, the YCS, for example, shows that young people with parents in manual occupations are significantly more likely to be in government-supported training or not in education, training or work (Pearce and Hillman 1998). Whereas 56 per cent of 16-year-olds have fathers in manual occupations, 79 per cent of those not in education and training and 80 per cent of those not in employment have such backgrounds. Recent work on support for young people on social housing estates found that over a fifth (23 per cent) of 16–17-year-olds in council housing and 28 per cent of housing association tenants were 'status zero' (Coles *et al.* reported in Pearce and Hillman 1998). Similarly, YCS data show considerable differences by parental occupation (2 per cent of 16-year-olds with parents in managerial/professional occupations are NEET compared with 13 per cent of 16-year-olds whose parents are in unskilled manual occupations) and by housing tenure (4 per cent of 16-year-olds living in accommodation owned by self or parents are classified as NEET compared with 15 per cent of 16-year-olds living in council rented accommodation) (DfES 2000).

While Istance and Williamson's study shows considerable variation in the proportion of NEET young people in different geographical areas, the areas used are not finely graded enough to map particular concentrations of NEET youth. The Northern Ireland study (Armstrong *et al.* 1997) divided communities into three categories: 'high', 'average' and 'low' NEET communities. The conclusion of this admittedly crude mapping exercize was that the high NEET areas were the urban areas of Belfast and Derry, the low NEET areas being in the rural west parts of the province. This geographical spread, they suggest, is similar to the differences in the distribution of adult employment and long-term employment in the province.

Conclusion

Focusing on poor performance and/or disruptive behaviour at school, and on absence in late teenage years from education, employment and training, some clear messages about youth disaffection emerge. First, though a minority, the numbers of young people that might be said to be disaffected is quite substantial. Secondly, there is a clear social patterning to such youthful disaffection. Low socio economic status appears to be related to poor school performance, to truancy and disruptive behaviour and to the likelihood of school exclusion. There are also some quite entrenched differences by ethnic origin – with African-Caribbean pupils being at greatest 'risk'. Predictably, those at greatest risk of such disaffection are also most likely to be found in the NEET group in the post-compulsory education years. This patterning of risks is now well established. Yet, of course, it is not in itself an explanation. At the outset of this chapter we noted that youthful transitions are now both more extended and more complicated than they were say 20–30 years ago. It is to such youthful transitions that we turn next.

Notes

1 We are grateful to Andy Furlong, Anne West and Howard Williamson for advice and help in tracing some of the more recent literature.
2 Some 17 per cent of the sample were absent on the days the questionnaires were administered.
3 Described as follows: 'To get an accurate measure of the full scale of Status 0, it is essential to add to the 'registered' Status 0 figures (ie those registered with the Careers Service as being available for employment, training or both) the number of the even more marginal young adults who are out of contact with the Careers Service. Their numbers are calculated – on the basis of well-informed assumptions – that most of the "known unavailable" (ie a grouping sub-divided into: "sick", "moved", "deceased", or "other" – which is largest category and refers to situations such as pregnancy, caring responsibilities, being in detention etc) remain out of education, training or employment for the periods that are counted as such by the Careers Service and that many of the "unknown" are also in Status 0' (Istance and Williamson 1996: 11).

Chapter 3

Youth transitions and the meaning of disaffection

In the previous chapter, following the bulk of the literature on 'youth disaffection', we focused primarily on two 'groups': those young people who are absent from school through truancy or exclusion and those beyond school age who are not in education, employment or training. Most commentators appear to be agreed that in understanding youthful disaffection these two groups are of central importance. Nevertheless, it is also widely recognized that the 'disaffected' will also include some young people who, while apparently 'engaged' in education, training or work, display 'disaffection' or 'disengagement' in other ways – through, for example, criminal activity or problematic substance use. In addition to the fact that various forms of offending and substance use may of themselves be illustrative of youthful disaffection, there is now also considerable evidence that substance use and offending are linked with truancy, exclusion from school and unemployment. This chapter explores the existing literature on these links and then moves on to consider the changing nature of youth transitions. As we have already noted, there have been very significant changes to the nature of transitions to adulthood over the past 20 years. In thinking about disaffection and, more particularly, intervening positively to reduce disaffection, understanding these transitions is vital. Finally, and anticipating much that we will have to say about those involved in the mentoring programmes later in the book, we examine the literature on the views of 'disaffected young people'. That is, as a counterbalance to the lengthy consideration of the 'objective indicators' of disaffection that form the heart of this and the previous chapter, we conclude with a discussion of the 'subjective' experiences of disaffection.

Youthful drug use

Survey data in this area must be treated with caution. None the less, most surveys suggest that while younger children and young teenagers are fairly unlikely to report ever having taken illegal drugs, drug use increases markedly after the age of 14 or 15, and the highest incidence of drug use is found among young people in their late teens and early twenties (ISDD 1994, 1997). Estimates derived from the Youth Lifestyles Survey show that whilst no more than one child in thirty in the 12–13 years' age group reported having used an illicit drug in the last year, the figure rises to somewhere in the region of one in two for 18–21-year-olds (Flood-Page et al., 2000).

On the whole local surveys give an even starker picture. Among the highest figures to be produced in recent times are the school-based cohort surveys by Parker and colleagues conducted in the north west of England during the early 1990s (see Parker et al. 1995). When their respondents were mainly aged 16 they reported a lifetime drug use prevalence of 51 per cent. Cannabis is universally shown by surveys to be the most widely used illicit drug in the UK with, for example, the 2002/3 British Crime Survey indicating that 26% of 16–24 year olds report having used it in the last year (Condon and Smith, 2003). Amphetamines, cocaine and ecstasy are the next most commonly used illicit drugs with something like 5% of 16–24 year olds reporting their use during the last year. Use of crack cocaine and opiates is much rarer with fewer than 1% of 16–24 year olds saying they have used more drugs during the last year. Needless to say, estimates of prevalence within shorter time periods – say the last month – are significantly lower across the board.

Two key points should be drawn from this brief discussion. First, the use (at least occasional use) of illicit drugs by young people is a far from unusual activity. Secondly, the use (especially regular use) of the most harmful drugs remains comparatively rare (Lloyd 1998). As Plant and Plant (1992: 48) put it: 'available evidence suggests that, while a substantial minority of teenagers and those in their twenties have used such substances, only a small percentage do so regularly or with harmful consequences.' Two questions remain important for us here. First, to what extent is regular or harmful use associated with youthful disaffection?

Secondly, is there any evidence that living in poor neighbourhoods is a risk factor in itself?

First, drug use and 'disaffection'. In relation to truancy there are some limited data. A survey of school children in London in the late 1980s found that the use of solvents and/or illegal drugs was significantly higher among both boys and girls who truanted than those who did not (Swadi 1989). This was particularly so in relation to 'repeated' use of 'so-called hard drugs' (Swadi 1989: 111). This pattern is confirmed in other studies, particularly in the USA. Heightened prevalence rates are also found among school excludees. Powis *et al.* (1998), in a study of 14–16-year-olds attending a PRU, found that 78 per cent reported having, at some time, used an illicit drug. Almost two fifths (38 per cent) reported having used a drug other than cannabis; 9 per cent, for example, reported having used cocaine and 15 per cent reported having used LSD. Although none of the studies of NEET youth has considered drug use in any detail, the research by Istance and Williamson (1996) found that 24 of the 28 young people interviewed admitted to 'fairly regular use' of illicit drugs.

The links between youthful drug use and 'poor neighbourhoods' are more difficult to discern. However, there are a number of studies that throw some light on the issue. Thus, for example, the Advisory Council on Drug Misuse (ACMD 1998: 39) reports that 'if clear and unambiguous socio-economic variations in drug use are not always found at the *individual* level, it is equally important to recognize that they are consistently found at the *neighbourhood* or *area* level'. Research has shown consistently that the highest concentrations of drug-related problems are in the poorest urban neighbourhoods. A study by Parker and colleagues of opioid use in Merseyside in the mid-1980s found an overall prevalence rate of 18.2 per 1,000 among the 16–24 age group. However, this varied by area from a low of zero to a high of 162 per 1,000. Moreover, geographical prevalence was highly correlated with seven key indicators of background deprivation within a given area. Leitner *et al.* (1993) also found that what they called 'drug areas' tended to be represented in their sample by council and inner-city housing. Indeed, the ACMD, in its study of drug use and the environment, concluded that some key aspects of problematic drug use in present-day Britain are related to deprivation. Of course, the key question of *how* they are related to deprivation remains unanswered. It is undoubtedly the case that the clustering of different forms of social difficulty in particular urban environments is in part a product of the placement of particular people – for example, problem drug users – in poor neighbourhoods. However, studies of poor estates in decline and in recovery suggest that, important as they are, there is a considerably broader range of factors affecting them than housing policies alone (Power 1997).

Youth crime

A number of studies of disaffected youth have noted the connections between various forms of non-participation and offending by young people (Wilkinson 1995; Pearce and Hillman 1998). Before considering these links, a few introductory remarks are necessary. Echoing our earlier comments about drug use, it is important to recognize that committing a criminal offence is not an especially unusual activity. At least one quarter of all recorded crime is committed by 10–17-year-olds and self-report studies indicate that at least half of males and a third of females under the age of 25 admit to committing a criminal offence. The peak age of offending is currently approximately 18 for males and 15 for females. However, where once this was taken as an indication that the vast majority of young people would simply 'grow out of crime', recent research has begun to cast some doubt on such assumptions. What has long been clear, however, is that a relatively small minority of young offenders commit a disproportionately large number of offences (Farrington 1997). Again, two main questions remain. First, to what extent is offending, and frequent or persistent offending in particular, associated with youthful disaffection? Secondly, is there any evidence that living in poor neighbourhoods is a risk factor in itself?

First, in relation to truancy, the youth lifestyles survey (Graham and Bowling 1995) found that for both males and females the odds of offending of those who truanted were more than three times those who had not truanted. Those who persistently truanted from school were even more likely to admit to offending. Over three quarters (78 per cent) of males and over half (53 per cent) of females who truanted once a week or more committed offences. Although the study suggests that on average offending started slightly before truanting, it does not throw light on the relationship between the two. Numerous other studies (e.g. Farrington 1995; Robins and Robertson 1996) have shown truancy to be a significant risk factor in criminal careers. Although the numbers in the sample were relatively small, the Youth Lifestyle Survey also found a strong relationship between temporary exclusion from school and offending (Graham and Bowling 1995). Powis et al.'s (1998) study of young people in a PRU found that 94 per cent admitted committing an offence. Almost a quarter (24 per cent) had been cautioned by the police and just over a fifth (21 per cent) had been convicted – more than one third had been cautioned or convicted. Liddle's (1998) qualitative study of persistent offenders found that 23 of the sample of 39 had been permanently excluded. The Audit Commission (1996) found that 65 per cent of young offenders of school age who are sentenced in court have been excluded from school or truant regularly.

In addition, there are those not in education, employment or training. Here, as with drug use, the evidence is flimsier. Istance and Williamson (1996), in their interviews with 28 'Status 0' young people, report that 19 admitted involvement in crime and 'many' had a conviction. In its study, *Misspent Youth*, the Audit Commission (1996) conducted interviews with 103 young offenders on supervision orders. Almost three fifths (59 per cent) were not engaged in work, training or education. Thirty-six per cent were unemployed and 23 per cent were excluded from school or persistently truanting.

Finally, there is the question of the links between youthful offending, disaffection and 'poor neighbourhoods'. At the most basic level – of distribution – there is clear evidence from a number of sources of the geographic concentration of offenders (Bottoms and Wiles 1997). Moreover, much of the evidence points to links between particular geographical locations and social deprivation. An analysis by the Audit Commission (1996) found that neighbourhoods where large numbers of young offenders live are more deprived as measured by the DoE index of local conditions. Rutter *et al.* (1998) argue that social disadvantage and poverty are fairly robust indicators of an increased risk of delinquency. Crucially, however, it appears that such influences are not direct. Thus, although they are risk factors, they are mediated by other influences, particularly adverse parenting and other forms of family stress. Rutter *et al.* (1998: 202) conclude, however, that it is important to appreciate 'that the finding that most of the effects of poverty are indirect does not negate its role in the causal chain'. Coming from a more sociological perspective, Bottoms and Wiles (1997) concur with the view that one has to go beyond social class and social status in explaining differential offender rates within particular areas. Centrally, they argue, it is necessary to consider the role of the housing market, and the ways in which it may serve to maintain, reinforce and, occasionally, exacerbate differences between areas. As one example, Bottoms and Wiles examined two areas, separated only by a main road, which had vastly different recorded offender rates but which were largely identical on most demographic variables. They found that once one of the areas had 'tipped', local authority allocation rules had the unintended consequence of housing on the estate those with a greater propensity towards offending. This, together with certain physical features, changes to the reputation of the (poorer) estate and to its schools combined to increase the different levels of criminal activity in the two areas.

Changing transitions and disaffection

As we have already noted, both the youth labour market and the nature of 'transitions' to adulthood have been very significantly altered in recent times. Among the most important changes that have taken place have been the shift from the manufacturing to the service sector, especially knowledge services, together with the decline in demand among employers for unqualified 16-year-old school leavers (and, simultaneously, a rising premium on skills). Shifts in the labour market have also seen significantly increasing participation by women and, linked in part with this, the growth in part-time, temporary, low-paid and self-employment. Since the late 1970s/early 1980s labour markets have increasingly been deregulated with the aim of increasing flexibility and lowering costs. The dominance of neoliberal philosophies also led to more restricted access to income support and unemployment benefits – indeed, in some cases for young people, to remove entitlement entirely. In general terms, the consequence for youthful transitions has been a very significant growth in the numbers staying on in education - a significant increase in educational achievement among the majority of pupils, together with an increase in youth unemployment for the minority – and a general lengthening of, and increasing complexity in, the transition from 'school to work'.

Bentley and Gurumurthy (1999: 12–13) argue that 'while many are achieving more than their parents' generation, for others the choices and risks have become more stark ... those who have not kept pace with this trend (towards increased achievement) are relatively more disadvantaged'. One key issue which appears to emerge from previous research is the existence of a small number of particularly important transitions experienced by vulnerable young people. Moreover, recent qualitative research on marginalized young people suggests that these are precisely the points in these young people's lives where they felt that they were 'let down' and that 'whatever support they have been offered has not fitted into any coherent framework which helps them give structure and meaning to their lives' (Bentley and Gurumurthy 1999: 127). In the section below we identify five sets of transitions that are potentially extremely problematic and very frequently have a profound impact on the life chances of the young people concerned.

Leaving home – into care

Children in care are one of the most vulnerable groups in terms of various forms of social disadvantage, educational under-achievement, risk of alcohol and drug misuse and psychiatric ill-health. Bebbington and Miles (1989), in a study of 2,500 children admitted to care, found that before admission only a quarter were living with both parents; almost three quarters of their families received income support, only one in five lived in owner-occupied, and over one half were living in 'poor neighbourhoods'. Other factors which increased the likelihood of admission were over-crowding (linked with large families), young mothers and a child's parents being of different racial origins. The cumulative effect of these factors – and the resultant odds of entering care – is illustrated in two 'ideal types' (see Table 3.1).

Furthermore the researchers found that deprivation was more closely associated with admission into care in the 1980s than it had been in a previous study (cited in Department of Health 1998a). As a result of their material and emotional deprivations young people entering care are significantly more likely to have major educational deficits as well as problems with their health. A study comparing young people aged 13–17 years in the care of one local authority with a control group of young people living with their families found particularly high levels of psychiatric disorder in the former group (McCann *et al.* 1996). Over a quarter (28 per cent) of the children 'in care' were diagnosed with conduct disorders and a similar proportion (26 per cent) with overanxious dis-order, compared with 0 and 3 per cent respectively in the control group. As the Department of Health (1998b: 7) notes, however: 'far from remedying existing deficiencies, research is showing that periods in public care have further impaired the life chances of some children and young people because of poor educational achievement, uncorrected health problems and maladjustment.' Several different studies illustrate the ways in which the disturbance and stress related to damaging pre-care experiences together with the experience of care have a major impact on these young people's educational careers' (Biehal *et al.* 1995: 58; see also Heath *et al.* 1994; Stein 1994) and therefore on their later life chances.

Table 3.1 Bebbington and Miles' (1989) 'ideal types'

Child 'A'	Child 'B'
Aged 5 to 9	Aged 5 to 9
No dependence on social security benefits	Household head receives income support
Two-parent family	Single-adult household
White	Mixed ethnic origin
Owner-occupied home	Privately rented home
More rooms than people	One or more persons per room
Odds are 1 in 7,000	*Odds are 1 in 10*

It is not just the transition into care that is problematic. It appears that one of the reasons that the experience of care exacerbates rather than ameliorates the difficulties faced by many children is the number of transitions that take place within care. Several research studies have pointed to the fact that a high number of placement moves is an integral part of the care experience for many young people (DHSS 1985; Stein 1990). This was confirmed by the more recent work by Biehal *et al.* (1994). They found that fewer than one in ten of their sample remained in the same placement throughout their time in care. Nearly one third made between four and nine moves and one tenth moved more than ten times. Though not based on a representative sample, the data presented by Shaw (1998) tend to reinforce this picture. Of the 200 young people in care who responded to her survey, 11 per cent had experienced eleven or more placements. The general messages emerging from the research are fairly clear. They are, first, that experience of care is associated with a range of poor 'outcomes'. Secondly, the transition 'into care' is itself problematic; it is highly disruptive and demoralizing and approximately half of children in care report this transition as being both 'scary' and 'confusing'. Finally, further significant transitions while in care – which are themselves relatively common – are associated with a negative impact on educational achievement, on identity formation and friendship networks (Millham *et al.* 1986; Stein 1990; Social Services Inspectorate 1991; Stein 1994; Biehal *et al.* 1995; Wilkinson 1995[1]).

Leaving home – homelessness

One of the areas of young people's lives that has altered significantly in recent times is that of 'leaving home'. Marriage patterns have changed with cohabitation increasingly becoming an intermediate stage. By the 1980s, according to Jones (1995), young people were increasingly leaving their parental homes and moving into 'independent' living situations prior to marriage or cohabitation, though the 'extended transitions' many face often makes leaving home problematic. Transitional housing has become a more visible feature of young people's household careers. However, some of those who cannot obtain such housing become 'homeless' – either on the streets or in other people's houses. Who is at risk?

Clearly, young people leave home for a wide variety of reasons. 'Traditional' reasons include marriage and setting up a new home and, increasingly, to pursue full-time education. However, there are a series of other reasons which are more 'problematic' (Ainley 1991; Jones 1995). These include an absence of jobs locally (Furlong and Cooney 1990), and problems in the family of origin. Young people who leave home at the age of 16 are more likely to do so because of problems at home, or because of the constraints of the local labour market. Moreover, those who leave home aged 16 or 17 because of problems at home are more at risk of homelessness (compared with others who are older but leave for the same reasons). Overwhelmingly, Jones found, homeless young people leave home because they do not get on with the people there. She concludes: 'Leaving home under the age of 18 should not be regarded as *per se* problematic. However, more housing provision and support is needed for young people who leave home under the age of 18 for "problem" reasons' (1995: 46).

Bentley and Gurumurthy (1999) note that for many participants leaving home was less about taking a willing step towards adulthood and more about family breakdown or strife. Indeed, one of their respondents when asked what advice they would give to other young people said 'don't leave home unless you absolutely have to'. As Jones (1995) argues, however, one of the key problems is that some of the people who face the greatest risks are those who are least able to avoid them (see also Carlen 1996). These include: 'young people having to deal with parental conflict or family breakdown (including many of those leaving care), and those from families experiencing unemployment and poverty, or deprived areas where there are no local opportunities for work, training or education' (Jones 1995: 144).

Though, as with other forms of 'disaffection' considered in this review, data on the possible influence of 'poor neighbourhoods' are largely absent, there are some useful indications. Thus, for example, Jones' (1995) analysis of the Scottish Young People's Survey found that large families (three or more siblings), unemployment in the family, and a young person's own unemployment were associated with leaving home earlier – 'indicators of family disadvantage or poverty which appear to operate as push factors' (1995: 48). Linking up with observations made before about particularly vulnerable groups, it appears that a significant proportion of young homeless people have 'care histories'. Research by Centrepoint (1996) found over half (57 per cent) of young homeless people aged 16–19 have been 'in care'. In Jones' Scottish study, one third of the young homeless had been in local authority care since the age of 14. The young homeless are particularly likely to have been absent from school for significant periods. In the Scottish study, 63 per cent of homeless respondents reported truanting for a day or more, and Centrepoint found that three quarters of 16–19-year-old homeless people were long-term non-attenders or had been excluded. Finally, and predictably given the above figures, their employment prospects are equally poor. A study of 56 homeless young people by the Family Policy Studies Centre (Smith *et al.* 1998) found just under half to be unemployed or long-term sick. Similarly, over half (56 per cent) of Jones' (1995) sample were currently unemployed.

Leaving care – going where?

Young people who are, or have been, accommodated by local authorities constitute one of the most vulnerable groups in our society. They are, as the government recognizes, very much at risk of social exclusion. Moreover, they are not a small group. Over 59,000 children were looked after at 31 March 2002 (Department of Health 2002). Of these, many return home after a relatively short period of time. However, in the previous year just under 9,000 young people aged 16 and above ceased being looked after in order to live independently. There is now considerable research evidence that: 1) on many measures these young people constitute a 'high risk' group; 2) that 'outcomes' for these young people are poor; and 3) that provision in terms of leaving care schemes and other forms of support is highly variable (see, for example, Stone 1989; National Children's Bureau 1992; Biehal *et al.* 1994, 1995).

Based on data from three studies, Stein (1994: 356) describes the 'common career trajectory' for the great majority of care leavers as 'leave school at 16 without qualifications, employment training and unemployment' though he goes on to note that this apparent simplicity masks complexities associated particularly with pre-care and care 'careers'. Research reported earlier in this review pointed to the extraordinary proportion of young people likely to leave care without any educational qualifications. As if attempting to enter the labour market under these circumstances weren't problematic enough, many of these young people are also expected to attempt to enter the housing market at the same time (Baldwin *et al.* 1997). More than perhaps any group, care leavers require intensive and continuing support through these transitions.

Respondents in Bentley and Gurumurthy's (1999) study said that the transition to leaving care was not well managed by the authorities. Indeed in many cases they claimed that the care system had ceased to provide support for them long before they left. Similarly, respondents to Shaw's (1998) survey who had left care were particularly likely to report feeling lonely and unsupported and Shaw concludes that 'clearly not enough is being done to support and assist these young people in their transition to independent life' (1998: 72). As a result of the increasing realization of this state of affairs, growing attention is now being paid both to the safeguarding of children living away from home (Utting 1997; Quality Protects 1998) and to support for young people 'leaving care'. The available research evidence shows that outcomes for these young people are affected by a combination of factors. The key starting points are the social networks these young people inhabit (and in particular the quality of family support they receive), their ability to make and sustain relationships, their self-esteem, motivations and care and pre-care histories (Biehal *et al*. 1995). Thereafter, major life events once they leave care, combined with variations in local housing and employment markets, together with the quality of support available, appear to play a key part in determining outcomes.

Missing school – going where?

Strictly speaking this is not a 'transition', although it may mark an important 'transitionary' stage in a young person's development. The Cambridge Delinquency Study (Farrington 1980) shows that truancy is associated with lower-status jobs and unstable employment histories after leaving school. An analysis of the data from the National Child Development Study (Hibbett *et al*. 1990) confirms this pattern. Using a crude measure of truancy (with no measure of frequency of traunting) Hibbett *et al*. found truants to be 2.4 times as likely to be unemployed as in work at the age of 23 (bear in mind that this cohort left school around 1974 – well before the major changes in the youth labour market). Again using the same source of data, Hibbett *et al*. (1990: 174) found truants to be 'progressing more rapidly through the major events and transitions of early adult life.'[2] Thus, they were significantly more likely to be married at the age of 23. Male truants were over three times as likely and female truants over six times as likely as non-truants to have two or more children by the age of 23. This is partly accounted for by social class differences, but only partly. NCDS data also indicate that truants are both considerably more prone to smoking and to smoking heavily although they do not reveal significant differences in drinking habits (defined as over 30 cigarettes a day) (see also Charlton and Blair 1989). No significant differences in drinking habits were found.

Lack of exam success at the age of 16 tends to be translated into relatively poor achievement later on. Using YCS data, Casey and Smith (1995) also explore whether truancy influences later outcomes other than through its relationship with Year 11 exam results. Truancy was found to be 'strongly related to education and labour market outcomes after allowing for the effect of other variables such as social class and exam results in the fifth year of secondary school' (Casey and Smith 1995: 15). Young people who had truanted were more likely to be 'unemployed or inactive' up to three years after the end of compulsory education. Data from the YCS show a clear relationship between truancy and educational attainment at GCSE (see Figure 3.1).

Leaving school (at 16) – going nowhere?

Crudely speaking, three main options are open to young people at the end of compulsory schooling: leave school; return for less than two years and then leave; or stay on for the full two-year period. Of course there is, within this, a multitude of alternative combinations which young people may follow. For the purposes of this review – focusing on disaffected youth – the final key transition is that taken by those young people who, largely without qualifications, leave school as soon as they are able (if they have not absented themselves, or been excluded, already). Studies of NEET youth include very variable estimates of the proportions taking different routes after compulsory schooling.

The discussion of NEET in the previous chapter looked at the proportions of young people who it is estimated occupy such a position. However, both the Mid Glamorgan and Northern Ireland studies contained a more dynamic element and allow estimates to be made not only of the proportion of young people that spent some time in Status 0, but also the length of time spent in such a position, and the frequency of occupation of that status. Although the studies categorize the length of time spent in Status 0 differently, they allow a distinction to be made between those occupying that status for six months or more in the two years since the end of compulsory schooling from those who have occupied that position for less time.

The data from the different studies produce contrasting results (though again the different methodologies need to be taken into account). The Northern Ireland study found that just over three quarters of 16–17-year-olds experienced no spells of being NEET. By contrast, in Mid Glamorgan

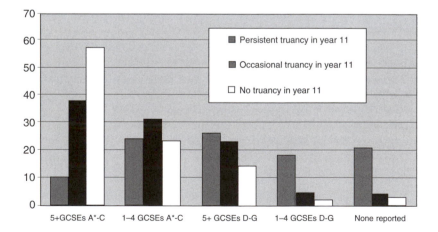

Figure 3.1 Young people's attainment of GCSEs (or GNVQ equivalents) by level of truancy from school (2000) (per cent of each category)

only 10 per cent of the age group made the transition straight into continuous training or work and a little over one third of the overall sample (36 per cent) had 'short term' experience of being NEET. In the South Wales study only 44 per cent stayed in education for the full two years after the end of compulsory education. Of the remainder, 54 per cent were NEET for six months or longer. Overall, therefore, just under one third of the 16–17-year-olds in the Mid Glamorgan study (30 per cent) had 'long term' or 'very long term' experience of being NEET. Nine per cent of the sample had been NEET 'most or all the time' since leaving school. The figures are lower in Northern Ireland. This study suggests that only 22 per cent of the sample experienced being NEET overall and, of these, just over one third (35 per cent or 8 per cent overall) experienced being NEET for over six months. A little under half of the latter had been NEET almost continuously since leaving school.

Most studies of NEET young people suggest that this is a difficult status to change. However, the evidence seems to suggest is that those not in education, employment or training for relatively short periods of time (under six months) are much more likely to move back into education or, more likely, into training or work, than are those who are NEET for longer. Thus, in the Mid Glamorgan study, of those who spent over six months in that position, two fifths did so in one spell. Bentley and Gurumurthy (1999) point out that the YCS shows that over half those not in education, employment or training at 16 were in the same position at 17, and a third still remained there at 18. A similar pattern appears to apply to the impact of experiencing unemployment into later life. Analysis of the NCDS suggests that young people with no experience of unemployment between 16 and 23 were unemployed for less than 2 per cent of the following ten years. By contrast, among those unemployed for more than a year between 16 and 23, the proportion rises to 23 per cent (Gregg 1999 reported in Bentley and Gurumurthy). Interestingly, Gregg (1999) found that 'about two thirds of the raw correlation between higher early unemployment and higher late unemployment is down to the unemployment itself, and one-third because of area or individual variation'.

Experiencing disaffection

Our focus so far has been on various forms of behaviour, or the occupation of a particular status, which are in some way taken to indicate 'disaffection'. Put another way, we have concentrated on 'objective' indicators rather than subjective experiences. By contrast, the primary focus of the remainder of this chapter is on the views of disaffected young people and, more particularly, their views of, or attitudes towards, those individuals or agencies that are tasked with providing services for them. The bulk of the literature focusing on the views of 'disaffected' young people – which is in itself relatively small – is qualitative in character and, in most cases, based on small numbers of interviews. The first point to make is that the qualitative literature provides ample evidence in support of the general points made earlier in this chapter and the preceding one, particularly in relation to what might be thought of as the key 'risk factors' for 'disaffection'. Thus, the literature is replete with references to, or descriptions of, disrupted family backgrounds, family conflict, the experience of growing up in 'poor neighbourhoods', the trauma of entering care and the difficulties experienced on leaving, early use of alcohol and drugs, trouble with the law, and boredom, bullying and 'failure' at school. In addition, however, there are three other, possibly less predictable, themes that appear in the literature. They are the ubiquity of 'trauma' and 'loss' in the lives of the 'disaffected', the value placed on family and, linked with this, the 'traditional' nature of the aspirations of the 'disaffected'. We look at each of these three rather less discussed issues in greater detail below, before moving on to consider young people's views of the professionals they encountered during the course of their lives and of the transitions they had negotiated.

Trauma/loss

Although based on a relatively small sample of young people, a study by BMRB (1999) draws attention to something that is often alluded to in the rest of the literature but is rarely discussed at length: the 'traumatic events' that appear with regularity in the lives of the disadvantaged young people (another exception is Wilkinson 1995). They identified three sets of traumatic events which, they suggest, appear to be instrumental in a young person 'going off the rails'. These were the death of a close friend or relative; the disappearance or reappearance of a mother; and sexual abuse. However, this rather minimizes the evidence they present. Some of the traumatic events – including potentially traumatic loss – experienced by the young people who are the subject of their four case studies are summarized in Table 3.2.

It is not suggested that these life histories are necessarily typical of the backgrounds of highly disaffected young people. However, there is sufficient evidence from studies of other 'disaffected' young people to suggest that experience of significant trauma and loss is a frequent part of such lives.[3] As one example, work by Demos (Bentley and Gurumurthy 1999) found that many homeless young people have suffered severe trauma or disruption both prior to, and during, homelessness. The authors conclude from this that while both the provision of accommodation and

Table 3.2 Trauma and loss in the backgrounds of young people not in education, training or employment

Case study 1	Case study 2	Case study 3	Case study 4
• Father left home (age 6) • Beaten by mother • Bullied at school (inc. death threats) • Raped • 'Put' into prostitution by mother • Early use of drugs • Brother dies • Early pregnancy	• Father dies Attempted to murder 'step-father' • Attempted suicide • Thrown out of family home • Enters care • Early pregnancy	• Father left home (age 8) • Beaten by step-father • Bullied • Assaulted • Thrown out of family home • Sleeping rough • Breakdown • Bedridden • Serious (drug-related) illness	• Behavioural problems • Expelled from primary school • Expelled from secondary school • Arrested twice • Early pregnancy • Miscarriage • Post-natal depression

Source: Summarized from BMRB (1999).

skills training are important to young homeless people, they may well also need intensive support to overcome 'pre-vocational' needs that may have contributed to their homelessness.

Centrality of family

As Table 3.2 indicates, it is the family that is the source, or the location, of many of the traumatic events experienced by these young people. Bentley *et al*. in their work on marginalized young people found that many of the traumas experienced at home made young people unable to focus on work at school. This, they felt, was a significant factor in their poor achievement levels. Partly as a consequence many of the young people in the study were of the view that counselling and support services for young people of school age should be better and more easily available. Despite the obvious difficulties that these young people faced, what comes shining through many of their accounts is the continuing positive views many held of their own families, and of the idea of 'the family' in the abstract. Generally positive attitudes towards families were found in several studies of marginalized young people (see Loudon *et al*. 1997). In many cases in the Northern Ireland study, it was a family member who was the single most significant person in the young person's life. The importance of these ties is both practical and emotional. Thus, many young Status 0 young people report receiving some financial support from their families (Istance and Williamson 1996; Loudon *et al.* 1997). More interestingly, perhaps, Istance and Williamson report that most parents appeared to 'tolerate' their children's behaviour. However, this is one of the few references to parents' views in the literature – they are almost entirely absent from most studies.

Aspirations

The clear message from the work on the views of 'disaffected' young people is that in the main they have 'traditional' aspirations. Thus, for example, the majority of interviewees in the Demos 'Real Deal' study 'appeared to aspire to a "normal life": for most this was to have "a home, a family and a job" ' (Bentley and Gurumurthy 1999: 43). Most wanted to work: 'They wanted to "stimulate their brains", they wanted to be "useful to people" and interact with people, but most of all they wanted to earn money so they could be independent' (1999: 104). The research by BMRB (1999) found that future aspirations did not vary between the different groups of 'disaffected' young people in the study. Again, their aspirations were largely traditional and mainstream. Similarly, data from the YLS show that those who truant at school are more likely to stress the need to improve their qualifications than those do not truant (Casey and Smith 1995). Moreover, 'those who have truanted typically want to get straight into a job and earn some money, whereas those who have not truanted are more ready to defer their immediate financial rewards' (1995: 10).

A slightly different picture emerges from interviews with Status 0 young people in South Wales. Here, although their primary aspiration remained fairly traditional – they wanted to work – this was overlain by a sense of despondency and a lack of clear aspirations. Williamson (1997) reports the 'two common threads' running through the behaviour of these young people as being 'short-termism' and 'opportunism'. The research is clear, however, that it is work, not training, that these young people desire (Istance and Williamson 1996).

Professionals and transitions

What then are the views of 'disaffected' young people of those individuals and agencies whose role it is to provide support? Perhaps predictably, their opinions are not entirely positive. First, teachers. For most of the young people in the Real Deal initiative, teachers were identified as a problem and one of the main barriers to improving education. Many felt that teachers were not interested in them (Bentley and Gurumurthy 1999). Wilkinson (1995: 23) identifies 'getting on badly with teachers' as one of the key reasons given for dropping out of school, though he also lists boredom, the influence of friends and 'drugs, alcohol and substance abuse'. In considering 'disaffection from school', the BMRB (1999) study identified three factors: tedium of schoolwork; difficulty of concentration; and dislike of teachers. The reasons for the latter took numerous forms including labelling by the teacher or failure by the teacher to care sufficiently about the young person concerned. The bottom-line message appeared to be that teachers should 'have a better understanding about what life was like for some of them and to treat them as individuals' (1999: 10). This picture is reinforced by the research by Kinder *et al.* (1997) on disaffected school pupils. They found that a significant proportion of pupils experienced a strong sense of being let down and rejected, or of suffering an injustice. Approximately half their sample suggested that the problem of relating successfully with teachers was a cause of both classroom disruption and truancy. Their explanations clustered around three main issues: lack of respect or consideration to pupils; a sense of injustice – being unfairly blamed, singled out or punished; and negative reactions to teacher 'self-presentation'. Finally, but importantly, the BMRB report says that it was at school that young people felt most let down and unsupported. Although there were isolated cases of important relationships developing, 'the evidence … suggests that there was little in place to provide the support that many school children needed, especially during those first years at secondary school' (1999: 50).

If anything, social workers come off worse. The BMRB study found that disaffected young people tended to be most critical of social workers:

> They rarely seemed to get the respect and trust of the young person so they would not confide in them. They often went through several social workers and each new one would say the same thing. They were often seen as boring and interfering and not to be trusted (1999: 48).

Similarly, the report suggests that young people were critical of the way in which it was often expected that they would seek help, rather than those in key positions coming forward to offer help. The most critical comments are generally reserved for the police. Respondents in the Real Deal study voiced general hostility to the police. The 'homeless' respondents, for example, argued that the police were unsympathetic to them, treating them as 'animals'. The sense that the police 'hassled' rather than 'helped' was widespread (1999: 111).

What emerges very clearly from the literature is the sense that many 'disaffected' young people feel that they have been let down at critical points in their lives. There is also considerable discussion of the process of becoming adult, something that is held to be becoming increasingly complex for many young people, and problematic for the marginalized. In many cases there appears to be confusion about what 'being an adult' means. Bentley and Gurumurthy (1999) suggest that it appeared 'that different elements of becoming an adult did not fit together in any straightforward way' for their respondents. One of the conclusions of the Demos Real Deal report is that many of the most vulnerable young people feel unsupported in preparing for life in the adult world – particularly those who have lived in the care system or experienced homelessness.

Many disaffected young people are critical of the limited way in which they perceive education to have prepared them for surviving away from home and out of the educational system (Wilkinson 1995; Istance and Williamson 1996). Having to undertake this difficult transition is often done under circumstances not of the young person's choosing. Thus, for many Real Deal participants, leaving home was less about taking a willing step towards adulthood and more about family breakdown or strife. Not surprisingly, money looms large in the accounts given by disaffected young people of their lives. They report one of the key barriers to further and higher education to be (lack of) money (see Wilkinson 1995; Istance and Williamson 1996; Bentley *et al.* 1999). This is, of course, especially the case for 16- and 17-year-olds who have, at best, very limited benefit entitlements. Carlen (1996: 91), in her study of the young homeless, says that 'most responses to questions about the DSS were characterized by sheer rage, as the young people talked about their battles (verbal and physical) for benefits'. Bentley and Gurumurthy (1999: 127) conclude from their qualitative work that an 'inescapable conclusion is that poverty and material disadvantage have a profound and damaging effect'. Concern about money also appears to impact on attitudes to training. Istance and Williamson's (1996) interviews with 28 young Status 0 men and women uncovered 'deep cynicism about training' and a 'determination to avoid it' (1996: 44). The primary reasons given for avoiding or abandoning training were the usual claims of 'slave labour' and 'crap allowances' (see also Loudon *et al.* 1997; Bentley and Gurumurthy 1999; BMRB 1999). Wilkinson (1995: 69) concluded from his study of 'drop-outs':

Significant numbers have negative reasons for not taking on a training programme in the first place: some feel it is a waste of time and others, a much larger proportion, feel the wage is poor. Others do take the initial step of accepting a place on a training programme but then fail to complete it, because of dismissal, because of what they consider to be poor training, and because of the poor wage.

Lack of money is, predictably enough, a common element in the discourse of disaffected young people. As 16 and 17-year-olds they have little likelihood of being able to claim benefits, are frequently unwilling to take part in 'slave labour' training schemes or the few available jobs ('shit jobs and govvy schemes' – Coffield *et al.* 1986), and are rarely able to rely to an appreciable extent on family for money. It should not be a surprise, therefore, that the 'illegal' or 'informal' economy is frequently mentioned by these young people. Unfortunately, attempting to estimate the nature and extent of their involvement in this area is almost impossible from the literature. The authors of The Real Deal Report that 'most [marginalized young people] have also worked at some time in the informal and illegal economies' (Bentley and Gurumurthy 1999: 88) and that most young people had worked cash in hand at some time or other: 'For some it was the only type of work they had had' (1999: 92).

Istance and Williamson (1996) also found that 'some' of their sample of 28 Status 0 young men and women 'had left training schemes for more occasional, but better paid, work in the informal economy' (1996: 51). Nineteen of the 28 admitted involvement in a wide range of criminal activity – most of whom said that their offending was largely to get money. Indeed, Williamson (1997: 75) suggests that one of the key findings of this research was the 'fact that all had slipped, or were slipping steadily along a continuum of "income generation": from benefit fraud (if it was possible), through casual employment and opportunistic petty crime, to more calculated and organized criminality'.

Yet, as was described above, in the main these young people do want to work. Work advice, however, is generally seen to be poor. Unlike their education choices, very few people mentioned their parents as sources of either information or advice on jobs. Information about employment tended to come from more formal sources such as schools, Careers Service and the Employment Service: 'However, there was criticism of most of these systems. Many young people felt that, in the case of the Employment Service, in particular, better integration would help' (Bentley *et al.* 1999: 95). Very few felt they had been well served by careers advice in school, but others said they had not taken advantage of the system either. Wilkinson (1995) confirms this general view, suggesting that what almost half his respondents (49 per cent) wanted from the Careers Service was more information about jobs and help with getting jobs.

Respondents in the BMRB study were reported as having found the attitude of some careers officers condescending: 'they wanted to discuss their situation but felt they were being told what to do, which they resented' (1990: 62). Loudon *et al.* (1997) in their interviews with 25 Status 0 young men and women found that few could remember much of detail about the school's careers service. No hostility was expressed towards the service, but few disaffected young people appear to feel that they are well served by careers advice in school or, indeed, thereafter. Istance and Williamson uncovered 'a deep cynicism of the professional world established to support young people' (1996: 59) among the NEET young people interviewed in South Wales.

Success, where it is reported, is more likely to be a result of serendipity than planning. Thus, Loudon *et al.* (1997: 50) found that among NEET youth that 'there were so many experiences of the connections they made being "by chance". Many of the young people did not experience being held or guided by structures, procedures or policies around them in the school or in the different agencies, post school leaving age'. In a similar vein, only 57 per cent of young people in care responding to Shaw's (1998) survey were able to state with any certainty that they had a care plan. As the author acknowledges, one assumes or hopes that the true figure is much higher. Even if it is, however, the response to her survey indicates that young people in care display a worrying lack of knowledge about, and therefore perhaps involvement in, planning their own futures.

This, indeed, is the primary conclusion of much of this literature: marginalized young people feel let down at critical points in their lives. In many cases they appear not to get proper support or advice from those whose responsibility it should be to provide it. 'One of the most striking themes,' Bentley *et al.* (1999: 109) report, 'was the criticism that people within specific organisations had failed to understand their problem or listen to their viewpoint.' Alternatively, young people simply don't know where to find the information, support and advice they require. Bentley *et al.* (1999: 111) again: 'another frequent comment was that young people were often unaware of what help was available; they did not know the "system".' The BMRB (1999) study also identified insufficient support as a major issue for marginalized young people. Personal support, they suggested, 'someone to confide in, someone to seek advice from at times of crisis and even to help cope with ongoing insoluble problems – was often glaringly absent from these young people's lives' (1999: 15).

> Those who had benefited from support at a crucial time were in no doubt about how it had helped them turn around their lives. Lack of continuous and pro-active support was likely to be a major barrier to these young people successfully moving, and remaining, out of social exclusion (BMRB 1999: 69).

This is, in the opinion of the young people concerned, a key component in their process of disengagement. Re-engagement often depends on chance. Will the young person concerned find someone, anyone, who will provide him or her with the support and guidance he or she requires? Loudon *et al.* (1997: 52) conclude with the depressing observation that 'so many of these young people's chances of succeeding at school were "hanging on a thread", depending on a relationship with one significant adult, perhaps a teacher or YTP tutor, or even the nature of their peer group'.

Conclusion

A minority of young people, primarily from disadvantaged and disrupted family and social backgrounds, will encounter significant problems in navigating one or more of the key transitions from dependent childhood to independent adulthood and will fare particularly badly in the education system and/or the labour market. It is clear that a great many of the most disaffected young people experience an absence of parental (and other) support. They are highly likely to hold very negative views of authority figures such as police officers, teachers and social workers and to perceive there to have been an absence of guidance from family and others – such as teachers and social workers – at critical points in their lives. Despite this, a great many still have positive views about the importance of family and education and continue to harbour traditional aspirations about work. Though one should not underestimate the difficulty of working with such young people, one of the key messages of the literature on youthful disaffection is that a great many of these young people are keen to change their lives – even if they are sceptical about the likelihood of achieving change and deeply ambivalent about the sincerity of anyone wishing to help them. It is at this point that we turn to mentoring, as the latest in a long line of what have been hoped or anticipated to be promising interventions with this particular group of young people.

Notes

1 Wilkinson (1995: 25) also notes that 'absenteeism from school is strongly correlated with residential insecurity as measured by the number of respondents who said they had never been without a fixed abode'.

2 Hibbett and Fogelman (1990: 178) conclude that 'an explanation might be that the difficulties encountered by the former truants are the result of their more

accelerated rate of progress through the major events and transitions of early adulthood'.

3 See, for example, the case histories of persistent young offenders in Hagell and Newburn (1994).

Chapter 4

Young people and mentoring

What is mentoring?

Mentoring has a long history which can be traced back to the Ancient Greeks. According to Homer, Mentor was the name of the friend chosen by Odysseus to act as guardian and tutor to his only son Telemachus. Natural or informal mentoring, along the lines of this classical Homeric version, is generally thought of as a relationship

> between an older, more experienced mentor and an unrelated young protégé. The mentor typically provides on-going guidance instruction and encouragement aimed at developing the competence and character of the protégé. Over the course of the relationship the mentor and protégé develop a bond of mutual commitment, friendship, respect and loyalty which facilitates the youth's transition into adulthood (Rhodes 1994: 189).

As such, the term mentoring describes an act of guardianship and guidance that occurs in a very broad range of settings and circumstances, practised by people the world over (Darling *et al.* 2002), though only a minority of such activities are likely to be called 'mentoring'. Rather, the term has become associated with a more formalized version of this relationship; a formal or 'artificial' form of mentoring which, though possibly informed by the same principles as naturally occurring mentoring, operates in different circumstances and settings. Such mentoring is generally thought of as being 'a relationship between two **strangers**, instigated by a third party, who intentionally matches the mentor with the mentee according to the needs of the younger person as a part of a planned intervention programme' (Freedman 1993: 176). As Freedman implies, mentoring in this form is generally designed as an intervention with young people who, for varying reasons, are perceived to require some form of guidance, direction and/or support above and beyond that they are already receiving. In particular, mentoring has increasingly been used with young people perceived to be 'at risk' – most usually in relation to disruptive behaviour in school, offending and substance use – though as an approach it is associated with the broad range of characteristics related to social exclusion. More specifically still, mentoring has come to be seen as the latest in a long line of 'silver bullets'[1] in relation to tackling youth crime.

Mentoring as a formalized response to social exclusion or social welfare problems originated in the USA and, indeed, has also operated successfully there for many years in the business environment. Mentoring became well established in the USA in the 1970s and 1980s, though some schemes started considerably earlier. As Philip (1999: 25) puts it, 'mentoring appeared to offer the potential to tackle some of the massive problems facing inner-city youth, educators and other professionals in the USA but within a highly localized, small-scale operation'. Mentoring spread rapidly and, in a situation not entirely unlike that of recent years in the UK, its promise was often viewed as being extraordinarily broad and its potential almost limitless. The key focus of many of the schemes was vulnerable young people, and was underpinned by the view that some of the problems of inadequate socialization and personal dysfunction and disaffection could be offset by the support of a mentor. The bulk of the literature on mentoring is, rather atheoretical. That is, it appears to make assumptions about the process and the value of mentoring. The classical model, Philip (http://www.infed.org/learningmentors/mentoring.htm) argues, involves a rather uncritical acceptance of traditional developmental theories about youth, has somewhat gender-bound assumptions about family and organization, and tends to neglect structural features of poverty and exclusion. This, she suggests, has three core characteristics. First, it is individualistic, having at its heart a relationship that is essentially private and isolated from young people's social environments. Secondly, it is highly gendered, being based on models of development that privilege white male experience (Brown and Gilligan 1992) and, finally, it is a relationship that pays relatively little regard to the young person's stated needs.

One of the difficulties with mentoring – and with assessing its value – is the difficulty of pinning down precisely what it means; a process complicated by the variety of the practices included under the rubric of mentoring, which may be held to cover at least one or more of the following: facilitating, coaching, buddying, befriending, counselling, tutoring, teaching, life-styling and role-modelling (Philips 1999; Clutterbuck 2002). The problems of definition, and the absence of agreed theoretical models underpinning practice, complicate any attempt to assess the impact of such interventions.

Mentoring in practice

One of the earliest, and now one of the best known mentoring programmes, is Big Brothers, Big Sisters of America (BBBSA). The original concept is attributed to a Cincinnati man in 1903, and a formal scheme was established by a court clerk from New York City, Ernest Coulter, in 1904. Initially simply called Big Brothers, it is said that Coulter was influenced by a New York Children's Court Judge who recruited influential men to mentor delinquent boys who came before him (http://www.bbbsa.org/about/about_faqs.asp). On their website, BBBSA recount the tale of Coulter becoming increasingly appalled by the fate of the thousands of children passing through the court, and quote from a speech he gave to a group of civic and business leaders in which, talking about a boy about to be jailed, he said:

> There is only one way to save that youngster, and that is to have some earnest, true man volunteer to be his Big Brother, to look after him, help him to do right, make the little chap feel that there is at least one human being in this great city who takes a personal interest in him. Someone who cares whether he lives or dies. I call for a volunteer!

Apparently, everyone in the room volunteered. In 1905, Catholic Big Sisters, the first known Big Sisters programme in the USA, was also formed in New York. BBBSA now describes itself as the biggest mentoring programme in the world covering not only much of North America, but also operating in Africa, South America and Europe, including the UK.

The general approach in BBBSA is to seek to pair unrelated adult volunteers with young people from single-parent households. The adult and young person agree to meet between two and four times a month for at least one year, with an average meeting lasting approximately four hours. The programme is not aimed at specific 'problems' but rather at developing the 'whole person' (Tierney and Grossman 1995). It is also, as we shall see, one of the few programmes that has been the subject of rigorous evaluation. BBBSA has a national office that publishes standards and procedures governing the screening of volunteers and young people, training and the creation and supervision of 'matches' between volunteer and young person. Screening of volunteers is time consuming and research found that after having been under consideration for between 3 and 9 months only about 35 per cent of volunteers had been matched (Roaf *et al.* 1994). The screening process for young people involves an interview with parent and child. The young person must have no more than one parent or guardian actively involved in his or her life, and may be aged between 5 and 18 years old. BBBSA's intensive and extensive infrastructure is in fairly sharp contrast with the *laissez-faire* approach of many of the other mentoring programmes established in the 1980s in the USA, many of which argued that adults could 'naturally' work with young people (Tierney and Grossman 1995) with the result that the achieved levels of interaction were often much lower than BBBSA (Tierney and Branch 1992; McCartney *et al.* 1994).

In the UK, mentoring is a somewhat more recent development with some of the best known programmes such as the Dalston Youth Programme (DYP) and Big Brothers, Big Sisters UK starting in the late 1990s and, indeed, in some cases drawing heavily on USA experience. DYP remains the best known of the UK programmes, despite the fact that it is located in a single London borough. Rather like BBBSA within the USA, however, it has been a highly influential model for the development of mentoring programmes in the UK. Established by Crime Concern and a number of partner agencies, it was designed as a creative response to problems of youth crime in Hackney. Focusing on 'at risk' young people aged between 11 and 18, DYP begins with a residential phase attended by young people, mentors and staff, followed by an almost year-long programme at the heart of which is a one-to-one relationship between mentor and mentee together with an ongoing educational/personal development component (O'Sullivan 2000; Tarling *et al.* 2001). In fact, DYP is one of the mentoring programmes that forms the focus of the empirical study in this book, and we return to its form and functioning in greater detail below.

Despite what are often considerable differences in understanding and practice, mentoring holds great appeal for policy-makers and there now appears to be increasing agreement that mentoring, natural or artificial, is an enabling strategy which can be used successfully in different settings with a variety of people. As DuBois *et al.* (2002) note, mentoring is used for the general purpose of youth interaction and development or more specifically to achieve progress in more instrumental areas such as education and or/employment. It is used with specific groups of people, i.e. disaffected young people and those deemed at risk of offending and other anti-social behaviour, to reduce risk and encourage the young person to embrace positive life goals or, more importantly, promote the internalization of positive expectations by young people (Steward 2000: 5).

Mentoring and New Labour

Mentoring appeared to be growing rapidly in popularity in the UK in the late 1990s; indeed a survey by the National Mentoring Network in the UK in 1996 discovered over 4,000 people acting as mentors to pupils in 400+ educational establishments, and research by the National Foundation for Educational Research identified over 70 separate mentoring schemes (Skinner and Fleming 1999). Mentoring also received a massive boost from the very considerable attention it was given by the New Labour government in the aftermath of the 1997 general election. In the lead-up to the election the Labour Party had signalled that, once elected, it intended to make youth justice reform the centrepiece of its Home Affairs policy (Newburn 1998). In its 1996 consultation paper, *Tackling Youth Crime: Reforming Youth Justice* (Labour Party 1996), it set out its critique of the existing youth justice system and, in particular, identified the failure to provide challenging community-based interventions for young offenders and those at risk of offending. Young offenders were to be made more personally responsible for their actions; the problems of poverty, educational failure and family dysfunction were no longer usable as 'excuses' for offending and anti-social conduct. An array of new orders, including Reparation Orders and Action Plan Orders, were introduced as were a number of non-criminal orders, such as Parenting Orders and Anti-Social Behaviour Orders. Responsibility for crime control was held to lie not only at the feet of the young offender or his or her parents, but was increasingly presented as a 'multi-disciplinary' endeavour in which the aim was to encourage *all* members of the community into contributing to the Home Office's newly established mission statement of 'building a safe, just and tolerant society'.

Of the community-based initiatives adopted by New Labour in the attempt to tackle youthful offending and anti-social behaviour, mentoring quickly became established as one of the most popular. Like so many other New Labour initiatives, its North American origins were undoubtedly something of a selling point (Newburn 2001). The range of locations in which mentoring was adopted by New Labour was extremely broad. One of the most significant was the New Deal initiative that focused on unemployed young people aged 18 and over. The New Deal had a number of key elements including assessment, job preparation, job search, work experience and personal support. The latter was provided from two sources: a personal advisor and a mentor. In a speech on New Deal Mentoring, then Minister for Employment, Welfare to Work and Equal Opportunities, Tessa Jowell, said:

> we know, because young people have told us, that it is sometimes difficult for them to confide in people on some matters. This is often because they have been trying to stand on their own two feet, and also because they find it easier to talk to someone who is independent ... Mentoring is becoming the new 'buzz' word for so many of our radical social justice programmes. If we look across government, at Sure Start, early years, learning mentors, ConneXions and the New Deal, all rely on the central contribution of mentors or advocates (www.newdeal.gov.uk/english/partners/mentoring.pdf).

New Labour's very explicit concern with social exclusion, particularly in its first term, led to numerous recommendations for the use of mentoring and expansion into new areas of activity. The Social Exclusion Unit (SEU), established soon after the 1997 election victory, recommended the use of mentoring in a number of its reports. Thus, in relation to tackling exclusion from school, it suggested that the particular problem of the disproportionate rates of exclusion among African-Caribbean boys might, in part at least, be responded to through the promotion of community mentoring in minority ethnic communities (SEU 1998b). Similarly, the Policy Action Team on Rough Sleepers suggested that mentoring could potentially have a major impact in helping overcome the social isolation experienced by the homeless (SEU 1998a). Other reports from the SEU, including those on reducing reoffending by ex-prisoners (SEU 2002), the PAT on Young People (SEU 2000) and on neighbourhood renewal (using mentoring to support young entrepreneurs) (SEU 2001) also made positive recommendations about the potential role of mentoring.

The other very significant area in which mentoring took off in the late 1990s was youth justice. In particular, the newly established Youth Justice Board issued guidelines for mentoring with young offenders in the aftermath of the passage of the Crime and Disorder Act 1998 and subsequently moved quickly to use its financial muscle to stimulate considerable activity in that area. By 2000, the Youth Justice Board had funded almost 100 mentoring schemes. In addition, the Home Office via a capital grants scheme became a significant funder of local mentoring programmes. The stated priorities for applications for this funding were mentoring

- offenders, ex-offenders and those at risk of offending;
- young people excluded from school;
- individuals with addictions; and
- refugees.

In spite of the growth of mentoring practice across the UK, there is little empirical documentation of the effectiveness of this approach in reducing disaffection or of benefits to participants in other ways – be they young people or the mentors. Research on mentoring is relatively scarce and the few rigorous studies are of a few large-scale programmes in North America. Evaluation in the UK has generally been absent, or when present has been slight. In reality, much of the expansion of interest in mentoring, and the financial investment made in it by bodies like the Youth Justice Board and the Home Office, has been an act of faith. Pitts (2001: 12) is especially critical of the current evidential base:

> Unsurprisingly, perhaps, the evaluations of mentoring cited by the Youth Justice Board … are remarkably upbeat, deriving as they do mainly from studies undertaken by members of the US-based National Mentoring Association. As such, they may tend, for under-standable reasons, to 'accentuate the positive' and overlook, or underplay, areas where no change occurs or where problems actually worsen.

Evidence of promise? Mentoring and research evidence

Evaluations of mentoring in the USA

By far the most thorough review of US mentoring research was that conducted on behalf of the Department of Justice by Sherman and colleagues (Sherman *et al.* 1999).

The first thing they note is that mentoring provides the highest 'dosage' of adult–child interaction of all formal community-based programmes. As a consequence, 'compared to street workers and recreation program supervisors, mentors can develop much stronger bonds with juveniles at risk'. The results from extant research are, however, far from un-equivocally positive. One of the problems is the paucity of rigorous research. In their review of community-based programmes (including mentoring) Sherman *et al.* argued that a large proportion of the evaluations were 'unscientific' and failed to stand up to basic assessments of 'methodological rigor'.

A total of seven of the more rigorous evaluations of mentoring programmes were assessed, each being assigned a 'scientific methods score' ranging from 1 (no reliance or confidence should be placed on the results of this evaluation because of the number and type of serious shortcomings(s) in the methodology employed) through 3 (methodology rigorous in some respects, weak in others) to 5 (methodology rigorous in almost all respects). A summary of the studies is provided in Table 4.1.

Sherman *et al.*'s review begins with the controlled experiments – these in principle being taken to have greater plausibility than research not based on random assignment. The earliest controlled experiment started in 1937 and involved visits paid by two recent college graduates to half, randomly assigned, of a sample of 650 'at risk' boys aged under 12. The visits involved academic tutoring, trips to cultural and sporting events and general support. The programme finished in 1942 when the counsellors joined the armed forces. No differences in criminal histories were found between the experimental and control groups in 1942 (Witmer 1972) or in the mid-1970s (McCord 1978). However, the longer-term follow-up did find significantly higher levels of diagnosed alcoholism, serious mental illness and stress-related physical health problems among the group that had received mentoring. Though on the surface such results are hardly good news for proponents of mentoring, as Sherman *et al.* point out, there are a number of other possible reasons – such as greater exposure to professional and medical services – that might explain the measured differences.

A more positive set of results – and indeed one of the few in relation to mentoring – were drawn from a controlled experiment evaluating the Big Brothers, Big Sisters America programme in eight cities (Tierney and Grossman 1995). The study, described as 'tightly randomized', found that although it was unclear as to whether BBBSA reduces criminality in later life, it was positively associated with substantial benefits for young people after one year:

> After spending around 12 hours monthly with their volunteer adult mentors, the treatment group children had 45% less reported onset of drug abuse than the control group children, who had been put on the waiting list. They also had 27% less onset of alcohol use, and 32% less frequency of hitting someone. The program also reduced truancy: treatment group children skipped 52% fewer days of school and 37% fewer classes on days they were in school (http://www.ncjrs.org/works/chapter3.htm).

Table 4.1 Community-based mentoring evaluations (USA)

Primary source (secondary)	Scientific methods score	Programme content	Programme effects
McCord 1978, 1992; Powers and Witmer 1972	5	2 visits monthly by paid male counsellors for 5.5 years with 253 at-risk boys under 12 in 1937–42; WW2 end	No effect on criminal record; treatment group did worse on diagnosed mental health
Tierney *et al.* 1995	5	Big Brothers and Sisters, 1 year for 10–14-year-olds, 60% minority and 27% abused; 3 hrs wkly	46% reduction in drug use onset, 32% reduction in hitting people, relative to controls
Green 1980 (Howell 1995)	4	Big Brothers for fatherless white boys 1/2 day weekly for 6 months	No effects on disruptive class behavior; no measures of drug use
Goodman 1972 (Howell 1995)	2	College student mentors of 10–11-year-old boys 6 hrs wkly over 2 years	High control group attrition; program effects on crime unknown
Dicken *et al.* 1977 (Howell 1995)	3	College student mentors for 6–13-year-olds, 6 hrs wkly, 4 months	No difference in teacher-rated behavior of mentees
Fo and O'Donnell 1974 (Howell 1995)	5	12 weeks of paid community mentors with at-risk 11–17-year-olds; *n* = 26	Truancy reduced significantly under some conditions
Fo and O'Donnell 1974 (Howell 1995)	5	1 year of paid community mentors meeting weekly with at-risk 10–17-year-olds	Lower recidivism for treatment groups with priors, higher without

Source: Sherman *et al.* (1999).

Moreover, the programme appeared to be highly cost-effective. Its use of volunteer mentors kept the costs down, the major financial burden being the process of matching mentors and young people. Though the potential long-term savings have not been calculated, according to Sherman and colleagues even the short-term benefits might justify government support for the programme.

They report two other randomized experiments. Both involved paid mentors, one only lasting 12 weeks and with very small numbers (a total of 26 young people randomly assigned); the other a one-year experiment with a larger group (Fo and O'Donnell 1974, 1975). Neither has particularly clear results – the small experiment appearing to show some impact of contingent approval by mentors, the larger study finding higher rates of offending among mentees with no previous offending history (compared with their controls), yet reduced rates among those who had prior records (compared with their controls). The remaining research, based on non-experimental methods, is given short shrift which, given largely negative results, is perhaps fortunate for those who currently seek to promote mentoring.

However, we should note that four of the seven projects reviewed by Sherman failed to show any evidence of success and of those that did show 'promise', most were successful at curbing the propensity for drug use, but not delinquency or offending, in the 10–14 age group only. Moreover, success was linked to the level of 'dosage' that the young person received from his or her mentor. The evaluated programmes suggest that three/four or more meetings a month, with each meeting lasting at least several hours, were associated with success. Regular telephone contact must take place with mentees calling mentors. Thus, even in the USA, where there has been greater investment in experimental and quasi-experimental social science research in the last two to three decades, the research evidence on the potential of mentoring remains remarkably slim. We turn now to the research base in the UK Brewer *et al.* (1995: 99).

Evaluating mentoring in the UK

As in so much in the evaluation field the UK lags behind the USA in the work that has been undertaken on mentoring (Newburn 2001). Current research knowledge is hampered by the fact that very little evaluative work has been undertaken in the UK, and where it has been done it has tended to be small scale, qualitative and largely atheoretical. This is not untypical of the wider field of crime prevention evaluation for, as Ekblom and Pease (1995: 585–6) argue, such work tends to be dominated by 'self serving unpublished and semi-published work that does not meet the most elementary criteria of evaluative probity'. As a consequence, there is currently no solid foundation in the UK for any of the claims that are made on behalf of mentoring though, as we have seen, this has not hampered its emergence as a central plank in policies that seek to address social exclusion.

In the UK the available empirical evidence is restricted to evaluations of two main programmes: the Dalston Youth Project (DYP) and CHANCE. A lot of publicity has surrounded a third programme, Youth At Risk (YAR), but to date it has not been subject to independent published research and any claims to the contrary should be treated with considerable scepticism. As we have noted, the widely acclaimed Dalston Youth Project (DYP) was one of the first mentoring projects in the UK and it is this project, like that of BBBSA in the USA, which is held up as the shining example of successful mentoring in the UK. Many projects have been modelled on the DYP format and since its creation the number of mentoring programmes has mushroomed in the UK, though they work with a variety of different social issues in a number of different ways, using a range of services.

Working with young disaffected youth from one of the most deprived boroughs in England and Wales, DYP runs programmes for 11–14-year-olds and 15–18-year-olds. Both sets of programmes have been the subject of small-scale evaluative research. Research on the older age group suggests some possible impact on self-reported offending and truancy – though not drug use – but, unfortunately, the numbers involved in the study are far too small to allow for the results to be treated with anything other than considerable caution (Webb 2001). Further evaluative research (Tarling et al. 2001) on the DYP 11–14 programme produced mixed results. Using fairly broad criteria of 'success' and 'failure' (relating to engagement with the programme and subsequent functioning), small numbers of interviews with participants, and no comparison or control, the authors suggest that DYP worked successfully with about half those involved. However, about half 'did not engage with the project in any meaningful way' and perhaps not surprisingly therefore the impact on offending behaviour was disappointing and gains in other areas such as behaviour, attitudes and learning were modest.

The second significant UK mentoring programme subject to evaluation – over three years – was CHANCE, established in 1996 to work with primary school-aged children with behavioural problems. The evaluation was again extremely small-scale, involving interviews with only 16 children and similar numbers of mentors and parents (St James-Roberts and Samlal Singh 2001). The authors report that those children who completed the project showed some improvement in self-confidence, social awareness, self-control and relationships. However, equivalent improvements were found in a matched comparison group of children with no mentors leading the evaluators to speculate whether mentoring can be expected to achieve significant generalized behavioural change in disadvantaged children within a year (St James-Roberts 2001: viii).

The final programme worthy of mention at this stage is Youth At Risk (YAR) which, like DYP, works with 'high risk' young people. This mentoring programme has claimed high rates of success with young people it describes as 'extremely alienated from society' (YAR undated). In its advertizing material it claims that 'independent American surveys' show that for young people that had attended YAR, truancy rates fell by 70 per cent, the number of arrests decreased by 50 per cent and drug use fell by 30 per cent (Utting 1996: 78). However, there is no published evidence that would support such claims, and the tendency for such 'results' to be repeated uncritically is somewhat typical of the current state of affairs in relation not just to mentoring but to many interventions with disaffected young people in the UK. It may be that mentoring is not only a 'promising approach' but has real potential to improve individual functioning. However, the spread of programmes without rigorous evaluation runs a number of risks. One is simply that in the same way that the stock of mentoring rose so it will fall; in the short to medium term the fashion may change and attention may turn away from mentoring towards another unproven intervention. The opportunity to assess the benefits of mentoring will have been lost. Secondly, and more dangerously, it is possible of course that interventions such as mentoring do more harm than good. It is this possibility, at least as much as the positive potential, that should concentrate the mind of the policy-maker and practitioner on the need for rigorous evaluation. It was partly as a result of such concerns that the evaluation of Mentoring Plus, which forms the substantive core of this book, was designed.

Evaluating Mentoring Plus

The empirical core of this book is based on a large and complex research study conducted over a period of approximately three years (July 2000– September 2003). As we outlined earlier, the study of mentoring has been characterized by a general absence of rigorous research evidence, especially in the UK. We were particularly concerned therefore that this study should be carefully designed and be capable of assessing impact as well as understanding the processes involved in mentoring. In this chapter we outline the study design, the methods used, and provide an overview of the fieldwork and the methods of analysis. In doing this we offer a critique of some previous research in the field and argue that much current research funding in this area is wasted on small-scale, poorly designed studies and would be better spent on larger-scale research based upon partly experimental, or quasi-experimental designs.

Aims and objectives

The research focused on ten mentoring projects run by the charity Crime Concern. These projects, known collectively as Mentoring Plus, works with particularly disaffected young people. In order to provide a comprehensive picture, the research focused on both the *process* by which the programme was implemented and the *outcomes* that it achieved. The research had five principal objectives. The first was to examine the process by which vulnerable young people become involved in a mentoring programme and the reasons why other, apparently similar, vulnerable young people, decide not to participate. Secondly, and related to this, we were interested in young people's perceptions of participating in a mentoring programme. How did they experience mentoring and how did they relate to their mentor? Thirdly, we were concerned to assess the experiences of the staff and those who work as volunteer mentors. What in turn were their experiences of attempting to work with disillusioned and disaffected young people? Fourthly, as we have said, this research had a very clear focus on outcomes as well as processes and we sought to gauge the impact of mentoring by examining the meanings that mentors and mentees attribute to the processes and, finally, by identifying the medium-term impact of mentoring on those young people involved through an assessment of levels of social engagement (education, training and work), levels of offending, drug use and general psychological functioning.

An overview

The research was built around a longitudinal survey of a group of young people who participated in the Mentoring Plus programme. At the outset of the study, we envisaged this element of the study would include 320–400 young people. These young people were to be recruited to the cohort as they joined the programme and were to complete three questionnaires as part of the evaluation: one as they joined the programme, one as the programme came to an end (the 12-month follow-up) and another six months later (the 18-month follow-up). The surveys were augmented by quantitative information collected directly from the programmes (such as that relating to the frequency with which young people attended the project or met with their mentor). In addition, the study included a substantial qualitative component – depth interviews were conducted with project staff, mentors, young people and referral agents and detailed observations were made of the key elements of the programme.

One of the key issues facing the evaluation was how to measure success. Put simply, how could we attribute any changes that were observed in the young people to the programmes? To provide the basis for rigorous assessment a series of comparisons were built into the design of the study. First, internal comparisons: 10 programmes were included in the evaluation and this offered an opportunity for partial validation as it meant that we could compare outcomes for individuals passing through different programmes. Another potentially useful comparison was that between mentoring relationships that appeared to be 'successful' and those that did not. This model is close to what Pawson and Tilley (1997: 43) describe as realistic evaluation: one in which 'the best way to get at the crucial causal harmonies is to hypothesize and test within-program variation in the success rate of different subgroups of subjects'.

In addition to these important internal comparisons we also established an external group to the main cohort. This was considered important in order to allow us to attempt to isolate the effect of participating in the Mentoring Plus programme. Our initial hope was that we could adopt an experimental design with young people being allocated, on a random basis, to the programmes and to a 'non-treatment group'. For a number of reasons this proved impossible – primarily because of insufficient numbers, but also because of the deep resistance to random allocation that currently exists within much professional work with young people. As a consequence, our preferred option then became to recruit a comparison group from those applicants who were excluded from the programme because of over-subscription. However, given that the rate of over-subscription could not be predicted with any certainty we recognized that it might be necessary also to recruit from those that expressed an initial interest in the programme but who decided not to participate for *whatever* reason. Using these methods we estimated that we would be able to recruit a comparison group of between 160 and 200 young people. The comparison group was to be recruited at the same time as the main cohort and we envisaged that the young people in the comparison group would complete the questionnaire on two occasions: once during the recruitment process/at the beginning of the mentoring programme and again as part of the 12-month follow-up. There were a number of reasons why the comparison group was included in the 12-month follow-up but not the 18-month follow-up. *First*, and most important, the end of the programme was considered to be the most appropriate time to assess impact; *secondly*, while the study was well resourced, resources were limited and it was not feasible for three sets of interviews to be undertaken with individuals in the comparison group; and *thirdly*, it was anticipated that inclusion of the comparison group in the 18-month follow-up would not be cost-efficient given the likely level of attrition and associated relatively low response rate.

Attrition is a particular difficulty in longitudinal research; that is, loss of contact with respondents as the study progresses. We felt that this was going to be especially acute for our evaluation as the samples were made up of 'at risk' young people who, in our experience of similar research, are not easy to stay in contact with and locate (see for example, Hagell and Newburn 1994). In order to minimize the degree of attrition, incentives – in the form of £10 vouchers – were given to the young people who completed a follow-up questionnaire.

While the survey provides the basis for a robust assessment of outcomes, depth interviews and observation played a crucial role in illuminating the processes through which mentoring might work. Our plan was that a minimum of two members of staff would be interviewed in each of the 10 programmes included in the evaluation, that between 20 and 30 interviews would be conducted with representatives from referral agencies and that approximately 40 mentors and 40 mentees would be interviewed across the 10 programmes. Our aim was to conduct interviews with 'pairs' of mentors and mentees – that is, with the mentor and the young person he or she was mentoring – who would be selected to represent the groups on key dimensions such as sex, ethnicity and programme. In addition, we envisaged that the research team would observe key elements of the programme – the residential, training sessions, mentor support evenings and programme activities. While all the programmes were included in the basic evaluation, detailed case studies were conducted in four of them and these programmes provided the focus for the bulk of the qualitative work.

The surveys

Although the programmes provided some information about the young people, the survey had to cover a wide range of areas, including demographic characteristics, education, training and work, offending and contact with the criminal justice system, substance use, attitudes and lifestyle. Wherever possible we included questions from other surveys, partly because they were tried and tested and partly because they provided a basis for comparison with the general population. Much of our questionnaire was derived from the 1998/9 *Youth Lifestyles Survey (YLS)* although it also included three formal scales to measure self-esteem (Rosenberg 1965), locus of control (Robinson *et al.* 1991) and readiness to change (McConnaughy *et al.* 1983; Rollnick *et al.* 1992).[2] The questionnaire that was developed for the first phase of the survey provided the basis for those that were used in subsequent phases and all these questionnaires were designed as self-completion forms (that is, they were to be completed directly by the respondents themselves).

As we have said, drawing on existing questionnaires has the advantage that comparisons can be made with other data sets. This consideration was particularly important in relation to the *YLS* which, as a nationally representative survey of nearly 5,000 young people (Stratford and Roth 1999), provides a robust benchmark against which we could compare the Mentoring Plus cohort. Some caution is required in making such comparisons as there are notable differences between the surveys. First, there is the question of timing, as interviews for the *YLS* were carried out between October 1998 and January 1999 while the first Mentoring Plus survey was administered from September 2000 to February 2002. Secondly, there is the question of administration. While the Mentoring Plus survey took the form of a pen-and-paper survey the *YLS* was administered via Computer Assisted Personal Interviewing which has been shown to be particularly well suited to asking questions about sensitive issues (Flood-Page *et al.* 2000). Finally, there are differences in coverage, for while the *YLS* was administered across the whole of England and Wales and included young people aged 12–30, our survey was limited to the ten areas in which the Mentoring Plus programmes were based and included young people age 12–19. In order to improve the comparability of the two surveys data from the *YLS* were weighted to reflect the age and sex profile of the Mentoring Plus cohort.[3] Even allowing for these differences, however, the *YLS* provides a useful basis for comparison and allows us to distinguish more clearly than we would otherwise be able to what it is that is distinctive about the lives of the young people involved in the Mentoring Plus programme.

The initial questionnaire was piloted by six of the programmes. Some important changes were made as a result of this process: the number of response categories was reduced as this was identified as a problem for some of the young people who participated in the pilot exercise. As well as providing useful feedback about the contents of the questionnaire this exercise confirmed that it was realistic to administer the survey through the programmes as part of the recruitment process. Though such detail may seem rather prosaic, in our experience research in this area is frequently met with scepticism at best, and downright hostility at worst. In particular, it is not uncommon to be told by practitioners that 'the young people won't want to participate', 'they certainly won't answer all these questions', 'you'll never get them to give up half an hour' and so on. Thus, in addition to checking that the questions were meaningful, it was vital for us to pilot the survey in order both to satisfy ourselves that it could be administered successfully and to demonstrate to others that this was a group of young people that we could work with successfully.

The fieldwork

The evaluation was originally designed around two waves of recruitment to the programmes but it quickly became apparent that this would not yield the numbers we had envisaged. Some programmes were postponed or cancelled, some recruited fewer young people than expected and some staff were unclear about the procedures for including young people in the evaluation. Consequently, the study was extended by six months which allowed us to include a third wave of recruitment and the process of data collection was clarified with the programme staff.[4]

In total, 378 young people were recruited to the cohort group and 172 were recruited to the comparison group. These figures compared well with our original estimates of 320–400 and 160–200 respectively. The comparison group was made up primarily of young people who expressed an interest in the Mentoring Plus programme but did not, for whatever reason, go on to participate in it. In a small number of cases all applicants were included on the programme and project workers recruited members of the comparison group via visits to the schools, youth clubs and YOTs with which they worked (32 young people were recruited to the comparison group in this way). Although the numbers recruited into the cohort and comparison groups provided a solid foundation for the evaluation, we had to take account of the closure of three projects during the lifetime of the evaluation.

The follow-up questionnaires were designed to measure change in relation to a variety of key areas – including employment, education, offending behaviour, substance use, self-esteem, locus of control and readiness to change – and to explore the young people's attitudes to mentoring and Mentoring Plus. We maintained contact with the young people by sending them a 'season's greetings' card in December 2001 and, in order to administer the follow-up questionnaires, the team attended project graduation evenings, organized specific sessions at the projects, sent flyers to the young people, telephoned the young people and made appointments with them outside the project. In a small number of cases questionnaires were administered by the mentors and a few young people asked us to send them a questionnaire which they completed and returned by post. The numbers of young people who participated in the follow-up surveys are shown in Figure 4.1.

The 18-month follow-up concentrated on those members of the cohort who had responded to the 12-month follow-up and successfully included more than half these young people (54 per cent). However, some young people who had not responded to the 12-month follow-up attended meetings for the 18-month follow-up and were included in the survey. The response rate for the second follow-up shown in Figure 4.1 is a slight

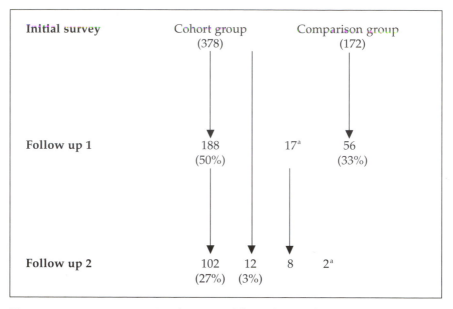

Initial survey	Cohort group (378)		Comparison group (172)
Follow up 1	188 (50%)	17[a]	56 (33%)
Follow up 2	102 (27%) 12 (3%)	8	2[a]

Note: a = no responses previously received from these individuals.

Figure 4.1   Response to the surveys

underestimate as a small number of cases could not be included due to slippage in the programmes.[5]

As predicted, attrition rates were fairly high. However, there is good reason to consider that non-response was fairly random which would mean that the sample remained broadly representative of the wider group. The main difficulty we faced in following up the young people was making contact, as the details we had for many of them were often out of date by the time of the follow-up. Once contact had been made very few young people refused to participate in the survey although a small number did fail to keep appointments.

The majority of programmes were reasonably well represented in the follow-up surveys although there was some variation. The follow-up rate for the second survey stood at between 44 and 53 per cent for all but one of the programmes, for which it stood at 72 per cent. For the third survey the follow-up rate stood at between 23 per cent and 29 per cent for three programmes, 30 per cent and 38 per cent for four programmes and 57 per cent and 64 per cent for two programmes (for one of the programmes none of the participants were successfully included in the second follow-up). More importantly, perhaps, there was less variation according to how well the programmes had been implemented[6]: for the second survey the follow-up rate stood at 49 per cent for those programmes which were judged to have a high degree of integrity, 55 per cent for those with a moderate level of integrity, 48 per cent of those that were considered to be problematic and 46 per cent for those that were judged to be in crisis; for the third survey the figures were 34 per cent, 35 per cent, 29 per cent and 15 per cent respectively.

Across the ten projects the follow-up rate varied quite markedly according to the degree to which young people had engaged in the programme (see Table 4.2).[7] Those who engaged most actively in the programme were also the most likely to have been successfully followed up. Although this is a form of 'bias' it actually helps to mitigate the implications of the fairly high levels of attrition. We may suppose that the impact of a programme is likely to be at its greatest among those who have been most actively involved. Thus, the high follow-up rate for those who were most actively engaged in Mentoring Plus means we can be reasonably confident about assessing impact in relation to these young people. Moreover, as we have information about level of engagement for *all* the young people in the cohort[8] we can generate robust estimates of overall impact by weighting the data.[9] Finally, in assessing impact the 'not engaged' category was combined with the comparison group as the young people in this category had not attended the programme and had not met with a mentor.

Table 4.2 Follow-up rate by level of engagement with Mentoring Plus

	Follow-up rate 1 (%)	Follow-up rate 2 (%)	n
Non-engaged	27	17	48
Minimally engaged	33	20	105
Moderately engaged	59	31	99
Actively engaged	71	54	97

In addition to the surveys, depth interviews were conducted with over 100 individuals involved in the programmes – including project workers, mentors and young people – and observations were carried out at almost 150 project sessions and events (see Table 4.3 for details). Of the young people who were interviewed as part of this element of the study, 12 were interviewed on two separate occasions as it was felt this would provide the basis for more detailed insights than one-off interviews.[10] Interviews and observations were spread across the 10 programmes although they were concentrated in the case study projects.

Table 4.3 Fieldwork carried out across the Mentoring Plus programmes

Observations	Type of session	No. of sessions observed
Mentees		
Recruitment	Induction/information session	2
Education/training	Education/numeracy classes	10
	Other workshops (drugs and crime, identity, etc.)	17
Entertainment	Activities (sports, games, video nights, etc.)	4
Residential	Pre-residential meeting	1
Mentors		
Recruitment	Information session	5
Training	Compulsory mentor training days	15
	Other (basic skills, etc.)	5
Residential	Pre-residential meeting	2
Support	Mentor support evening	22
Joint activities	Pre-residential meeting	7
	Residential	9
	Mentor–mentee matching meeting	13
	Entertainment	7
	Education/training	2
Other	Managers/mentor co-ordinator meetings	12
	Project staff meeting	5
	Parents' evening	4
	Exhibition	1
	Visit to local YOT	1
	Steering group meeting	1
Total		**145**

Interviews	Type of respondent	No.
	Project workers	25
	Mentors	40
	Mentees (+ follow-up interviews)	36 (+12)
	Referrers	20
Total		**133**

Considerable thought was given to the way in which mentors and mentees were selected for the depth interviews. Twelve 'pairs' of mentors and mentees were interviewed (separately) and a series of guidelines were developed to ensure that the sample reflected a range of issues which might be influential in determining the nature of the mentoring relationship. Pairings where male mentors were matched with male mentees, where female mentors were matched with female mentees and where female mentors were matched with male mentees[11] were included in this component of the study and relationships where the partners shared a common ethnic heritage and where they did not were also included. Profiles of the mentors and young people who were interviewed are provided in Table 4.4.

Table 4.4 Profile of qualitative sample – mentors and mentees (no.)

Individual characteristics			
Mentors		Mentees	
Sex		Sex	
Males	14	Males	22
Females	26	Females	14
Age		Age	
20–29	13	12–14	5
30–39	14	15–16	20
40+	12	17+	11
DK	1	DK	–
Ethnicity		Ethnicity	
White	21	White	16
Black and minority ethnic	19	Black and minority ethnic	20

Conclusion

As we outlined in some detail mentoring, like so many interventions with disaffected young people, has gathered considerable momentum without there being especially convincing evidence as to its efficacy. For any number of reasons this is an approach that is intuitively attractive. The idea that a friendly and responsible adult, mature and yet possibly still relatively young, might take a disaffected young person 'under their wing', providing advice, wise counsel and support, is something which there is good reason to suppose will be beneficial. There is ample evidence that many young people, often the most disaffected, lack forms of social support from which the majority benefit (Hagell and Newburn 1994). Moreover, our culture (and quite often our personal biographies too) contains powerful examples of the positive influence that a role model can have on callow youth. That mentoring should have flourished in recent times, and have gained considerable political support, is perhaps not so surprising therefore. However, there are dangers in this sudden flowering of popularity. In particular, mentoring has developed and spread without any solid research foundation. It is, in short, unproven. Under such circumstances, one danger is that it will be 'talked up' in ways, and with supposed outcomes, that it can never hope to achieve. In the longer term this will almost inevitably lead to a sense of disappointment among policy-makers, with consequent withdrawal of funding as the search begins elsewhere for the next 'silver bullet'. Under these circumstances there is a real danger that mentoring will become unfashionable in almost the same way that it first became fashionable. The greater danger of the spread of unevaluated mentoring programmes is that, far from having a positive outcome, it is always possible – until proven otherwise – that the intervention does more harm than good. Such programmes, after all, are intervening in the lives of already highly disadvantaged young people. Moreover, much of the intervention relies upon the skills and attributes of volunteer, largely untrained, members of the public. Under such circumstances, the potential for harm should not be ignored.

What is undeniable therefore, as Sherman and colleagues noted some years ago, is that rigorous evaluation of such programmes is required urgently. It was to this end that the study that forms the core of this book was designed and conducted. As we reported above, our initial ambition was to use random allocation as a means of maximizing the robustness of the measurement of outcomes. However, we were unable to do this and, consequently, opted for the best option available which was to include a sizeable comparison group within the study. Though not our ideal, we nevertheless regard this as a comparatively rigorous method of checking the strength of our outcome measures and, in particular, consider this research to be significantly more methodologically robust than any research previously carried out in this area in the UK.

Notes

1 For a lengthier discussion of this notion, see Marx (1995).
2 To measure self-esteem Rosenberg's (1965) scale was included in the questionnaire. To measure locus of control the abbreviated version of the Nowicki–Strickland Internal-External Control Scale for young people (grades 7–12) was used. Items which referred to parents and life at home were dropped, however, on the advice from Mentoring Plus/Crime Concern (it was felt that these areas would be particularly sensitive for the young people involved in the programme). This scale was, moreover, slightly reworded to reflect the age of the respondents (e.g. the term 'kids' was replaced with young people). Existing Readiness to Change scales – most of which relate to tobacco and alcohol consumption – were used as a basis from which to develop a generic scale. We are grateful to the Psychology Department at Goldsmiths College and to Professor Nick Emler (Surrey University) for their help and guidance regarding the use of psychological scales.
3 This was done by adapting the weights provided with the *YLS*.
4 The survey was discussed with managers and staff during visits to the programmes and at a specially convened one-day event which was dedicated to the evaluation.
5 Three projects experienced some delay in the implementation of the final programme included in the evaluation: consequently, by the end of the fieldwork period, 18 months had not passed since the start of these programmes. If we exclude the young people involved in these programmes from the calculation we have an adjusted cohort-response-rate for the 18-month follow-up of 34 per cent, with 30 per cent having responded to both follow-ups.
6 Programme integrity was assessed as being high, moderate, problematic or in crisis. For more on how this classification was developed, see Chapter 5.
7 Young people were classified as non-engaged if they did not attend the project and did not meet their mentor, as minimally engaged if they had attended the project and/or met their mentor rarely or infrequently (i.e. every couple of months or less), as moderately engaged if they had attended the project or met their mentor frequently/very frequently (i.e. monthly or more often) and as actively engaged if they had attended the project and met their mentor frequently/very frequently (i.e. monthly or more often).
8 Information about levels of engagement was provided by the projects.
9 The term weighting refers to a process of adjustment whereby more weight is given to cases with certain characteristics than others. In this way the balance of a sample may be altered to reflect more accurately the population from which it is drawn. Thus, through weighting, we can ensure that respondents to the follow-up surveys reflect the levels of engagement that are evident in the overall sample.

10 We had hoped to carry out repeat interviews with 20 young people but, because of difficulties contacting the young people and refusals, this proved not to be possible.

11 As a matter of policy Mentoring Plus does not match male mentors with female mentees.

Chapter 5

Mentoring Plus

Introduction

Having examined the nature of youthful exclusion, and the existing research evidence on mentoring, we begin, in this chapter, to focus specifically on Mentoring Plus. While serving as an introduction to Mentoring Plus, this chapter also raises a number of substantive issues which help to illuminate the mentoring process. Consideration is given to the structure and content of the programme, the social and demographic backgrounds of the mentors and the mentees, patterns of recruitment on to the programme and participants' reasons for becoming involved.

Mentoring Plus

The mentoring projects included in this study were run by Crime Concern and Breaking Barriers[1] and were modelled upon the widely acclaimed, and award-winning, Dalston Youth Project (DYP). Established in 1994 by Crime Concern, DYP was one of the first formal mentoring projects in the UK and is widely considered to have been a successful and pioneering project. It targeted disaffected young people and sought to build their basic education, employment skills and confidence through a one-to-one mentoring relationship with an adult volunteer drawn from the local community and a structured education and careers programme. Within two years DYP was identified by the Audit Commission as an example of good practice (Audit Commission 1996) and a period of expansion followed as Crime Concern established a series of new projects, known as Mentoring Plus, based on the DYP model. By 2000, projects had been established in eight London boroughs, Manchester, and Bath and northeast Somerset.[2] These projects aimed to reduce youth crime and other at-risk behaviour, help at-risk young people back into education, training and employment, and enable community members to get involved in solving community problems through volunteering.

All ten projects shared a similar structure (see Figure 5.1; also Benioff 1997). Steering committees, comprizing representatives from local agencies with an interest in combating disaffection and reducing crime (e.g. Social Services, Education Welfare, police, probation, Local Regeneration Programmes and Training and Enterprise Councils), played a key role in monitoring the projects and supporting their development. Each project was linked to Crime Concern by a consultant who was responsible for strategic and thematic-based support which covered issues such as funding, staff employment, training and support, policy decisions and changes to programme content/structure. The core staff team was typically made up of four distinct posts – Project Manager, Education Co-ordinator, Mentor Co-ordinator and Administrator – although, in practice, the roles of Education Co-ordinator and Mentor Co-ordinator were sometimes combined.[3] In many of the projects youth workers were employed on a sessional basis to deliver and support components of the education programme.

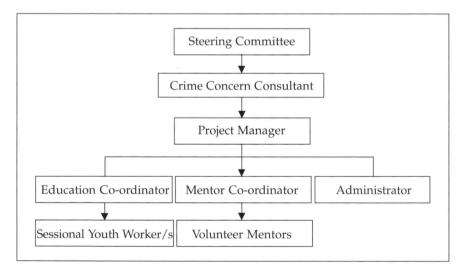

Figure 5.1 Organizational structure of Mentoring Plus

Seventy-five members of staff were employed across the 10 Mentoring Plus projects during the period covered by the study. The programme included a particular focus on black and minority ethnic communities, particularly those of black African/Caribbean heritage (Crime Concern undated b), and this was reflected in the composition of the staff teams. Slightly more than half (54 per cent) of those employed by the projects were black African/Caribbean; just over a third (37 per cent) were white; less that one in ten (8 per cent) were mixed race and the remaining 1 per cent were Asian.

The projects recruit young people (aged between 15 and 19 years) twice a year on to cycles spaced six months apart, usually in the autumn and then again in the spring. They provide a mentoring service alongside an education/training component and this 'Plus' element of the programme covers issues such as literacy, numeracy and basic life-skills (e.g. job search and interview skills). Each programme runs for 10 to 12 months and typically starts with a residential course.

Residential courses

Residentials last for three days and the aim is to build trust between young people and mentors through a mixture of physical outdoor activities and indoor sessions. Outdoor activities are designed to help establish relationships and co-operation while indoor sessions aim to enable young people to develop positive, achievable goals for the coming year. At the end of the residential young people are matched with volunteer mentors.

One-to-one mentoring

Following the matching, the young people and mentors are expected to meet once a week for the duration of the programme. The aim is to provide positive and supportive role-models to young people who have previously experienced very difficult relationships with adults. Mentors are trained to help young people work towards their new personal objectives and may also act as 'outreach workers' linking individuals with local services that they would otherwise fail to access.

An education/training programme

This part of the programme aims to provide the young people with the complementary practical life-skills and educational/training opportunities needed to support their new personal goals. The education component concentrates on improving the young people's interpersonal and presentation skills, literacy and numeracy, and personal motivation and effectiveness. Classes are designed and led by both in-house project staff and in partnership with existing local providers. Young people have the option of receiving accreditation for their work. During the period covered by the evaluation most projects ran at least one education/ training session a week although some ran up to three such sessions a week.

Each new cycle starts with a recruitment drive for mentors and young people. Young people are recruited on to the project in several ways, the most common being referral from statutory and community agencies and, less frequently, through outreach work in local communities and youth clubs or via friends and or family members. Once referred, each young person is subject to an interview and selection process and, if accepted, attends an induction session where he or she learns more about Mentoring Plus, mentoring, the education sessions and the commitment required by him or her. Participation in the project is voluntary. Young people are free to decline to become involved and, similarly, the projects may reject referrals they deem to be inappropriate although this rarely occurs in practice.[4]

Mentoring Plus has a structured process of recruiting mentors primarily through advertising in local, national and specialist (*The Voice, New Nation, The Big Issue*) newspapers, though the Mentor Co-ordinator responsible for the recruitment is free to employ other methods. Application forms are distributed to those volunteers who have expressed an interest in becoming a mentor, and they are invited to an introductory session to learn more about the project and to meet existing mentors. The introductory session is followed by a police search and an extensive training pro- gramme prior to the residential.

Until the residential, or at least until the pre-residential evenings, the young people and volunteers follow separate pathways into mentoring. The residential presents a pivotal point in the Mentoring Plus experience for both groups (see Figure 5.2). Henceforth they will start the process of familiarisation and begin working with each other to facilitate the mentoring component of the programme. Matching young people with a volunteer marks the beginning of the mentoring process which, it is intended, will continue throughout the following year or so. In addition to mentoring, the young people are encouraged to take part in other programme activities such as educational workshops, project group nights and social events which involve considerable input and support from project staff. Similarly, volunteer mentors are offered support – in the form of one-to-one and group sessions – from the Mentor Co-ordinator which is then supplemented by additional training.

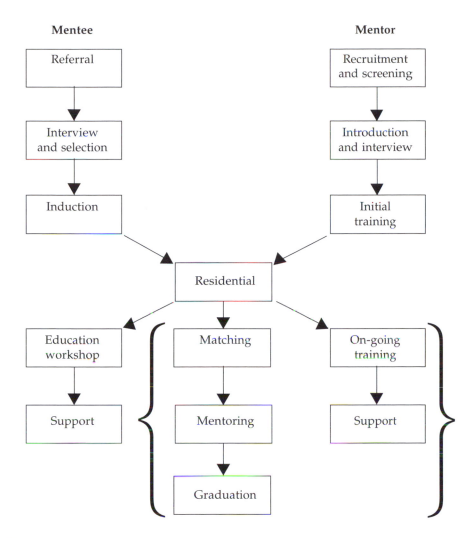

Figure 5.2   Programme structure

As each cycle of the programme approaches completion, the projects co-ordinate an 'ending session' for mentors which is designed to help them develop strategies for ending the relationship with their mentee and to discuss any future relationship they may have with them.[5] This session provides a platform for mentors to discuss any reservations they may have about ending their relationships and to receive guidance on how to terminate them successfully. The completion of the programme is marked by a graduation ceremony, which serves to recognise the achievements of both mentors and mentees and formally to end the programme for a particular cycle.

The mentors

Despite their obvious importance in the mentoring process, mentors have been given a rather cursory treatment in much of the research-based literature. In the search for evidence of success, research has focused largely on the experiences of those being mentored and on any changes that they may make as a result of the mentoring process (Freedman 1993; Utting 1996; Gilligan 1999; Skinner and Flemming 1999; Tierney *et al.* 2000). Mentors have generally been treated as minor members of the supporting cast, rather than as central actors, with the result that little is known about them and their motivations (Philip and Hendry 2000). This, it seems to us, is an important gap as mentors' characteristics and motivations raise important issues which go to the very heart of the mentoring process.

Mentoring, as we have already seen, fits comfortably with New Labour thinking and is often presented in terms of civic renewal and community responsibility. Thus, for example, Mentoring Plus aims to 'enable the community to get involved in solving community problems, through volunteering' (Benioff 1997: 8). This community discourse inevitably raises questions of affinity and belonging, which have been framed in terms of inclusion and diversity. Speaking at the Active Community Convention in March 2000, the Prime Minister, Tony Blair, issued a 'diversity challenge' to the voluntary sector: 'Everyone in this country has something to contribute,' he declared, 'but too many voluntary organisations have volunteers that all come from the same background, and their recruitment drives target the same group again.' Among the organisations to have responded to this challenge, the National Centre for Volunteering has emphasised (www.diversitychallenge.org): 'The population is changing and organisations need to reflect people's increasing diversity to be relevant and effective. By recognizing and accommodating *difference, organisations can ensure they meet individual needs.* [emphasis in original].' Issues of affinity and belonging are, perhaps, felt particularly sharply in the context of Mentoring Plus because of its focus on disadvantaged young people and because of the philosophy that surrounds this type of intervention. Mentoring programmes typically place considerable emphasis on 'role models' and 'role modelling' and these concepts require a degree of identification between mentee and mentor, which may be influenced by characteristics such as age, sex, ethnicity and shared life experiences. It is, in this context, worth noting that Crime Concern (undated b) claims to have developed particular expertise in mentoring black African/Caribbean young people. Such a focus reflects the particular vulnerabilities of these communities to processes of exclusion and marginalization and the 'double disadvantage' that comes with being concentrated in deprived areas and facing particular forms of racial discrimination (Cabinet Office 2000).

As a matter of policy, Mentoring Plus does not match male mentors with female mentees. Its position on ethnic matching is less clear cut. On the one hand, it is noted that black mentors may be particularly valuable in working with young black people who have a negative perception of their ethnicity as they 'may help a young person to enhance his or her self-concept by providing a relevant, positive role model'. On the other hand, it is suggested that 'cross cultural' partnerships can help to promote the value of diversity and that the importance of 'cultural' matching depends – too some extent – on the aims of the intervention (Crime Concern undated b: 4). In seeking to strike a balance, Crime Concern recommends that ethnic matching should provide a point for negotiation between the project, the mentor and the mentee. Ethnic matching was clearly a live issue within the projects and this was most apparent from the emphasis that was placed on the particular needs of young black men:

> At this moment in time, in this project we get predominantly black young boys and in terms of identity, in terms of role models – I'm not saying it's a thing that always works – but in terms of identity, we would give them, or we would like to be saying, that a young person could be mentored by somebody they can definitely identify with straight away. So, yes, if we can match a black mentor to a young black mentee, we would think that's advisable. It's the same way that we'd look to match a female mentor with a female mentee. We think that's advisable. Especially, when in the black community we know that there is not enough black role models and we know that we need to address that … I am not going to say now that a white mentor wouldn't be as good (Mentoring Plus project worker).

There are, of course, a number of potential dangers associated with this position. According to Noguera (1996: 2), for example, explanations which focus on 'race' and 'gender' and ignore other influences, such as social class and geographic location, result in 'an explanation of the crisis facing Black males that focuses almost exclusively on cultural rather than structural factors'. As a result, he argues, such an approach risks stigmatizing and marginalizing those whom it seeks to help. Far from being ignored, however, structural factors provided a key element of the Mentoring Plus programme – hence the emphasis on education, training and work. In addition, research in other areas of social welfare provision has highlighted the role of black workers in ensuring the 'cultural competence' of the service and in meeting the needs of diverse communities (Sangster *et al.* 2002).

Who volunteers to become a mentor?

The emphasis that the projects placed on the need to recruit male and/or black mentors appeared to be at odds with the archetypal image of the volunteer as a 'white, middle-aged, middle-class, highly educated god-fearing woman, with a secure income' (Davis-Smith 1997). This image has been broadly upheld by empirical research although some fairly specific revisions have also been suggested. A recent national survey of voluntary behaviour in the UK indicated that males are just as likely as females to become volunteers although they are attracted to different forms of volunteering (Davis-Smith 1997). Females are more than three times as likely as males to be involved in volunteering connected with education, school, social welfare, the elderly and religion, while males are twice as likely as female to be involved in sports-related volunteering, the arts or politics. In keeping with the traditional image of the volunteer, this survey confirmed that volunteers are disproportionately recruited from among middle-aged, white professionals.

While the traditional image of volunteers has largely been upheld by research a couple of caveats and provisos are required. Claims have been made, for example, that individuals from working-class and black and minority ethnic backgrounds are more likely to be involved in informal volunteering (Leat 1983; Bhasin 1997). For black and minority groups, moreover, it has been suggested that such involvement reflects a history of self-help which is driven by the needs of the community that are largely unmet by mainstream organisations. It follows that individuals from these groups are unlikely to volunteer for such organisations and where they do, they tend to support organisations that tackle particular issues which reflect the needs of the community in which they live (Bhasin 1997).

The sociodemographic characteristics of the mentors involved in the programme were simultaneously similar to, and different from, the national profile for volunteers (see Table 5.1). As we would expect from the national profile, female mentors outnumbered male mentors by a ratio of two to one. Given the emphasis that was placed on recruiting black male mentors, it is worth noting that the ratio of males to females was almost

Table 5.1 Profile of mentors (per cent)

Sex	
Males	31
Females	69
	100
Age	
18–24	13
25–34	47
35–44	29
45–54	9
55+	3
	100
Ethnicity[1]	
White	44
Black African/Caribbean	47
Asian	4
Mixed race/dual heritage	4
Other	1
	100
Occupational status[2]	
Managers and senior officials	6
Professionals	14
Associate professionals and technical	21
Administrative and secretarial	13
Skilled trades	3
Personal service	9
Sales and customer service	6
Process, plant and machine operatives	1
Elementary occupations	4
Unemployed	11
Students	12
Other economically inactive	2
	100

Notes:

$n = 453$.

[1] Most of the mentors who were classified as white described themselves as white British. Overall, only 2 per cent of the mentors were classified as white Irish and only 3 per cent were classified as white European; 5 per cent were classified as white other. Most of those included in the African/Caribbean category were classified as black Caribbean (this category accounted for 20 per cent of all mentors) or black British (this category accounted for 18 per cent of all mentors). The categories black African and black other accounted for 9 per cent and 1 per cent respectively. None of the specific Asian categories accounted for more than 2 per cent of the mentors – Indian (2 per cent), Pakistani (1 per cent), Bangladeshi (less than 0.5 per cent) and Asian other (0.7 per cent). No detailed information was available for those classified as mixed race.

[2] This information is based on the Standard Occupational Classification 2000 (www.statistics.gov.uk).

Source: Mentoring Plus (project information).

identical for black African/Caribbeans and whites. Predictably, perhaps, given what is known about volunteering generally, a large proportion of the mentors held senior, professional or associate professional posts. Just over one in ten (13 per cent) of them reported having a criminal conviction, mainly for relatively minor offences such as shoplifting or traffic violations.

Marked differences in profile were evident in relation to age and ethnicity. While the peak age for volunteering nationally is 45–55 (Davis Smith 1997), the mentors in Mentoring Plus were somewhat younger than this. Their average age was 34 years and relatively few of them were older than 45 years. In general terms, black and minority ethnic groups were well represented within the programme, accounting for more than half the mentors. There were, however, notable differences between groups. Large numbers of black African/Caribbean mentors were recruited on to the programme, reflecting the particular emphasis that Crime Concern places on working with such communities (see above). Very few south Asian mentors were recruited, however, and this pattern could not wholly be explained in terms of the location of the programmes. While comprizing one third of the population in Newham[6], for example, south Asians only accounted for 7 per cent of the mentors in this area.

Why become a mentor?

Much of the literature on volunteering focuses on the motivations of the volunteers and, more particularly, the role of altruism. Several authors have challenged the idea that volunteering may be understood as an altruistic act, carried out for the good of others. Leat (1983) considers it naïve to think of volunteers as 'angelic humanitarians', arguing that volunteering provides a platform from which individuals can develop personally, progress in terms of their career and get involved with – and gain support from – the community. While altruism may be a necessary prerequisite for volunteering, she suggests, it does not provide its essence. A similar point is conveyed by Sheroff's (1983) distinction between normative and instrumental motivations. Normative or moral motivations are those that encompass the desire to do something, the right thing, or what is good and proper, while instrumental motivations are those that derive from a deliberate strategy; from this perspective, volunteering is seen as a means to an end, such as employment. The validity of instrumental motivations has become widely acknowledged and is reflected in the emphasis that is often placed on the role of reciprocity within volunteering. A recent report to the Parliamentary Hearing for the International Year of Volunteers (2001), for example, considered that the benefits accrued to the volunteer form a legitimate part of volunteering and community involvement.

The mentors in Mentoring Plus revealed a variety of motives for their involvement in the programme, which could be divided broadly into those that were instrumental and those that were normative (see Figure 5.3). Although the distinction between these different types of motivation is analytically useful, it is important to recognise that they are not mutually exclusive and are often intertwined. One of the main motivating factors for becoming a mentor was the opportunity Mentoring Plus provided for individuals to learn new skills, qualifications and gain experience of working with young people. This set of motivations was often framed in terms of future career prospects: 'I might want to pursue a career in working with young people, I thought that it would have been a good way to start … that's why I chose this' (mentor). From this perspective, the voluntary nature of the role was considered to be an advantage because it provided people with a platform from which they could enhance their career prospects without having to give up the security of their current position:

> I was always working with adults and I wanted a taste of working with teenagers. But I didn't want to leave my job just in case I hated it. So I thought if I could do it on a voluntary basis I can be working with teenagers, working with offenders, ex-offenders and that way I could do both. Kill two birds with one stone and still get paid (mentor).

Normative motivations included the desire to develop a better understanding of young people and the obstacles they faced. Some mentors expressed concerns that they were losing touch with young people, their lifestyles and what it meant to be young. While this set of motivations included an instrumental dimension (mentoring was seen as a way of developing a better understanding) it was also rooted in a desire to do the 'right thing':

> I just had to take a look at myself and I thought I could hear myself moaning, do what most people do, they always moan about young people on the bus on the way home from work … and I felt myself falling into that trap and I stopped and thought what are you doing? You swore that you was never gonna be like this! You were young once and that was how you acted! (mentor).

The mentors commonly talked about their concern for young people and the impact this had on their decision to become involved in the programme. Most emphasised the difficulties associated with the

Instrumental

Work experience and career progression:
- To enhance job prospects.
- To gain experience of working with young people.

Substitute for work:
- Unsatisfied in current job.
- Frustrated at work.
- Wanted reprieve from work.
- Wanted to work in area that made a difference.

Personal development or family circumstances:
- To be involved in an activity that would make them a better person.
- To gain insights into young people that would help them to raise their own children.
- To compensate for own negative experiences of family life as young person.
- To do something rewarding, challenging and more personal.
- To do something else in life besides going out and having fun.

Enhancement of social life:
- To fill spare time.
- To meet others as spend most of time alone.

Normative/moral

Societal concern or contribution:
- To get to know culture and society in local area.
- To do something or give something back to the community.
- To have impact on crime in local community.

Concern for young people:
- To learn about young people and lifestyle.
- To help and understand young people.
- To help delinquent young people.
- To work with black and minority ethnic young people, especially young black men.
- To compensate for not being able to foster a young person.

Sense of duty:
- To help people less fortunate.
- To provide people with a listening ear.
- To make a contribution to the disadvantaged.
- Had a mentor when they were young and wanted to continue tradition.

Figure 5.3   Mentors' motivations for volunteering

transition through the teenage years and spoke of wanting to help young people in their journey through this turbulent time by listening to or supporting them. The particular difficulties that some young people faced because of cultural, racial, physical, sex and class differences formed an important part of such avowed motivations. Once again, the need for positive black (male) role models to combat negative stereotypes was an important feature of the way in which people talked about the programme:

> I wanted to go to the heart, so to speak, into the heart of trying to do something positive and it said about role models … I often hear negative things about black men. I'm a black man and if they say black men then that doesn't exclude me that puts me right in it. So that was the real reason the depth of why I went into mentoring and why I felt I had something to offer (mentor).

The young people

The design of Mentoring Plus assumes that disadvantaged young people, who are at risk in some way, can be actively engaged in a programme which aims to bring about 'positive' changes in their lives. While the realism of this assumption is open to question, it can be assessed in a variety of ways. We begin by considering the demographic characteristics of the young people who were recruited on to the programme and the reasons that they gave for joining.

Who joins a mentoring programme?

The demographic characteristics of the young people recruited to Mentoring Plus are shown in Table 5.2. At the time of joining the programme the vast majority of the young people were 15 or 16 years old. Males outnumbered females by about two to one and most of the young people were from black and minority ethnic groups, although whites made up approximately two fifths of the cohort. Most of the black and minority ethnic young people recruited to the programme were from black African/Caribbean or mixed-race backgrounds, reflecting the claims of the programme to have developed specific expertise in working with these groups. Very few Asian young people were recruited on to the programme: only one of the projects recruited any young people from these communities, and even here the proportion recruited was low compared with their demographic representation in the local borough.

Table 5.2 Demographic characterisics of the young people (per cent of the cohort)

Age	
12–14	17
15	44
16	25
17–19	13
	100
Sex	
Male	68
Female	32
	100
Ethnicity[1]	
White	43
Black African/Caribbean	41
Asian	2
Mixed 'race'/dual heritage	14
	100

Notes:

$n = 373$.

[1]Most of the young people who were classified as white described themselves as white British. Overall, only 3 per cent were classified as white Irish, only 1 per cent were classified as white European and only 1 per cent were classified as white other. Most of those included in the black African/Caribbean category were classified as black Caribbean (this category accounted for 18 per cent of the young people) or black British (this category accounted for 13 per cent of the young people). The categories black African and black other accounted for 9 per cent and 2 per cent respectively. None of the specific Asian categories accounted for more than 1 per cent of the young people – Indian (0.5 per cent), Bangladeshi (1 per cent) and Asian other (0.5 per cent). There were no Pakistani young people on the programme. Although an attempt was made to collect detailed information about those in the mixed race category, it proved to be unsuccessful.

Source: Mentoring Plus cohort (first survey).

Comparing the demographic profiles of the mentees and mentors highlighted some potentially important features of the mentoring process. The ethnic profiles of the two groups were remarkably similar. Whites and black African/Caribbeans each accounted for approximately two fifths of the mentors and the mentees, while very few Asians were included in either group. Based on these figures it would seem that the projects could realistically have pursued a policy of ethnic matching if they had so chosen. The one group for whom this does not appear to have been a viable option, however, was mixed-race mentees as there were many more mentees than mentors in this ethnic category. Nor does the prospect of strictly matching same-sex pairs appear to have been a viable option as the profiles of the mentors and mentees were diametrically opposed to one another. While slightly more than two in three mentors were female, a similar proportion of mentees were male.

Why join a mentoring programme?

Young people are primarily recruited on to the Mentoring Plus programme through a formal referral process. While the projects do advertise their services using posters and leaflets, the early experience of DYP indicated that disaffected young people tend not to read publicity materials placed in 'mainstream' locations (Benioff 1997). It was found to be much more productive to have a social worker or teacher speak to the young person about the programme and refer him or her directly. As a result, recruitment drives tend to concentrate on agencies that work with the types of young people that the programme wishes to attract. Two in three of the young people recruited on to the programme during the research were referred by Youth Offending Teams (YOTs), schools, educational welfare, specialist educational providers (including Pupil Referral Units) or Social Services (see Figure 5.4).

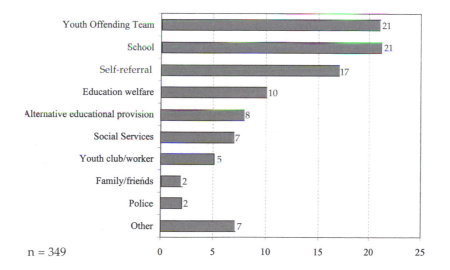

Figure 5.4   Route into Mentoring Plus (per cent of the cohort)
Source: Mentoring Plus cohort (project information).

The referrers we interviewed tended to feel that the young people they referred to Mentoring Plus did not differ, in any obvious ways, from those they worked with generally. They did note, however, that referrals were made largely on the basis of the interests expressed by the young people and the accessibility of the programme to them. Moreover, the young people were described as being in need of constructive adult role models or advocates, and as needing to feel accepted, to be listened to and not preached to, to be respected and to be helped to move towards achieving certain goals. Within this context, Mentoring Plus was seen as providing a useful service as there was generally considered to be a shortage of appropriate places for the young people to go to.

While most of the mentees were formally referred to the programme by another agency, a sizeable proportion referred themselves. The importance of informal processes was confirmed by the way in which the young people had heard about Mentoring Plus. In response to the first survey, more than one in four (27 per cent) mentees indicated that they had heard about the programme from friends and more than one in ten (13 per cent) indicated that they had heard about it from a family member. The importance of 'word of mouth' was also highlighted by the depth interviews:

> My friend used to attend mentoring; she said to me that they was looking for more people, and so she put my name down and I come here for the induction day … because my friend thought that it might help me, because she knew what I was like (young person).

The way in which the young people talked about the programme revealed two distinct, and potentially competing, sets of motivations. Many of them described Mentoring Plus in ways which invoked the image of a traditional 'youth club' and they saw the project as providing a place to have fun and to 'chill out'. This emphasis was particularly marked in relation to the residential, which was often talked about as a 'holiday' and was clearly an important incentive for many of those who joined:

> I just come along because it is a weekend away, so I thought that I might as well, but I didn't actually know about you getting yourself a mentor and everything – I just thought that it was an activity weekend kind of thing (young person).

Alongside this theme, however, it was generally recognised that Mentoring Plus offered more than opportunities for recreation. While some of the young people were attracted by the prospect of the one-to-one confidential relationship, and expected to be 'sitting down and having a chat with someone', many were motivated by the desire to change some aspect of their lives:

> If you come here they can put you on little courses and stuff, things to do instead of getting into trouble. So I started coming ... Because I thought like going on the way that I'm going on I'm going to go in prison soon, so I thought I don't want to go down that route, I've got to sort myself out ... I just thought that [Mentoring Plus] was going to be about like, a place to chill out and people to talk to, people to help out with problems and keep you off the streets (young person).

A similar pattern was evident from the first survey. On the one hand a sizeable proportion of the young people indicated that escaping boredom had been a factor in their decision to join Mentoring Plus and this confirmed the importance of general entertainment-based activities (see Figure 5.5). On the other hand, specific goal-oriented objectives were also an important source of motivation and considerable congruence was evident between the aims of the programme and the young people's reasons for joining: the desire to stop getting into trouble and gaining access to employment and/or training were key motivational factors, while the desire to get back into school/college and to improve relationships were also significant for a sizeable minority of participants.

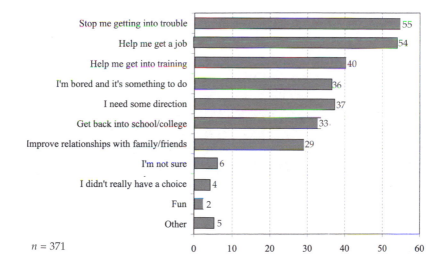

Figure 5.5   Reasons for joining Mentoring Plus (per cent of the cohort)
Source: Mentoring Plus Cohort (first survey).

Conclusion

Mentoring Plus fits comfortably with much of the recent discourse about mentoring. It may, for example, be interpreted as an attempt to promote civic responsibility by encouraging 'the community' to get involved in solving its own problems. While politically appealing, such a discourse raises important – and elusive – notions of affinity and belonging. Mentoring Plus consciously targets disaffected young people through agencies which work with some of the most challenging and challenged of the nation's youth. And the question arises, with whom are these young people likely to feel a sufficient sense of affinity to be able to strike up a meaningful mentoring relationship? There are, we would suggest, various points of potential affinity which may make such relationships possible (Shiner and Newburn 1996; Shiner 2000). Demographic affinity may emerge from shared characteristics such as age, ethnicity and sex; motivational affinity may emerge from a shared sense of purpose; and experiential affinity may emerge from shared experiences. The emergence of affinity is likely to be a complex process, however, which can play out in a number of different ways. Demographic affinity may be a necessary, but insufficient, condition for producing positive relationships between mentors and mentees. Alternatively, successful relationships may be established where there are no obvious points of demographic affinity, possibly because of the over-riding influence of motivational or experiential affinity.

The characteristics and motivations of the mentors and mentees suggest a number of potential points of affinity. There were, for example, marked similarities in their ethnic profile and a desire among the mentees to make positive changes was matched by a desire among the mentors to help them do so. At the same time, notable differences were apparent, which may result in dynamics that threaten to undermine the relationship between mentor and mentee. Most of the mentees were male, for example, while most of the mentors were female. And many of the mentees appeared to be at considerable risk of social exclusion (the extent to which this was the case provides the focus of the next chapter), while many of the mentors were employed in high-status occupations. The potential tensions associated with this asymmetry are evident in Gilroy's (1990: 117) claim that:

> Class relations are changing profoundly and new antagonisms are being created in urban areas between a pauperized, permanently workless layer and the young urban cadres of the professional and managerial class who are colonizing the inner city as gentrifiers. The

fear of crime speaks above all to the anxieties of this latter group. It offers a spurious means to connect their experiences of vulnerability and victimage to the lifeworld of other inner-city residents with whom they have absolutely nothing in common.

The extent to which such tensions were evident on the programme, and the degree to which they were overcome, will be something to which we will return in later chapters.

Notes

1 Crime Concern is an independent national crime reduction charity which was set up in 1988 with the help of the Home Office. Breaking Barriers was a regeneration initiative run by Crime Concern from 1998 to 2003 in the London boroughs of Camden, Islington, Hackney and Islington (http://www.crime.concern.org.uk).
2 The eight London boroughs were Bexley, Brent, Camden, Hackney, Islington, Lewisham, Lambeth and Newham.
3 The Project Manager was responsible for local fund raising and day-to-day management of the project. The Education Co-ordinator was primarily responsible for recruiting the young people, for implementing a range of social and educational activities and monitoring contact between the young people and their mentor. The Mentor Co-ordinator was primarily responsible for recruiting, training, supervizing and supporting the mentors. The Administrator was primarily responsible for managing the office.
4 Referrals may be considered inappropriate if the young person falls outside the age range on which the projects focus (i.e. 15–19 years old); if the young person has issues which the project feels unable to deal with (e.g. serious mental health issues); or if he or she is judged to be a threat to other people in the project.
5 In some cases the mentor and mentee may decide to continue the relationship on an informal basis by meeting less frequently or continuing telephone contact.
6 This figure was taken from population projections for 2001
   (see http://www.newham.gov.uk/Statisticsprofile/population.htm).

Chapter 6

Mentoring Plus and youthful exclusion

Introduction

Most of the young people recruited on to the Mentoring Plus programme had recently left school or were in the final few years of their compulsory education and faced important decisions about their future. The programme was designed to ease the transition into early adulthood and one of its key aims was to help at-risk young people (back) into education, training and employment. This focus, and indeed this language, reflects the now well established empirical evidence which suggests that there are a number of readily identifiable 'risk factors' in childhood and adolescence that heighten the likelihood of problems later in life. These include parental conflict and separation, early involvement in offending, drinking and drug use, and disruptive behaviour at school.

The prevalence of such risk factors among the young people recruited on to the Mentoring Plus programme provides the main focus of this chapter, alongside some consideration of attitudes and future orientations. This enables us to establish how successful the projects were in targeting 'at risk' young people and also allows us to start considering how appropriate the programme was to those who were recruited on to it. The findings from this chapter, we suggest, also provide important insights into the nature of youth disaffection more generally. Such a claim is not unproblematic, as the Mentoring Plus cohort does not provide a representative sample of a known population.[1] Given the obvious difficulties of establishing a representative sample of disaffected young people, however, the characteristics and experiences of specific popula- tions (such as the Mentoring Plus cohort) are an important source of information, particularly when set against the broader context provided by other research (for example, in Chapters 2 and 3).

Social exclusion?

A key question which we sought to address was the extent to which the young people's lives could be understood in terms of social exclusion. This concept provides a central plank of recent government thinking and is essentially concerned with the negative impact of multiple forms of disadvantage and deprivation. According to the Centre for Economic and Social Inclusion (2003), social exclusion may be defined as a process by which individuals and groups become isolated from mainstream economic, social and cultural life. Unemployment, poverty, low skill levels, lack of qualifications, poor housing, high-crime environments, bad health and family breakdown are all considered to put people at risk of social exclusion, while education, training and work are considered to offer the solution to this downward spiral (Centre for Economic and Social Inclusion 2003; Social Exclusion Unit 2003). The causes of social exclusion have been much debated and different schools of thought have emerged which variously emphasize the role of globalization, the state and its institutions, issues of discrimination and the role played by excluded individuals themselves. In considering these different perspectives, Hills *et al.* (2002) highlight the interplay between the following types of in- fluence: individual (e.g. age, gender, race, disability, preferences, beliefs and values), family (e.g. relationship breakdown and caring responsi- bilities), community (e.g. social and physical environment, schools, health and social services), the locality (e.g. labour market and transport), nation (e.g. cultural influences, social security and legislative framework) and globalization (e.g. international trade, migration and climate change).

While social inclusion implies a complex web of causal influences, our interest is restricted to the fairly straightforward idea that various forms of disadvantage are compounded and reinforced by one another. Following on from our discussion in the opening chapters we focus mainly on four specific areas: education, training and work; offending; substance use; and family relationships. Personality factors, such as self-esteem and locus of control, provide a secondary focus. In order to judge the position of the young people recruited on to the Mentoring programme, comparisons with the general population were required and the 1998/9 *Youth Lifestyles*

Survey (YLS) facilitated precisely this type of comparison (Stratford and Roth 1999). Based on a nationally representative sample of nearly 5,000 young people, the *YLS* covered many of the same issues as our questionnaires and provided a robust benchmark.[2]

Family background

Although conventionally considered a stabilizing influence and provider of emotional support, the family has been identified as a significant source of instability and distress for young disaffected people (Bentley and Gurumurthy 1999; BMRB 1999). The implications that this has for their future development have also been well established. During the mid-1970s, for example, the Cambridge Study of Delinquent Development reported that poor parenting was an important predictor of youthful delinquency (West and Farrington 1973, 1977). And this conclusion was broadly confirmed some 20 years later, when Graham and Bowling (1995) reported that family breakdown, poor family relationships and a lack of parental supervision were important predictors of youthful offending.

The difficult nature of family relationships formed an important theme in the interviews with the young people on the programme. Some of the young people we spoke to said they did not get on with, or even see, their parent(s); some said they had been 'kicked out' of the family home and/or described being passed from one relative to another; and others talked of being involved in arguments and physical confrontation with their (step) parent(s). An early indication of these difficulties was provided by project workers who expressed concerns about the content of the survey. In a questionnaire that covered such issues as drug use and offending, it was questions about family circumstances which were thought to be most sensitive. While clearly important, these sensitivities did not result in large-scale non-response, however, as the vast majority of the young people (more than 90 per cent) answered the questions about family circumstances and relationships.

The domestic circumstances in which the young people were living implied a strong degree of family disruption and breakdown (see Figure 6.1). Slightly over half were living in single-parent families (50 per cent were living with their mother and 4 per cent with their father) and this was, by some distance, the most common household structure within the cohort. As a point of comparison, the *YLS* indicated that this household type accounted for approximately one in five (19 per cent) similarly aged young people in the general population. In other words, the young people on the programme were almost three times as likely as those in the general

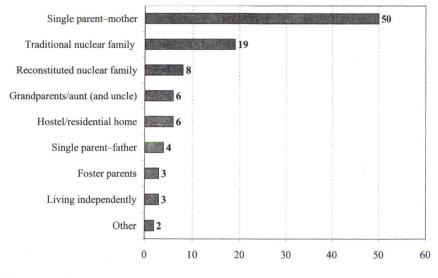

Note: *n* = 365.

Figure 6.1 Family/household structure (per cent of the cohort)[4]

Source: Mentoring Plus cohort.

population to be living in a single-parent family. A similar pattern was evident in relation to traditional nuclear families: while one in five (19 per cent) of the young people in the cohort were living with both biological parents, this was less than a third the rate found in the general population (65 per cent).[3] Some of the young people in the cohort were living in reconstituted nuclear families or with extended family members but, for others, the care networks associated with their biological family appeared to have broken down completely (6 per cent were living in residential homes or hostels and 3 per cent were living with foster parents).

Family dynamics within the cohort had particularly serious implications for the young people's relationships with their fathers. As many as two in five (40 per cent) of the young people appeared not to be in contact with their father, compared with one in thirty three (3 per cent) who appeared not to be in contact with their mother.[5] The absence of fathers was most apparent in relation to black African/Caribbean young people and mixed-race young people although the differences in this regard were not particularly marked (45 per cent of Black African/Caribbean young people and 46 per cent of mixed race young people were not in contact with their father and this compared with 34 per cent of white young people).[6] Family difficulties were also apparent in the quality of the young people's relationships with their parents. Overall, approximately one in six of the young people in the cohort indicated that they did not get on 'at all well' with either or both of their parents (17 per cent did not get on at all well with their mother and 15 per cent did not get on at all well with their father). In total, therefore, nearly three in five (55 per cent) of the young people in the cohort indicated that their relationship with their father was either non-existent or problematic and one in five (20 per cent) indicated that their relationship with their mother was either non-existent or problematic.

Engagement in education, training and work

There can be little doubt that the young people who joined the Mentoring Plus programme were a highly disaffected group. The particular difficulties they experienced in relation to education and work were, once again, put into sharp focus by comparisons with the *YLS* (Table 6.1). Two in five of the young people on the programme were disengaged from education, training and work and this was ten times the rate that was evident in the general population. More specifically, while the young people on the programme were more likely than those in the general population to be on a training scheme they were much less likely to be attending school, studying at college or university or to be working. They were, in addition, much more likely to have truanted from school on a regular basis and this was reflected in the relatively high proportion who reached the school-leaving age without any GCSEs.[7] The qualifications profile of the young people in the Mentoring Plus cohort suggests that many of those who went to college did so, initially at least, to compensate for their lack of GCSEs: hence the relatively large proportion with NVQ Foundation/Intermediate qualifications.

Within the cohort, levels of disengagement were most marked among those young people who had come to the end of their compulsory schooling. Almost three in five (57 per cent) of the 17–19-year-olds were disengaged from education, training and work, a much higher proportion than studies of young people in the general population, and indicating the very high level of disaffection within this group. Only modest variations were evident according to ethnicity and sex[8] (while, for example, 44 per cent of young white people were disengaged this compared with 36 per cent of black Africans/Caribbeans and 41 per cent of those who were 'mixed-race'.

The particular difficulties that the young people in the cohort experienced at school have far reaching implications. Compulsory education plays a crucial role in the transition into adulthood and negative

Table 6.1 Current status, orientation to school and qualifications (per cent)

	Mentoring Plus cohort	General youthful Population[1]
Current status[2]		
Attending school	46	74
Studying at college/university	8	13
On a training scheme	5	2
Working	1	7
Disengaged	40	4
	100	100
Truanting from school[3]		
Every week	34	5
Two or three days a month	18	1
Less often	17	14
Not at all	31	79
	100	100
Qualifications (17–19-year-olds only)[4]		
GCSE	47	82
NVQ Foundation/Intermediate	17	3
BTEC Certificate	2	4
City and Guilds	13	6
No qualifications	45	9

Notes

The 1998/9 YLS was adjusted to reflect the age and sex structure of the Mentoring Plus cohort.

1 Confidence intervals were produced for estimates based on the YLS and are shown in Table I.1 in Appendix I.

2 The 46 per cent of the Mentoring Plus cohort who were attending school included those who were attending a special education unit (10 per cent of the total cohort) and those who were truanting regularly (9% of the total cohort). The YLS did not distinguish special education units from schools and nor was it possible on the basis of the YLS to identify young people who were excluded from school or were truanting regularly. Young people in the Mentoring Plus cohort who were excluded from school were included in the disengaged category.

3 The figures given here relate to the cohort as a whole and include those who were in school at the time of the survey and those who had already left. Our question about truanting was not strictly comparable with the question used in the YLS. We asked about truanting during the last year or the last year that the young person attended school while the YLS asked about truanting in relation to 'secondary school'.

4 The percentages given here do not add up to 100 because people could have gained more than one type of qualification, in which case they would be double counted.

Source: Mentoring Plus cohort (first survey, $n = 353$) and YLS (1998/9, $n = 1,680$).

experiences of school tend to be associated with a range of negative outcomes later on in life (Hills *et al.* 2002). Poor educational attainment at this stage is a powerful precursor of negative adult outcomes and young people who leave school with low levels of attainment are at a heightened risk of unemployment, low pay and social exclusion (Hobcraft 2002: 77; Sparkes and Glennerster 2002). While truanting has also been found to be associated with such outcomes, it has, in addition, been linked to a range of personal problems, including high rates of marital breakdown, heavy smoking and depression (Sparkes and Glennerster 2002).

Future orientations and attitudes to education and work

Unsurprisingly, perhaps, given the difficulties they experienced, a sizeable proportion of the young people in the cohort appeared to be alienated from school. In response to the first survey, two fifths of the young people on the programme indicated that they actively disliked school (11 per cent disliked it a little while 30 per cent said they disliked it a lot) and slightly less than one in four indicated that they were ambivalent (21 per cent neither liked nor disliked school). The reasons given for truanting also pointed to a degree of alienation, with the two most frequently given reasons being the 'lessons were hard, boring or uninteresting' (given by 51 per cent of those who had truanted) and feeling frustrated at school (37 per

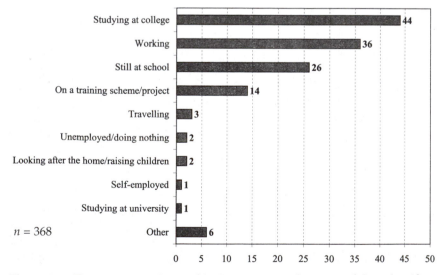

Figure 6.2 Future expectations – this time next year (per cent of the cohort)[9]
Source: Mentoring Plus cohort (first survey).

cent). In addition, one in four (26 per cent) of those who had truanted indicated that they had done so, in part at least, because they felt that school 'was a waste of time'. Other reasons given for truanting included problems with teachers – 29 per cent indicated they had truanted because 'the teachers did not respect me' and 13 per cent indicated they had done so because they were 'being bullied by teachers'; peer influences – 25 per cent indicated they had truanted because 'my friends did it'; and general difficulties – 16 per cent indicated they had truanted because of 'problems at home'.

The sense of alienation that was evident among the young people in the cohort tended to be fairly specific, however, focusing primarily on the *process* of schooling and only rarely extending to the conventional *goals* of education, work and training. When they joined the Mentoring Plus programme, the vast majority of the young people expected, in a year's time, either still to be in school or to be working or studying at college and very few expected to be unemployed or doing nothing (see Figure 6.2). Even when this analysis was limited to those who had already left school or were due to so in the next year the general pattern remained unchanged as nine out of ten (91 per cent) of these young people expected to be engaged in education, training or work.[10] A similar orientation was apparent in terms of the value that the young people placed on education and training. When they joined the programme, four out of five of them (79 per cent) indicated that education and training was 'very important' to their future, one in five (19 per cent) indicated that it was 'fairly important' and only one in fifty (2 per cent) indicated that it was 'not at all important'.

Even among those who appeared to be most alienated from school and/ or at most risk of social exclusion, there was widespread support for the conventional goals of education, training and work. While tending to place less emphasis than others on the importance of education and training, very few of the young people in such situations completely rejected these activities as being 'not important'. The differences that were evident in this regard tended to reflect the *degree* of importance placed on education and training. Thus, for example, while those who truanted every week were the least likely to rate education and training as 'very important' to their future, they were the most likely to rate it as 'fairly important' and very few of them rated it 'not important' (74 per cent, 24 per cent and 2 per cent respectively).[11]

Offending behaviour

Social disadvantage is associated with an increased risk of delinquency (Rutter *et al.* 1998) and various criminological theories have explored the nature of these links (see Smith and McVie 2003). Offending behaviour provided a key focus for our study and detailed questions about it were included in all three surveys. As part of the first survey, the young people recruited on to the programme were asked whether they had ever committed a range of offences and, if so, whether they had committed them during the previous 12 months. In order that comparisons could be made with the *YLS*, respondents were asked whether they had[12]:

- written or sprayed graffiti on walls, buses, train seats, bus shelters, etc.;

- stolen anything worth more than £5;

- taken a car, motorcycle or moped without the owner's permission, not intending to give it back;

- driven a car, motorcycle or moped on a public road, without a licence and/or insurance;

- driven a car, motorcycle or moped knowing that you have drunk more than the legal amount of alcohol;

- stolen anything out of or from a car;

- damaged or destroyed something – on purpose or recklessly – that belonged to someone else (e.g. a telephone box, car, window of a house);

- snatched anything from a person – a purse, bag, mobile or anything else;

- sneaked into a private house, garden or building intending to steal something;

- bought or sold stolen goods;

- carried a weapon such as a stick or knife to defend yourself;

- carried a weapon such as a knife to attack other people;

- threatened someone with a weapon or threatened to beat him or her up, in order to get money or other valuables from him or her;

- taken part in a fight or disorder in a group or in a public place (e.g. a football ground, riot or in the street);

- set fire, on purpose or recklessly, to something (e.g. car, building, garage, dustbins);

- beaten someone up (belonging to your family or not) to such an extent that you think medical help was needed; and

- hurt someone, on purpose, with a stick or other weapon.

At the point of joining the programme, the vast majority (93 per cent) of the young people had committed at least one of these offences at some point in their lives and most (85 per cent) had done so during the previous 12 months. On average, they had committed six offences, with four having been committed in the last year. No clear patterns were evident in relation to which types of offence were most widely committed (see Figure 6.3)[13]: while some violent offences, such as public disorder, were among the most widely committed others, such as carrying a weapon to attack someone, were among the least widely committed; similarly, while some property offences, such as stealing something worth £5 or more, were relatively widespread, others, such as snatching something from the person, were relatively unusual.

The young people on the programme can be characterized as generalist rather than specialist offenders (in line with other studies of persistent offenders, e.g. Hagell and Newburn 1994). There was, for example, very little evidence that their offending was organized around similar types of offence, although two distinct clusters were identified.[14] The largest cluster was made up of offences involving theft (i.e. those defined as property offences plus snatch theft) and this indicated that individuals who committed one such offence were more likely to commit another. A smaller cluster was also evident, which incorporated carrying a weapon to defend oneself, carrying a weapon to attack somebody and hurting somebody with a weapon. Those young people in the cohort who had carried a weapon with the intention of attacking somebody were the most likely to have hurt somebody with a weapon (70 per cent had done so). In addition, however, a sizeable proportion of those who had only carried a weapon to defend themselves had also hurt somebody with a weapon (42 per cent compared with 14 per cent of those who had not carried a weapon).[15] The generalist nature of the young people's offending was also evident from the way in which it cut across the broad categories of violent offences, property offences, criminal damage and traffic violations: less than a quarter (22 per cent) of those who had offended during the previous year had restricted themselves to one of these categories and nearly three in five (57 per cent) had committed offences across three or four of them.

The relatively strong association between carrying a weapon to defend oneself and hurting somebody with a weapon highlights an important point about youth offending. There is, among young people, a close relationship between offending and victimization (Smith and McVie 2003) and distinctions between these categories may be particularly blurred in relation to violent offences. It is, in this context, worth noting that more than twice as many young people in the cohort carried a weapon for the purposes of defence than attack (see Figure 6.3) and that, during conversations and interviews, many of them highlighted ways in which

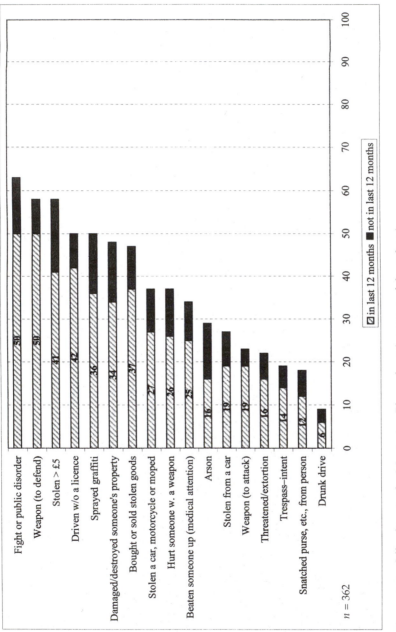

Figure 6.3 Offending in the Mentoring Plus cohort (per cent of the cohort)
Source: Mentoring Plus cohort (first survey).

they routinely managed the potential for violence associated with 'street culture', gang rivalries and territorialism. For many this involved carrying a knife and for some it meant carrying a gun. In some cases, the consequences were fatal or near fatal. During the course of the fieldwork two young people associated with the programme were stabbed to death and two of the young people on the programme were seriously injured as a result of knife attacks.

While the boundaries between victim and offender may be blurred, it is clear from comparisons with the *YLS* that levels of offending within the Mentoring Plus cohort were very high (see Table 6.2). The young people in the cohort were more than twice as likely as those in the general youthful population to have committed an offence during the previous 12 months and were between three and four and a half times as likely to have committed an offence within each of the broad categories during this period. Differences between these populations were even more marked in relation to persistent and serious offending[16]: the young people on the programme were nearly six times as likely as those in the general population to have offended persistently and were seven times as likely to have committed a serious offence during the previous 12 months. In view of this there can be little doubt that many of the young people recruited on to the programme were among the most prolific of young offenders.

The entrenched nature of offending within the cohort was confirmed by comparisons across the different age groups. Overall levels of offending were remarkably similar, regardless of age, and the youngest members of the cohort were just as likely to have offended as the oldest and had committed just as many offences – the average number of offences committed during the last year was four for each age group. Nor was there any suggestion that the youngest members of the cohort were committing less serious offences.[17] There was, however, some evidence that the nature of offending changed with age. As in the general population (Graham and Bowling 1995; Flood-Page *et al.* 2000), the young people on the programme appeared to grow out of criminal damage as they moved through their teenage years. The proportion who had committed such an offence during the last year decreased steadily with age, as the rate of desistence increased: within this offence category, the number of current offenders for every past offender fell from 5.5 among 12–14-year-olds to 3.9 among 15-year-olds, to 2.6 among 16-year-olds and to 2.2 among 17–19-year-olds[18]. No such patterns were evident in relation to any of the other broad offence categories.[19]

Levels of offending within the cohort did vary between males and females and these variations broadly replicated those that have been found in the general population (Graham and Bowling 1995; Flood-Page *et*

Table 6.2 Comparative rates of offending (per cent)

	Mentoring Plus cohort	General youthful population[1]
Committed an offence		
No, never	7	42
Yes – but not in last 12 months	8	20
Yes – in last 12 months	85	38
	100	100
Criminal damage		
No, never	31	67
Yes – but not in last 12 months	16	18
Yes – in last 12 months	54	15
	100	100
Property offences		
No, never	27	71
Yes – but not in last 12 months	14	13
Yes – in last 12 months	60	16
	100	100
Violent offences		
No, never	22	76
Yes – but not in last 12 months	14	10
Yes – in last 12 months	64	14
	100	100
Traffic violations		
No, never	50	78
Yes – but not in last 12 months	8	10
Yes – in last 12 months	42	13
	100	100
Persistent offender		
No	38	89
Yes	62	11
	100	100
Serious offence		
No, never	30	85
Yes – but not in last 12 months	13	7
Yes – in last 12 months	57	8
	100	100

Notes:
The 1998/9 *YLS* was adjusted to reflect the age and sex structure of the Mentoring Plus cohort.
  1 Confidence intervals are given in Table I.2 in Appendix I.
Source: Mentoring Plus cohort (first survey, *n* = 376) and *YLS* (1998/9, *n* = 1,254).

al. 2000). The young women on the programme were less likely to have offended than the young men and their offending tended to be less serious and less persistent. Twice as many of the young women as young men indicated that they had never offended (13 per cent compared with 5 per cent) and, on average, the young men had committed approximately twice as many offence types as the young women: while the former had committed a total of seven offence types, with four having been committed during the previous 12 months, the latter had committed a total of five offence types, with two having been committed during the previous 12 months. One and a half times as many young men as young women had offended persistently during the last year (71 per cent compared with 43 per cent) and twice as many had committed a serious offence during this period (69 per cent compared with 34 per cent).[20]

There was, in contrast, little variation between ethnic groups. Once again, this replicates the pattern in the general population, as levels of self-reported offending have been found to be broadly similar among white and African/Caribbean youth (Graham and Bowling 1995; see Newburn 1997). The proportion of young people who had ever offended and had done so in the last 12 months was broadly similar across ethnic groups, as was the proportion who had committed a serious offence. There was, however, some suggestion that African/Caribbean members of the cohort were offending less persistently than white or mixed-race young people although the differences were modest: while African/Caribbeans had committed an average of five offences, with three having been committed in the last year, this compared with figures of six and five for whites and seven and five for mixed-race young people. Thus while two in three white and mixed-race members of the cohort (66 per cent and 67 per cent respectively) had offended persistently during the last year this compared with a little more than one in two African/Caribbeans (54 per cent).[21]

Contact with the criminal justice system

Given their level of offending it is, perhaps, unsurprising that most of the young people in the cohort had received some kind of sanction from the criminal justice system (see Figure 6.4). Nearly two in three had been cautioned by the police, nearly one in two had been arrested and charged with an offence, more than one in four had been convicted of an offence in court and one in eight had spent time in a Young Offenders' Institution or in Local Authority Secure Accommodation. The bulk of this contact with the criminal justice system had occurred during the last year. As a point of comparison, the *YLS* indicates that approximately one in twenty (5 per cent) young people in the general population had been cautioned during

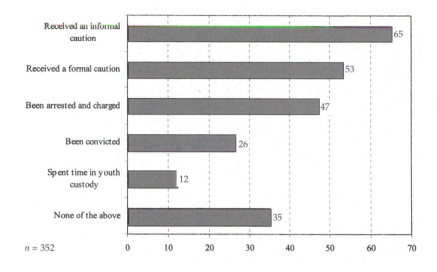

Figure 6.4 Contact with the criminal justice system (per cent of the cohort)[23]
Source: Mentoring Plus cohort (first survey).

the last year, one in fifty had been taken to court during this time and one in two hundred (0.5 per cent) had ever spent time in a Young Offenders' Institution or in Local Authority Secure Accommodation.[22]

Reflecting their greater levels of offending, male members of the cohort had had markedly greater contact with the criminal justice system than females and this was most evident in relation to custody (15 per cent of young men compared with 5 per cent of young women had spent time in custody). The youngest members of the cohort had had the least contact with the criminal justice system (42 per cent of 12–14-year-olds had avoided any kind of criminal justice sanction compared with 21 per cent of 17–19 year olds). And, where they had been sanctioned, they tended to have been treated more leniently (8 per cent of 12–14-year-olds had spent time in custody compared with 32 per cent of 17–19-year-olds). As these differences could not be readily explained by levels of offending, they point to escalating criminal justice responses. Very little variation was evident according to the young people's ethnicity.[24]

Drinking, smoking and drug use

Although underage drinking and illicit drug use are often considered to be forms of delinquent or deviant behaviour such a view has been increasingly challenged in recent years. Alternative perspectives have been developed which view adolescent drinking as essentially normal behaviour (Wright 1999; Brain *et al*. 2000) and suggest that illicit drug use is undergoing a process of normalization (Parker *et al*. 1998). There is, however, strong empirical evidence linking (excessive) consumption of alcohol and drugs to a range of anti-social and 'risky' behaviours, as well as a series of negative health outcomes (for an overview, see Lloyd 1998; Newburn and Shiner 2001). While establishing the precise nature of these links has proved extremely difficult, it has been suggested that there may be a degree of circularity here, with certain forms of substance use leading to exclusion and exclusion providing greater opportunities for substance use (Hammersley *et al*. 2003).

The vast majority of young people on the programme had drunk alcohol and smoked cigarettes at some point in their lives and many continued to do so (see Figure 6.5). Comparisons with the *YLS* suggest that while rates of smoking in the cohort were very high, rates of drinking were *relatively* modest. The proportion of daily cigarette smokers in the cohort was approximately three times that in the general population (48 per cent compared with 15 per cent). By contrast, the proportion of regular (weekly) drinkers within the cohort was lower than in the general population (21 per cent compared with 33 per cent).[25] Rates of drunkenness within the cohort also appeared to be unremarkable. At the time of joining the programme, one in ten (10 per cent) of the young people had been drunk at least once a week during the previous year, a further one in six (17 per cent) had been drunk at least once a month and a further two in five (40 per cent) had been drunk less often than this, leaving one in three (33 per cent) who had never been drunk.[26]

To some extent, the relatively moderate rates of drinking that were evident in the cohort reflected its ethnic composition. There is some evidence that young people from black and minority ethnic groups drink less than white young people (for an overview, see Newburn and Shiner 2001) and this pattern was evident in the cohort. Twice as many black African/Caribbean and mixed-race young people as whites were non-drinkers (26 per cent and 29 per cent respectively compared with 14 per cent). And twice as many whites as African/Caribbeans and mixed-race young people were getting drunk on a weekly basis (15 per cent compared with 8 per cent and 7 per cent respectively). Even among the white young people, however, levels of drinking within the cohort appear unremarkable when compared with the general youthful population. As well as drinking less, black and minority ethnic members of the cohort also tended to smoke less than their white counterparts (61 per cent of whites smoked on a daily basis compared with 31 per cent of black African/ Caribbeans and 60 per cent of mixed-race young people). Nevertheless,

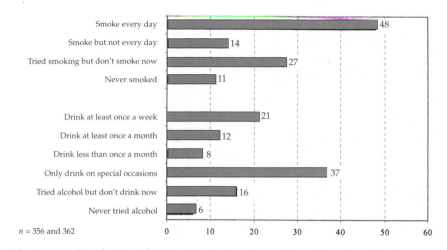

Figure 6.5 Drinking and smoking in the Mentoring Plus cohort (per cent of the cohort)
Source: Mentoring Plus cohort (first survey).

rates of smoking in all these groups were high when compared with the general youthful population. Only minor variations in smoking, drinking and drunkenness were evident according to sex and age.[27]

Most of the young people on the programme had used an illicit drug at some point in their lives and most had done so within the last year (72 per cent and 62 per cent respectively). As in the general population, cannabis was by far the most widely and intensely used illicit drug. Three in five (60 per cent) members of the cohort had used cannabis during the last year and more than a third (38 per cent) had done so on a weekly basis (it is likely that around half of this group were daily users).[28] Some way behind cannabis, cocaine was the second most widely used illicit drug followed by ecstasy and amphetamines – these substances were included in the hallucinant category[29] and solvents (see Table 6.3). These substances were not widely used, however, and their regular use was limited to a very small minority. Only 2 per cent of the cohort had used cocaine on a weekly basis during the last year and a further 1 per cent had done so on a monthly basis. Similar rates of use were evident in relation to the hallucinants (2 per cent had used one of the substances on a monthly basis and the same proportion had done so at least once a week). Any use of heroin and, to a lesser extent, crack cocaine was very unusual and only 1 per cent of the cohort had used *either* of these substances on a weekly or monthly basis during the last year. This is particularly noteworthy given the emphasis that is often placed on these drugs as a cause of crime (Drugs Strategy Directorate 2002).

Comparisons between the cohort and the *YLS* highlighted some notable differences in levels and patterns of drug use (see Table 6.3). Predictably, perhaps, levels of use tended to be higher among the young people on the programme than among those in the general population but this was not always the case. The extent to which the hallucinants and solvents were used within the cohort was, for example, unremarkable when compared with the general population. Marked differences were evident in relation to other substances, however. The young people in the cohort were two and a half times as likely as those in the general population to have used cannabis during the last year; and were five times as likely to have done so on a weekly basis (38 per cent compared with 7 per cent). They were also seven times as likely to have used cocaine during the last year and thirteen times as likely to have ever used crack or heroin.[30]

Within the cohort use of *some* illicit substances, namely cannabis and cocaine, increased markedly with age. The oldest members of the cohort were, for example, three times as likely as those in any of the other age groups to have used cocaine in the last year (15 per cent of 17–19-year-olds compared with 5–6 per cent of each of the remaining age groups). Such variations were not universally apparent, however, and no clear patterns were evident in relation to the hallucinants, solvents and crack/heroin. Levels of use tended to be higher among female than male members of the cohort, although these variations were generally fairly modest. Most markedly, females were twice as likely as males to have (ever) used cocaine and crack/heroin (11 per cent compared with 5 per cent for cocaine and 6 per cent compared with 3 per cent for crack/heroin).[31] Consistent ethnic differences were also evident, with white and mixed-race members of the cohort showing higher levels of use than black African/Caribbeans. This trend was most marked in relation to hallucinants and solvents. White and mixed-race young people were more than two and a half times as likely as black African/Caribbeans to have used hallucinants during the last year (17 per cent, 11 per cent and 4 per cent respectively), and were also ten times as likely to have ever used solvents (11 per cent, 11 per cent and 1 per cent respectively). Finally, use of heroin and/or crack was most marked among mixed-race members of the cohort (11 per cent had ever used these substance(s), compared with 6 per cent of whites and 4 per cent of black African/Caribbeans).[32]

Psychological characteristics

Various attempts have been made to explain delinquency in terms of individual psychological traits such as self-esteem and locus of control.

Table 6.3   Comparative rates of illicit drug use (per cent)

	Mentoring Plus cohort	General youthful population[1]
Cannabis		
Used in the last 12 months	60	24
Used but not in last 12 months	10	6
Never used	30	70
	100	100
Hallucinants		
Used in the last 12 months	10	9
Used but not in last 12 months	5	5
Never used	85	86
	100	100
Solvents		
Used in the last 12 months	4	4
Used but not in last 12 months	3	4
Never used	93	92
	100	100
Cocaine		
Used in the last 12 months	7	1
Used but not in last 12 months	3	1
Never used	90	98
	100	100
Crack and/or heroin[2]		
Used in the last 12 months	4	0.3
Used but not in last 12 months	3	0.5
Never used	94	99
	100	100

Notes
The 1998/9 *YLS* was adjusted to reflect the age and sex structure of the Mentoring Plus cohort.
  1 Confidence intervals are given in Table I.3 in Appendix I.
  2 These substances have been combined because of the small number using them and because they provide the basis for what is typically thought of as being 'problematic' use. Recent analysis has also shown that use of these substances tends to go together (Parker and Bottomley 1996; Shiner 2003).
Source: Mentoring Plus cohort (first survey, n=345) and *YLS* (1998/9, n=1,630).

Although self-esteem has, in particular, come to be seen as a kind of 'social vaccine' against a range of social ills, it does not appear to be causally linked with offending behaviour, substance misuse or academic failure (Emler 2002: 2). This does not mean that low self-esteem is not harmful, however, and it has been found to be associated with a heightened risk of depression, teenage pregnancy, suicide attempts, unemployment and difficulties in forming and sustaining close relationships. Many mentoring programmes aim to raise the self-esteem of the young people they work with and this provided an important focus for Mentoring Plus. The potential value of mentoring in this regard has been highlighted by a recent evaluation of a project working with young care leavers, which concluded that the programme helped to improve the young people's prospects by building self-esteem and opening up new social relationships (Gilligan 1999).

We were interested in self-esteem and locus of control as important dimensions in themselves and as potential mechanisms for change. Both traits were measured using well established scales[33] (Rosenberg 1965; Robinson et al. 1991) and we were initially concerned with establishing whether they were associated with delinquency within the cohort at the time that the young people were recruited on to the programme. This possibility was assessed by focusing on offending and truancy. The young people's self-esteem scores were very similar, regardless of the frequency with which they had truanted (average scores varied from 21 to 22) and regardless of the extent of their offending (the average score was 21 regardless of whether or not they had ever offended and, if they had, regardless of whether or not they had done so persistently). A broadly similar picture was evident in relation to locus of control (average scores varied from 6 to 7 according to levels of both truancy and offending).[34] As such, our findings are consistent with the conclusion that low self-esteem (and an external locus of control) is not a significant cause of delinquency among young people.

The web of exclusion

The young people recruited on to the programme had experienced multiple forms of disadvantage and were at considerable risk of becoming isolated from mainstream social, economic and cultural life. Many of them had experienced substantial disruption in their schooling and family lives. Truancy and disengagement were widespread and many of those who had left school had done so without any qualifications. In addition, levels of offending, illicit drug use and contact with the criminal justice system were much higher than in the general youthful population. Because these different forms of disadvantage tend to reinforce one another, they may provide the basis for enduring patterns of social exclusion. In order to illustrate this point we will consider the links between truancy, offending and drug use and will then consider the ways in which these forms of behaviour are linked to family circumstances.

Truancy, offending and illicit drug use were all linked with one another. Members of the cohort who had truanted most frequently also tended to have offended most actively. On average, for example, those who had truanted on a weekly or approximately fortnightly basis had committed twice as many offences as those who had not truanted at all (see Table 6.4). In addition, the young people who had not truanted at all were more than three times as likely as those who had done so to have never offended (14 per cent compared with 3 per cent or 4 per cent of those who had truanted, regardless of how often they had done so). Truancy was also associated with heightened rates of drug use. Approximately three in four of the young people who had truanted on a weekly or approximately fortnightly basis had used an illicit drug during the last year, compared with half those who had truanted no more than once a month or had not done so at all (74 per cent and 71 per cent compared with 46 per cent and 52 per cent). While this general trend was evident in relation to most substances, it is worth noting that there were particularly marked differences in the use of crack and/or heroin: weekly truants had used these substances at approximately three times the rate of those who had truanted infrequently or not at all (11 per cent of those who had truanted on a weekly basis had used crack and/or heroin at some time in their life, compared with 5 per cent of those who had truanted on an approximately fortnightly basis, 4 per cent of those who had truanted once a month or less often and 3 per cent of those who had never truanted).[35]

Drug use was, in turn, associated with heightened rates of offending. Recent drug users within the cohort had, on average, committed twice as many offences during the last year as past users and three times as many

Table 6.4 Average number of offences committed by rate of truancy

Rate of truancy	Median no. of offences ever	Median no. of offences in the last 12 months
Every week	7	5
Two or three days a month	7	4
One day a month or less	5	4
Not truanted	4	2

as non-users (they had committed an average of six, three and two offences respectively). The highest rates of offending were associated with the use of solvents and crack/heroin: current users of these substances had committed an average of nine offences during the last year.[36]

While truancy, offending and drug use provided the basis for a distinct pattern of delinquency, they were also linked to the family circumstances of the young people. Although differences in this regard were generally fairly modest they tended to be consistent. Delinquency was most marked among those young people who appeared to have experienced greatest disruption in their family lives. Those living in residential care, hostels or with foster parents were, for example, twice as likely to have truanted from school on a weekly basis as those living in traditional nuclear families (48 per cent and 25 per cent respectively; compared with 35–36 per cent of those living in reconstituted families, single-parent families or in other circumstances). They had, on average, also committed twice as many offences during the last year (six and three respectively; compared with four among those living in reconstituted families or single-parent families and five among those living in other circumstances). In addition, while general levels of drug use were broadly similar across the range of family circumstances, marked differences were evident in relation to the most problematic substances. Once again it was the young people living in residential care, hostels or with foster parents who appeared to be at greatest risk: they were, for example, four times as likely as those living in nuclear families to have used crack/heroin at some time in their lives (13 per cent and 3 per cent respectively; compared with none of those living in reconstituted families, 6 per cent of those living in single parent families and 9 per cent of those living in other circumstances).[37]

Conclusion

At the outset of this chapter we proposed to address three themes – the success of the programme in recruiting disaffected young people, the apparent appropriateness of the programme and the nature of youth disaffection. There can be little, if any, doubt that the programme was highly successful in its attempts to target disaffected young people and those who were recruited on to the programme clearly reflected its aims. They were much more likely than young people in the general population to be living outside traditional nuclear families and a substantial number had no contact with their father; they were much more likely to have truanted from school and to be completely disengaged from education, training and work; most of those who had left school had done so without qualifications; many of them were, by conventional standards, fairly prolific offenders and their rates of contact with the criminal justice system were much higher than in the general population; and they were much more likely to have used illicit drugs, including crack and/or heroin.

Given these patterns it is, perhaps, difficult to avoid the conclusion that the young people on the programme formed what may be described as 'delinquent subcultures'. There are, however, well-known difficulties with such a perspective. It is, of course, by no means unusual for young people

---

Case study: Solomon's story

We first interviewed Solomon when he was 17 years old. Describing himself as a 'thug', he talked of his involvement in local gang-life and how he had been to court for a series of violent incidents, including stabbings and shootings. Solomon felt he had been surrounded by trouble since he was young. During his childhood the police had regularly come to the house looking for his cousins and an older brother who was sent to prison when Solomon was 13 years old. He said: 'My cousins raised me and I picked up their thug mentality.'

Solomon initially went to the same secondary school as his older brother and felt that his family's reputation had made school life difficult for him. He felt his teachers expected him to behave like his brother and that the other pupils were scared of him. His education was disrupted when he was moved to another school, which he described as being 'thugged out' and 'a big ghetto'.

Solomon had mixed feelings about his family life. He said: 'I haven't really got a family, there is only my brothers and sister and my mum and it has always been broken; we have never been one.' His mother had tried to protect him when he was little and, although he did not got on well with her, he said he would always be grateful to her. It upset him to see her struggle on her own. When we interviewed Solomon for a second time, almost a year later, he said he was still unable to talk to his mother: 'because when I sit with my mum it is like I can feel her pain and I know when she is upset, and I would rather avoid it than see it, so I just can't be around my mum.'

By this time Solomon was at college and had come out of the gang scene although, he said, his former involvement still had repercussions. He said: 'I'd got myself into situations with big men and it has actually put me in my place because I thought I was bad but I got myself in situations and it could get very serious.' Solomon had seen people he knew go to prison and had suffered from sleeplessness and anxiety after being shot at. He felt that the birth of his niece had been a 'turning point' and he described feeling responsible for her and 'calm' when he was with her. Solomon was thinking about his future and was looking forward to having a family of his own.

---

in the general population to have been involved in various forms of delinquency. Much of it is typically petty, however, involving one or two offences (Graham and Bowling 1995). What we have seen among the young people on the programme is something quite different involving much more extensive and entrenched forms of offending. It is, moreover, wrapped up with considerable structural impediments and a degree of alienation. The high levels of truancy and low levels of qualifications within the cohort reflect widespread disillusionment with the process of schooling. In the longer term they carry the threat of unemployment, low pay, marital breakdown and depression.

And yet we must avoid the dangers of presenting an overly dystopian view. Delinquent subcultures do not exist in an antagonistic relationship with wider society and nor are they based on a deeply held oppositional morality (Matza and Sykes 1961; Matza 1964, 1968). The boundaries between delinquent subcultures and wider society are inevitably blurred and reflect general tendencies rather than absolute differences. Important points of contact remain. The sense of alienation that was evident among the young people on the programme was largely specific to the process of schooling, for example, and rarely extended to the general cultural goals of education and work. In the way they thought about their future, many of these young people revealed highly conventional attitudes and aspirations. They emphasized the importance of education, they saw themselves studying at college or working and many of them spoke about having a family. By providing opportunities for education and training the programme appeared to dovetail neatly with the aims and aspirations of the young people it recruited. Whether this provided the basis for meaningful engagement, and whether the young people made the most of this opportunity, remains to be seen.

Notes

1 For the purposes of the formal analysis the cohort has been treated as a population (made up of young people recruited on to the Mentoring Plus programme during a given period). As a result, confidence intervals have not been given and, when assessing relationships between variables, probability values have not been used. Measures of association have been used, however, as they are meaningful regardless of whether the data come from a sample or a population.

2 In order to facilitate these comparisons many of the questions in the survey were taken from the YLS. Some degree of caution is required, however, as there are notable differences between the surveys. Interviews for the YLS were carried out between October 1998 and January 1999 while the first Mentoring

Plus survey was administered from September 2000 to February 2002. While the Mentoring Plus survey took the form of a pen-and-paper survey the *YLS* was administered via Computer Assisted Personal Interviewing which has been shown to be particularly well suited to asking questions about sensitive issues (Flood-Page *et al.* 2000). Unlike the *YLS* which was administered across the whole of England and Wales and included young people aged 12–30 our survey was limited to the ten areas in which the Mentoring Plus programmes were based and included young people aged 12–19. In order to improve the comparability of the two surveys data from the *YLS* were weighted to reflect the age and sex profile of the Mentoring Plus cohort. This was achieved by adapting the weights provided with the *YLS*. Confidence intervals (at the 0.05 level) were generated for *YLS* estimates and where figures for the Mentoring Plus cohort lie outside these confidence intervals, it follows that the young people in the cohort are different from those in the general population.

3 The 95 per cent confidence intervals for the general population estimates are, 62–68 per cent living in traditional nuclear family and 16–21 per cent living in single-parent families.

4 The term 'traditional nuclear family' has been used to describe households where young people were living with both natural parents. The term 'reconstituted nuclear family' has been used to describe households where young people were living with one of their natural parents and his or her partner.

5 Contact with parents was assessed on the basis of respondents' answers to questions about whom they lived with and how well they got on with their parents. Respondents who lived with their parents were assumed to have contact with them. Those who did not live with a particular parent and gave a 'does not apply' answer to the question about how well they got on with them were judged not to be in contact with them. A large number of respondents did not answer the question about the nature of their relationship with their father ($n = 78$) and they were judged not to be in contact with them providing that they did not live with them and answered the question about the nature of their relationship with their mother.

6 Cramer's $V = 0.12$ (contact with father by ethnicity). The percentage has not been given for Asian young people because the number of cases was insufficient to support meaningful analysis ($n = 7$).

7 According to the *YLS*, 82 per cent of young people aged 17–19 had at least one GCSE and this is less than we might expect given the overall figures for school leavers (95 per cent – see Department for Education and Skills 2002). This discrepancy reflects the adjustments that were made to the *YLS*: the data were weighted to reflect the sex structure of the Mentoring Plus cohort (68 per cent male) and as girls outperform males in their GCSEs this reduces the estimated proportion of young people with at least one GCSE.

8 Cramer's $V = 0.33$ (current status by age), 0.14 (current status by ethnicity) and 0.07 (current status by sex).

9 Respondents were *only* classified as expecting to be unemployed/doing nothing if they selected these options and did not select one of the following:

still at school, working, studying at college, on a training scheme/project, studying at university or self-employed. This restriction reduced the number of respondents who were classified in this way from 4 to 2 per cent.

10 This figure is based on those respondents who were aged 16 years and above at the time of the first survey and those who were aged 15 and did not expect still to be at school in a year's time.

11 Kendall's tau-c = 0.07 (importance of education by truancy).

12 These items were selected from the 35 included in the *YLS* on the basis that they were most relevant: some items included in the *YLS* such as those relating to falsely claiming benefits or not declaring income tax were excluded on the basis that they were of very limited relevance – most of the young people involved in Mentoring Plus were too young to claim benefits or to pay tax. Some other items from the *YLS* were combined: thus, for example, we combined separate items from the *YLS* for having stolen something worth £5 from school, from a shop, from home, from work or anything else as we did not require this level of detail. Similarly we combined items relating to having ever beaten up a family member and a non-family member.

13 Violent offences include the following – snatching something from the person, carrying a weapon to attack other people, threatening someone in order to get money or other valuables from him or her and taking part in a fight or disorder in a group or in a public place; property offences include – stolen something worth more than £5, stolen a car or motorcycle, stolen something out of a car, trespass with intent and bought or sold stolen goods; criminal damage includes – graffiti, damaged or destroyed something belonging to someone else and arson; and traffic violations include – driving without a licence and/or insurance and drunk driving. Unless stated otherwise the median has been used as the preferred measure of central tendency.

14 In order to identify any underlying patterns in offending, relationships between specific offences were examined. All the young people who had committed an offence were included in the analysis and, for each offence, distinctions were drawn between having committed it during the previous 12 months, having committed it but not during the previous 12 months and never having committed it. All possible comparison were made between offences.

15 112 out of the 136 comparisons between offences involved a fairly modest degree of association (Kendall's tau-b = < 0.3). Of the 24 pairs where there was a stronger relationship 10 were between offences involving theft and 4 were between carrying a weapon to defend oneself, carrying a weapon to attack somebody and/or hurting somebody with a weapon.

16 A persistent offender was defined as someone who had committed at least three of the specific offences during the previous year. Persistence was defined in terms of the range of offences committed because our survey did not include questions about the frequency of offending. The volume of young people's offending is, however, very strongly correlated with the breadth of their offending, so that those who commit the broadest range of offences tend also to commit the greatest number of offences (Smith and McVie 2003). Serious offenders were defined as those who had committed at least one of the

following offences: stealing a motor vehicle without consent, snatching a purse, etc., trespassing with intent, threats/extortion, assault resulting in medical attention, hurting somebody (on purpose) with a weapon.

17 Kendall's tau-c = 0.00 (offended by age); eta = 0.14 (total number of offences ever committed by age); eta = 0.07 (total number of offences committed in the last year by age); Kendall's tau-c = 0.04 (serious offence by age).

18 'Current offender' refers to those who had committed an offence during the last year and 'past offender' refers to those who had committed an offence but had not done so in the last year.

19 Kendall's tau-c = 0.16 (criminal damage by age); Kendall's tau-c = 0.01 (property offences by age); Kendall's tau-c = 0.02 (violent offence by age); Kendall's tau-c = 0.04 (traffic violation by age).

20 Cramer's V = 0.16 (offended by sex), 0.26 (offended persistently by sex), 0.36 (serious offence by sex); eta = 0.30 (total number of offences ever committed by sex); eta = 0.29 (total number of offences committed in the last year by age).

21 Cramer's V = 0.09 (offended by ethnicity), 0.13 (offended persistently by ethnicity), 0.08 (serious offence by ethnicity); eta = 0.10 (total number of offences ever committed by ethnicity); eta = 0.11 (total number of offences committed in the last year by ethnicity).

22 The 95 per cent confidence intervals for these estimates were: 4–7 per cent (cautioned), 1–3 per cent (court) and 0–1 per cent (custody).

23 We have assumed the following: those who had received a formal caution had previously received an informal caution; those who had been arrested and charged had previously received both types of caution; those who had been convicted had previously been arrested and charged and had received both types of caution and those who had spent time in a Young Offenders' Institute had previously been arrested and charged and had received both types of caution.

24 Kendall's tau-c = 0.15 (contact with the criminal justice system by age), 0.18 (contact with the criminal justice system by sex) and 0.01 (contact with the criminal justice system by ethnicity).

25 The confidence intervals for the YLS intervals are daily cigarette smoking, 12–17 per cent; weekly drinking, 30–37 per cent.

26 Differences in the questions between our survey and the YLS meant that this comparison was not straightforward. Our survey asked respondents whether they had been drunk while the YLS asked whether they had been *very* drunk. Estimates from the YLS indicated that, within the general population, approximately one in four young people had been very drunk at least once a month during the previous year and approximately one in twenty had been very drunk on a weekly basis (20–26 per cent and 3–7 per cent respectively).

27 Cramers V = 0.18 (cigarette smoking by ethnicity), 0.24 (alcohol consumption by ethnicity) and 0.16 (drunkenness by ethnicity). Cramer's V = 0.17 (smoking by sex), 0.07 (drinking by sex) and 0.05 (drunkenness by sex). Kendall's tau-c = 0.02 (smoking by age), 0.05 (drinking by age) and 0.07 (drunkenness by age).

28 The estimate that half of these young people had used cannabis on a daily basis is based on recent research we conducted in two London YOTs. More

than four in five (83 per cent) of the young people included in this study had used cannabis during the previous 12 months and two in three (66 per cent) were using it on a weekly basis. Of those who were using cannabis on a weekly basis half (51 per cent) were doing so every day (Shiner unpublished).

29 This term was coined by Ramsay and Percy (1996) to describe stimulants and hallucinogens – amphetamines, LSD, magic mushrooms, ecstasy and amyl nitrate. Recent analysis has shown that, in terms of patterns on use, these substances form a meaningful grouping (Shiner 2003).

30 The confidence interval for weekly cannabis use within the general population is 5–8 per cent. The analysis presented here may overstate the heightened rate of cocaine use within the cohort because this type of drug use became more widespread within the general population during the period between the 1998/9 *YLS* and the first Mentoring Plus survey. According to the British Crime Survey the proportion of 16–59-year-olds who had used cocaine in the last year increased from 1 per cent in 1998 to 2 per cent in 2001/2 (Aust *et al.* 2002). Even if we double the estimate for the general youthful population based on the 1998/9 *YLS*, however, the resulting figure is still well below that for the Mentoring Plus cohort.

31 Kendall's tau-c = 0.11 (cannabis by age), 0.05 (cocaine by age), 0.01 (hallucinants by age and solvents by age) and 0.02 (crack/heroin by age). Cramer's V = 0.15 (cocaine by sex), 0.10 (crack/heroin by sex), 0.07 (cannabis by sex), 0.07(solvents by sex) and 0.06 (hallucinants by sex).

32 Cramer's V = 0.11 (cannabis by ethnicity), 0.18 (hallucinants by ethnicity), 0.17 (solvents by ethnicity), 0.11 (cocaine by ethnicity) and 0.09 (crack/heroin by ethnicity).

33 The scales are reproduced in Appendix II. Self-esteem scores varied from 10 to 37, with a mean and median of 21.0 and a standard deviation of 4.9. Lower scores indicated higher self-esteem. Locus of control scores varied from 0 to 15 with a mean of 6.7 and a median of 7.0 and standard deviation of 2.7. Low scores indicate an internal control locus, while high scores indicate an external control locus.

34 Eta = 0.17 (self-esteem score by truancy), 0.01 (self-esteem score by general offending), 0.03 (self-esteem score by offended persistently); Pearson's r = 0.11 (self-esteem score by number of offences ever committed) and 0.10 (self-esteem score by number of offences in last year); eta = 0.17 (locus of control by truancy), 0.04 (locus of control by general offending), 0.07 (locus of control by offended persistently); Pearson's r = 0.04 (locus of control by number of offences ever committed) and 0.08 (locus of control by number of offences in last year).

35 Eta = 0.25 (number of offences ever by truancy) and 0.25 (number of offences in last year by truancy). Cramer's V = 0.18 (general offending by truancy), 0.20 (general drug use by truancy), 0.13 (crack/heroin use by truancy).

36 Recent users are those who had used an illicit drug during the last year, past users are those who had used an illicit drug but had not done so during the last year and non-users are those who had never used. Eta = 0.34 (number of

offences in last year by general drug use), 0.27 (number of offences in last year by solvent use) and 0.23 (number of offences in last year by crack/heroin use).

37 Cramers' $V = 0.13$ (truancy by family circumstances), eta = 0.12 (number of offences in last year by family circumstances), Cramer's $V = 0.15$ (crack/heroin use by family circumstances).

Chapter 7

Mentoring in practice

As we have outlined, the mentoring programmes which lay at the heart of this study had two main components. They sought to establish a one-to-one relationship between the young people and an adult assigned to them – their 'mentor'. Alongside this relationship, the programmes also provided a significant educational/training element – the 'plus' bit of Mentoring Plus. In this chapter we examine both these elements of the programme, from the initial residential that the majority of young people attended, through to the end of the young person's relationship with the programme (at some point during the course of the year).

We begin by looking at the issue of programme integrity. Previous research on many forms of social intervention has highlighted the central importance of implementation in understanding how interventions work (and whether they have any impact). In particular, an unfortunately large body of research has shown how failed implementation often lies at the heart of the apparent absence of success in interventions. Understanding project integrity is important therefore in helping us make sense of young people's engagement with the projects, as well as providing crucial contextual information for our discussion of impact in the later chapters.

Programme Integrity

Programme integrity has recently been identified as a key influence on the development of successful interventions. This notion covers a range of distinct, but related, issues including programme design, management and staffing. For a programme to have a high level of integrity it must employ skilled practitioners, the stated aims should be linked to the methods being used and management should be sound (Hollin 1995; McGuire and Priestley 1995). In essence, programme integrity is less concerned with programme content than with the process by which it is implemented, delivered and managed: according to Hollin (1995: 196) it 'simply means that the programme is conducted in practice as intended in theory and design'.

The integrity of the Mentoring Plus programme varied markedly across the ten projects included in the evaluation. Although none of the projects implemented the programme exactly as it is outlined in the literature (there was, for example, very little evidence of college 'taster' courses, as was generally promised), we concluded that four of them had achieved a relatively high degree of programme integrity: staff turnover in these projects was low and/or well managed and the main elements of the programme were implemented as planned.[1] Three of the projects achieved a moderate degree of integrity (staff turnover was reasonably well managed and some of the key elements were implemented as planned) and three achieved a low degree of integrity (staff turnover reached problematic levels and elements of the programme were consistently delayed or did not occur at all).

Four factors stood out as key influences on the integrity of the programme. First, was *staffing*. While the majority of staff said they enjoyed working at Mentoring Plus they also commonly reported being 'overloaded', of having to work unreasonably long hours and of having to 'cram stuff in to each day'. These pressures translated into a high degree of 'burnout' as nearly half (49 per cent) the staff involved in the projects had left Mentoring Plus by the end of the evaluation. In some projects staff shortages meant that elements of the programme had to be postponed or cancelled and downward spirals were established in which staff turnover and implementation failure fed off one another to create a sense of crisis: staff shortages meant that elements of the programme were postponed or cancelled which undermined staff morale and, potentially, led to further departures. Although Mentoring Plus staff were, on the whole, well qualified and highly experienced for their roles, once projects were caught in a downward spiral they often appointed new members of staff who had little by way of relevant qualifications and experience:

> I think just recently with the recent cycle, it's probably been the most
> difficult cycle yet and ... having one member of staff on long-term

sick leave and having the manager away for a couple of weeks during the quite critical point of recruitment and not having an administrator at that time which meant there was just one full-time member of staff and three part-time sessional staff … I kind of made the decisions I thought were right for the project … and give ourselves a deadline, if we don't get the young people in and we don't get the mentors by that date then we are not going to do it (project worker).

The second factor is *longevity*. Newly established projects were particularly vulnerable to high staff turnover, to downward spirals and to low levels of programme integrity. Six projects were established in the year before the evaluation started and of these four experienced a high degree of staff turnover, three achieved a low level of programme integrity and four closed down before the end of the evaluation. Three projects which were established at the same time or one year earlier achieved a high degree of integrity and none of them experienced anything more than a low level of staff turnover. Only one project achieved a high degree of programme integrity in the face of moderate or high staff turnover and this reflected a robustness which it had developed over time: it is no coincidence that this project had been running the longest out of all those included in the evaluation.

Thirdly, the *location* of the projects formed a recurring theme in interviews with project workers. Only one of the projects occupied premises on its own and this was considered important by the workers: 'the young people are free to roam about here and that's been fundamental to the success of the project.' The remaining projects shared premises with other community groups and workers voiced concerns that the projects were inaccessible and/or unappealing because they were located a long way from where the young people lived and/or because they were based in unsafe and inappropriate locations:

I mean, I think the venue can be a problem, where we are, I think the venue … I've heard from young people that it's not safe around here at night and stuff like that really and it's an issue for the walking home and this sort of 'gang culture', and territorial, you know, you're in my area … that kind of issue as far as engagement goes (project worker).

One of the projects ceased to operate temporarily as it relocated from premises in an area which the workers considered to be unsafe. Another project had to postpone elements of the programme as its premises were flooded and another project had to vacate its premises when they were declared unsafe by health and safety inspectors.

The final, and linked, factor was *funding*. Financial difficulties were an important threat to programme integrity. Some of the project workers felt the programme would have been better implemented and would have a greater impact if funds had been available to provide additional specialist services. In more extreme cases it was suggested that elements of the programme could not be implemented because of insufficient funding and, on occasion, short-term difficulties had long-term consequences. One of the project managers felt that the project had never recovered from an initial shortfall in funding and while the more recently established projects were most vulnerable to funding 'crises', the longer-term projects were not immune from them: financial difficulties were heavily implicated in the closure of three of the projects before the end of the evaluation.

These influences combined to create what were often unstable and unpredictable environments in which to work. Considerable disruption was evident across the projects; many experienced high levels of staff turnover and some simply ceased to operate. By the end of the evaluation period four out of the ten projects had closed down, one faced an uncertain future as it had ceased to operate and two had withdrawn from the Mentoring Plus umbrella. Some such disruption is common, if not endemic, within the voluntary sector, particularly in circumstances where future funding is far from guaranteed and organisations are caught up in a merry-go-round of fund-raising. Although far from unique, this operating environment is of central importance in understanding the nature of the Mentoring Plus projects, for it affects every aspect of their operation and shapes the experiences of project staff, mentors and young people.

Engaging with young people

While programme integrity provides a useful framework for thinking about the relationship between the delivery and the impact of mentoring there are some more immediate questions which must be addressed first. We have already seen that Mentoring Plus successfully identified a highly disadvantaged, often disruptive, socially detached group of young people. The next question to consider is: to what extent did it engage them?

Approximately two in three (69 per cent) of the young people referred to Mentoring Plus were recruited on to the programme. Information about their levels of engagement was provided by the projects and was classified according to the following criteria:[2]

1 *Not-engaged*: did not attend the project and was not given a mentor.

2 *Minimally engaged*: attended the project and/or met their mentor every couple of months or less often.

3 *Moderately engaged*: attended the project or met their mentor at least once a month.

4 *Highly engaged*: attended the project and met their mentor at least once a month.

The vast majority of young people recruited by Mentoring Plus engaged with the programme on some level. Approximately one in seven did not engage at all, while the rest were divided fairly equally between the different levels of engagement (see Figure 7.1). Almost three in five engaged with the project and/or the mentors at least once a month and slightly more than one in four engaged with both elements of the programme on this basis. Overall, the project achieved a higher level of engagement than the mentors. Young people who engaged actively with the project outnumbered those who engaged rarely or not at all (46 per cent compared with 36 per cent respectively), while the opposite pattern was evident in relation to the mentors (40 per cent compared with 46 per cent respectively).[3]

Overall rates of engagement with Mentoring Plus varied according to the young people's demographic characteristics although differences

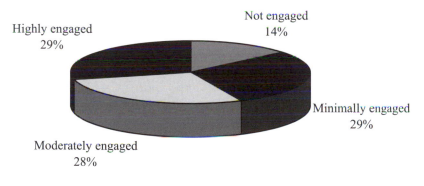

n = 391

Figure 7.1 Levels of engagement with Mentoring Plus (per cent of the cohort)
Source: Mentoring Plus cohort (project information).

between groups tended to be fairly modest. Young women tended to engage more actively than young men (46 per cent compared with 37 per cent) and young people from black and minority ethnic groups tended to engage more actively than white young people (47 per cent of black African Caribbeans, 43 per cent of mixed-race young people and 35 per cent of whites).[4] Going against the general trend, however, a very low rate of engagement was evident among south-Asian young people (only 10 per cent of those who took part in the recruitment process engaged actively with the programme).[5] Very little variation was evident according to age.[6]

Rates of engagement did vary according to the key dimensions of current activity and levels of offending. Crucially, Mentoring Plus appeared fairly effective in engaging those young people who were most at risk of social exclusion. In terms of current activity, the young people who were studying at college/university or who were on a training scheme or were in paid work were the least likely to engage actively with the Mentoring Plus programme (29 per cent), suggesting that they may have felt the focus on social exclusion was less relevant to their circumstances. While the highest rate of engagement was evident among those young people who were attending school or a special education unit (43 per cent engaged actively), similar rates of engagement were evident among those who were truanting regularly or were completely disengaged from education, training and work (38 per cent and 39 per cent respectively). In addition, those young people who offended persistently during the previous year were just as likely to engage actively as those who committed fewer offences (38 per cent of each group). Those who committed serious offences, however, were less likely to engage actively than those who had not done so (35 per cent compared with 47 per cent). Notable differences were also evident according to family structure, with the young people who had experienced greatest disruption being the most likely to engage actively (51 per cent of those living with foster parents or in a hostel; 44 per cent of those in reconstituted families; 42 per cent of those in single-parent families; 31 per cent of those in the 'other' category; and 26 per cent of those living in nuclear families)[7].

In seeking to explain these levels of engagement a number factors may be considered important. The projects did not assume that the young people would simply attend the programme and invested a considerable amount of time and energy building relationships, encouraging them to attend the programme and supporting them in various aspects of their lives: this involved frequent telephone calls, text messages, letters, passing messages on through friends, home visits, talking through problems and, in some cases, attending police stations and court. In addition, a range of incentives were built into the fabric of the programme which included money, vouchers, food and social activities/entertainment which would appeal to the young people (such as bowling and Laser Quest[8]). Within the London projects, moreover, the notion of 'cultural competence' may have been a key factor (Sangster *et al*. 2002). It seems likely that specific attempts to address the needs of black African/Caribbean youth, which included the recruitment of large numbers of black African/Caribbean staff and volunteers, contributed to the successful engagement of young people from these communities.

The mentoring relationship

At the end of the residential, mentors and young people were asked to nominate three people that they would like to work with and matches were announced at a 'matching meeting' one or two weeks later. Although the projects sought to match people who had chosen one another it was not always possible and some mentors and young people were matched with people they had not nominated. Matches were not made in any precise or scientific way and indeed the process varied across the projects. In general, young people were matched with people they 'got on with' or with mentors with particular personal characteristics, skills or experiences which were deemed to be appropriate and relevant: in one case, for example, a young person who wanted to work in the music industry was matched with a mentor who had strong connections in that area. Personal characteristics were also taken into account so, for example, male mentors were not matched with female mentees. Although the projects did not follow a policy of strict ethnic matching there was a tendency to match mentors and mentees with a shared ethnic heritage.

After the matching meeting the mentors and the young people with whom they had been matched were expected to identify the key issues on which they would focus and this provided the basis for an 'action plan'. Ideally the action plan should be developed by both partners and in most cases the areas identified reflected the programme's main aims and objectives: reducing offending or other anti-social behaviour or getting back into education, training or employment.

Numerous attempts have been made to understand and model mentoring relationships. By and large such models are linear in construction, following the relationship from its inception through different stages to its eventual conclusion. These models oversimplify the nature of mentoring and tend to overstate the centrality of goal-focused, instrumental activities. By idealizing mentoring in this way such models assume that young people will move relatively quickly into activities that either challenge some aspect of their behaviour or remedy some deficit in their social functioning (such as literacy and numeracy difficulties or other education or work-related issues). Though such models may have some didactic value, they do not reflect the complexity and diversity of mentoring relationships and tend to underplay the relatively mundane nature of much mentoring activity. Consequently, they may lead to unrealistic expectations among participants, funders and policy-makers. We offer an alternative way of looking at mentoring which is both more nuanced and realistic. In this model we describe the 'ordinariness' of much mentoring activity and offer a conceptual framework which highlights the cyclical and reactive nature of many mentoring relationships. We go on to consider how such relationships are managed by those involved before, finally, identifying a range of qualities which characterize 'successful' relationships.

Towards a model of mentoring

While mentoring relationships are often presented in linear form, our research suggests that in practice they are typically *cyclical* in nature. In its most basic form, for example, the mentoring relationship involves contact being made, a meeting being arranged and then undertaken. The activities involved when the parties meet are generally fairly mundane – having tea/coffee, playing pool, shopping, bowling, or perhaps going to the cinema. Almost all mentoring relationships will begin this way. Most will continue in this fashion for some time before they can progress further. Often, in fact, relationships do not progress much beyond this, if at all. This cycle of 'contact–meeting–doing' we refer to as the 'basic cycle'.

Much of what occurs in the mentoring relationship is *mundane*. Difficulties with the idealized action-oriented approach were evident very early on in most relationships as, in practice, constructing an action plan proved problematic. Many young people were unable to identify things that they wanted to change, while others simply did not turn up to the meeting. This is not to say that there were no examples of formal action planning between mentor and mentee at the outset of the relationship. And where such planning did occur, it tended to move the relationship beyond the 'basic cycle':

> Right from the beginning he wanted help finding a job. He wanted help with learning about skills for jobs. He wanted someone just to go round with him because at first he didn't have any confidence to go and ask if they had any vacancies. I used to go round with him. He used to pour out all of his problems and all of the things he has been through (mentor).

Such action-oriented behaviour so early in the relationship was rare, however, and contrary to the picture often held of mentoring, much of what happened had little obvious connection with responding to challenging behaviour or the causes or consequences of social exclusion. It was the mundane, humdrum stuff of basic human interaction which provided the staple diet for most mentoring relationships. This should not lead one to underestimate their importance, however, as it is precisely the repetition of such activities that helps to build familiarity and, with luck, eventually trust. And as studies of other quasi-therapeutic relationships have found (Newburn 1993; Mair *et al.* 1994) it is often vital that some form of practical engagement is established before any more substantial form of intervention can be attempted (if it is at all):

> I have told her stuff from a couple of times after meeting her and nothing has come back to me whatsoever, so then I brung it on a little bit more and nothing's come back to me and I brung it on more and more and then, in the end, I just let out everything and then nothing came back to me, do you know what I mean? And so, if she did go and say something like, to one of her mates, it wouldn't bother me, but if she told someone who like lives locally and then the word goes round that's when I would be really pissed (young person).

Given this, it is unsurprising, perhaps, that engaging in challenging, action-oriented activity in the context of mentoring relationships proved difficult. Moreover, while most relationships did not move beyond the 'basic cycle' this should not necessarily be considered problematic. And, arguably, only becomes so if there are expectations – on the part of the mentor, mentee or the project – that successful mentoring relationships will necessarily go beyond this stage.

Where relationships did progress, they often did so in response to a problem or crisis experienced by the mentee (e.g. homelessness, family breakdown, specific forms of offending, substance misuse, violent behaviour). As we have already suggested, proactive planning and action were relatively rare, particularly in the early stages of a relationship, and it was more often the case that problems emerged during the course of a meeting that the mentor needed to deal with. As such many mentoring relationships may be considered to be *reactive*. Because movement beyond the 'basic cycle' often involved reacting to a difficulty or problem that arose, we refer to this element in the relationship as 'fire-fighting'. Again, the relationship tended to be experienced cyclically with the emergence of an identifiable pattern where, in response to some problem or crisis, the contact–meeting–doing cycle extended into 'contact–meeting–doing–fire-fighting'. This fire-fighting element of the relationship came as a surprise to many of the mentors, especially those who held to the more ideal-typical model and, while some of them engaged actively with the issues that arose during this period, others were less able to cope and experienced difficulties around boundaries and emotions:

> I initially thought it would maybe mean meeting once a week for a couple of hours but the young person that I was matched with, it's been like, some weeks it's been like contact seven day's a week, you know if she's had a real difficult problem that she's had to deal with and it has meant, yeah, I've had to give her more support and I've had to go out and meet her. Sometimes I don't think the other volunteers understand that the contact is maybe a little bit more than what they actually think (mentor; see Cheryl's story).

Having progressed to the fire-fighting stage it is possible, as with the basic cycle, for a mentoring relationship to remain there for a considerable period. Once a particular problem had been dealt with, however, many relationships returned to the basic contact–meeting–doing cycle. That is to say there is no necessary progression on to a more advanced stage. Relationships may stay in the fire-fighting cycle, revert to the basic cycle or, in some cases, progress beyond the reactive fire-fighting stage, to become genuinely action-oriented and closer to what often appears to be the ideal-typical conception of mentoring.

More usually, where relationships did move into an action-oriented phase, this occurred fairly late on, once trust had developed and issues were identified. Then, more creative activities (with, say, time being spent engaged in job-hunting or in Internet cafes perfecting and sending CVs) could be identified and undertaken:

> [At first] she didn't really talk about family and stuff, and then it was only after that we sort of started, she started talking to me in little bits and bobs ... I suppose, definitely, she has learned to trust me, you know that must have been a big, really big thing for her ... In the first few months I didn't want to push it about her getting a career and this, that and the other, because basically she wasn't ready, you could just tell straight away, she was here, there and everywhere in her head, you know. I just wanted to befriend her really, I just wanted her to sort of just be able to come up and say, 'can we go out for a chat?' The first half of the year was definitely just more like going out every week and chatting, her getting to know as much about me as possible because I thought that would be quite important and then I'd slowly

try to bring a little bit of structure and we did our action plans (mentor).

Once again, this process was experienced, and may be presented, as a cycle of activity. The 'action-oriented cycle' tended to be either a four or five-stage process depending on whether fire-fighting was necessary (contact–meeting–doing–[fire-fighting]–action). As a means of simplifying and understanding the mentoring relationship we may therefore identify three potential cycles:

- The basic cycle: contact–meeting–doing.
- The problem-solving cycle: contact–meeting–doing–fire-fighting.
- The action-oriented cycle: contact–meeting–doing–[fire-fighting]– action.

In Figure 7.2 these cycles appear from left to right along an arrow indicating the start and end of the mentoring relationship. Though linear in appearance, this should not be taken to imply that we see there being any necessary progression from one cycle to another. Although possible, such progression is not inevitable and should not be expected. Mentoring relationships may never proceed beyond the basic cycle or, alternately, having reached either the problem-solving or action-oriented cycle may then revert to the basic cycle. As the surrounding box indicates, the basic cycle is in many ways the staple of the mentoring relationship, and even in those cases where the relationship has 'moved on' to problem-solving or to action it may revert at any time to the basic cycle. As with relationships more generally, there is no clear and simple path that can be charted in mentoring. Indeed, this is even more the case given the fragile nature of most mentoring relationships.

Starting and managing the relationship

At almost any stage the relationship between mentor and mentee may break down. Failure to keep appointments is frequently cited as a reason for breakdown (though it may also be a consequence of relationship breakdown of course) and there are many other potential sources of difference and even conflict. For both mentor and mentee, the relationship is one that requires considerable investment and trust, and is one that is experienced – perhaps particularly when it does not move beyond the basic cycle – as a rather fragile entity. This fragility is generally ever present in the mentoring relationship, though is especially visible in the early stages:

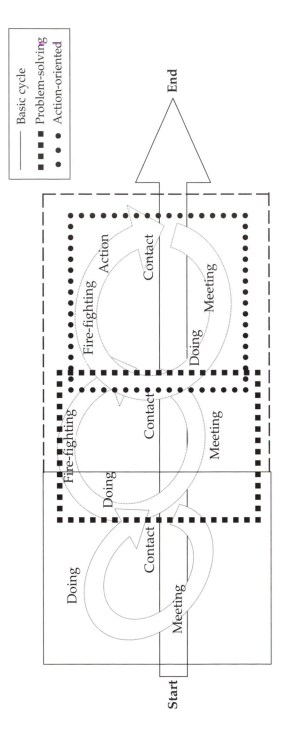

Figure 7.2 A model of the mentoring relationship

Well, I tried to make contact with him quite a few times and he didn't make contact back with me. And that is the truth. I lost motivation because I didn't want to feel as though I was stalking him and putting him under pressure to meet up. I did put quite a lot of effort into it (mentor).

I don't know, I never felt that I could really talk to her. It was just kind of a still atmosphere when I was with her. So I didn't really like it that much (young person).

In the early stages the projects were proactive in arranging interaction between the mentor and the young person. Structured activities were organised by the project with the aim of establishing basic contact and beginning a process of demystifying the idea of mentoring. The start of the mentoring relationship, however, signalled the point at which the mentors took greater charge of the relationship and what happened within it. Not many of the young people commented on their first meeting with their mentor (outside the residential setting). Those who had not been allocated the mentor of their choice or had not attended the residential (selection by proxy) reported having had a positive experience/impression of their mentor at their initial meeting, where they saw him/her as showing an interest in how they felt, as being 'understanding', or where their mentor appeared to be fun to be with:

She rang me up and said we would meet in McDonald's and that she would be wearing a red coat. I went there and I see someone in a red coat. I went to her and I said 'hello, is your name Jenny', and she said 'yeah' and from that day we just started talking. We went in the restaurant and had something to eat, we chatted for about two hours. She was a really nice woman, she was all right to talk to as well, she was understanding, that is why I got along with her I reckon (young person).

Generally, the young person and his or her mentor would arrange where to meet and what to do by mutual agreement, either from one session to the next, or over the telephone, depending on the schedules of both mentor and mentee. Unsurprisingly perhaps given the somewhat chaotic lives that many of the young people led, turning up for meetings was by no means guaranteed. Simply 'not being bothered' was one of the main reasons that young people gave for failing to keep appointments or, linked with this, that they felt they had other more important, or more attractive options:

I disliked the time I had to take. Sometimes I couldn't be bothered to meet her, sometimes I could be, but back then I was a little kid and I wanted to go out and play football. [But] my mum would find out; she would slap me on my head and say 'go' and I would just go (young person).

In addition, in response to the first, follow-up survey, approximately one quarter (27 per cent) of the young people said that they did not feel that they needed a mentor and a third (31 per cent) said that they could not really relate to their mentor. Under such circumstances establishing a relationship between mentor and young person was especially problematic. These are tricky human relationships which have considerable potential for rupture – and by no means just because of the behaviour of the mentee:

I was supposed to go to the job centre that day or something, but told her [the mentor] that I was feeling a bit ill. 'Oh any excuse' [she said], and I was telling her the truth … I told her to get off my fucking line and I switched off the phone (young person).

However, even when contact was made, and the basis of a relationship established, the failure to keep appointments was one of the key 'stress points', often leading the relationship to break down. The impact of such breakdown on the young person depended in part on his or her attitude to mentoring, and also on his or her relationship with the mentoring project more broadly. Where they felt supported by the project they sometimes felt that the mentor was less important. In practice, the majority of the young people developed quite strong and positive relationships with one or more project workers, and at times would see 'the people in the project (as) more like my mentors than my actual mentor'. Only a small minority (8 per cent) of the young people mentioned that they did not get on with the workers at Mentoring Plus. Where they had a less supportive relationship with the project, however, feelings that their mentor was not 'sticking with them' could be particularly upsetting:

My boyfriend went in jail and I did phone her a bit late, I think it was about half eleven. But I needed that support but even if she didn't pick up the phone she would have had a missed call and it would have said from Sara. And she didn't phone me back and I thought … that was a bit out of order because she could have phoned me to see if I was all right. She must have known that something was wrong with me because I don't normally phone her that late … I thought that I could rely on her because she told me that I could rely on her ... I have told her that I have lost weight, I lost a stone, that is how depressed I am, so the thing that she could do is at least phone me (young person).

Speaking to Sara five months later, she had not been in contact with her mentor since that point. On the whole, in relationships where project workers and/or mentors were clear about boundaries, and where the young people felt supported by the project, a telephone call not received or a meeting having to be rearranged was less problematic than it might be in other circumstances; the longer established the relationship the less likely it was to break down:

There are occasions when [the mentor] has not turned up but there are occasions she has had a really good excuse not to turn up. But having said that it doesn't really bother me because ... even when you first meet you're asked to understand that they have got to work and they have got their own life as well as being there for you, they've got their own lives and they have got their own things to sort out, so they can't be there with you 24/7 but they can be there the majority of the time. Sometimes, she doesn't phone me, but I don't think anything of it, that she has got her own life and that she will phone me when she is ready (young person).

Qualities of successful relationships

A number of characteristics of a 'successful' mentor, or mentoring relationship, were identified by the young people, of which five appeared to be key. First, 'being able to talk'. A significant element of any mentoring relationship revolves around fairly mundane everyday communication and conversation. As we described in relation to the 'basic cycle', the very act of engaging with the young person in this way, however mundane it may feel, is both a significant aspect of the mentoring relationship and potentially the basis for more far-reaching activity:

I could tell her anything, and there was a lot of things that I couldn't speak to other people including my friend and I spoke to [my mentor] about it and it helped me, because I got it all off my chest, you know speaking about it (young person).

The second characteristic we have termed 'reciprocity'. 'Success' demanded that the mentor give something of him or herself. Of course, much of this was simply time, and the opportunity to talk. In addition, however, a willingness to share personal information, particularly where that might involve difficulties that the mentor had experienced and possibly overcome, was perceived by the young people to be an important component in the developing relationship:

> I gave her the basics before I could get a bit deep – I have trouble at home with my mum and at school and this, that and the other, and she was like 'OK then'. And we spoke and stuff and then later … she told me stuff about her. Saying it made it easier for me to talk as well, because, I was like, 'OK then, she is not like a robot or anything like that'. So yeah it was all right. And then, just the other day I saw her and she was upset because her friend did commit suicide and she was the last one that he saw, so I was like 'OK then', and I was talking to her and that, not brought her out of her shell, but I was talking to her until she felt relaxed and that she could talk. And she said to me 'thank you' (young person).

Thirdly, and linked to the last point, successful mentoring relationships tended to be based on respect rather than authority. Typically of disaffected young people, many of the difficulties that the mentees faced concerned, to a greater or lesser degree, the relationships with authority figures – parents, teachers, social workers, police officers, etc. Building a relationship based on trust – however tricky and tenuous – in which the mentor avoided imposing his or her priorities on the young person was seen to be a significant element in creating a space or atmosphere in which constructive dialogue, and potentially activity, could take place: 'In our school structure, teachers are supposed to be higher than you, therefore you've got to respect them and they don't have to respect you, but with a mentor you have to respect them and they have to respect you, so it's completely different' (young person).

Fourthly, and perhaps predictably, it was absolutely vital that mentors were, and were perceived to be, understanding and interested in young people. The young people tended to have good 'bullshit detectors' and resented mentors that they felt were not genuine in their desire to provide help and support:

> [Mentors are] genuinely interested in what is going on in your life, and they are not just there because it is a job, because as far as I'm aware they are like volunteers so they are not getting paid, so they can't really pretend because there is nothing in it for them (young person).

Finally, and related to much that we have had to say so far about not underestimating the importance of activities that on the surface may appear ordinary or mundane, the other quality that mentees identified as crucial to the success of a mentoring relationship was 'having fun': '[Mentoring] is about people helping you, like giving you advice when you need it, someone to talk to, someone to confide in, someone to have a laugh with, someone to go out with and things like that' (young person).

Only a minority of young people saw their mentor all the way through until the official end of the mentoring relationship, one year later. In addition to the premature breakdowns of relationships, described above, in some cases, the relationship would come to a natural end during the course of the year because the young person felt that he or she did not really need his or her mentor any more, had moved on, or either the young person and/or mentor was too busy and involved in too many activities to keep up the relationship. The majority of those who saw their mentor for the full year said that they were hoping to keep, or were still keeping, in contact. For some this meant that they would still meet their mentor, albeit less frequently. Those who were still seeing each other mentioned that at this stage the nature of the relationship had changed:

> Our season is kind of over soon ... But we still carried on meeting each other over Christmas time, even like Mentoring Plus didn't have nothing going on. Now it is not even like mentor and mentee, it is just like big friend, little friend, that is what it is like after a while. I think that is the whole point of it like, you can go past a certain stage, so you can drop the barrier, so yeah (young person).

The Plus element

The young people's attitudes to the Plus element of the programme tended to be very positive. In response to the first follow-up survey almost all of those who had attended the project indicated that they liked going to Mentoring Plus and that they enjoyed the activities there (92 per cent in both cases). A recurring theme within the depth interviews centred around the idea that, by going to Mentoring Plus, the young people were 'killing two birds with one stone': that is, they were having fun and getting help at the same time: 'It's fun to be on the project', cos you do things that are good, it helps you deal with things, helps you with life, they can help you get into college and stuff and you have fun the same time' (male young person).

Case study: Cheryl's story

Cheryl was in her mid to late 20s when she volunteered to become a mentor, after seeing an advert in a local newspaper. She had children of her own and had considerable experience of working with young people but wanted to work with young adults and felt that being a mentor would help her to become a youth worker. At the residential Cheryl spent quite a lot of time with Dawn and the two of them were subsequently matched with one another:

> One of the things we particularly laugh about is that we were both frightened of heights and we were on this assault course, and I remember thinking to myself, there's no way I'm going there, forget that, and she was really terrified, and I was encouraging this young person, 'yeah, go on climb that tree, you'll be pretty safe up there'.

Dawn was was living in residential care and, although Cheryl was nervous about being a mentor, she felt well prepared: 'I've come to the project with my eyes open anyway', cause I'd worked with teenagers in care, and I'd dealt with teenagers that don't want to bond and don't want to speak to you.' Cheryl had also left home at a young age and felt she could relate to Dawn and understand her. After an initial 'testing' period Dawn began to 'open up' and told Cheryl how frightened she was of being alone:

> It took a bit of time for the young person to trust me, you know she was very inquisitive about why I was on the project, 'why do you want to do this when you're not getting paid?', you know, sort of them questions at first … At the beginning I think she was cautious as to what she was telling … we could have a laugh and joke about the residential and that was OK but when it comes to talking about problems that she had and things needed sorting she would tell me part of the story but she wouldn't tell me the whole story. And then maybe a couple of days later she'd phone and say, 'oh, I didn't tell you this the other day' … But over a period of time, the relationship has changed … and it's just now totally different and more trusting.

Over the course of the year Dawn went through some 'bad times'. She suffered a bereavement and was moved from one care home to another. During these times Cheryl spoke to Dawn most days and tried to help her understand what was happening. At Dawn's request Cheryl attended a Social Services case review. By the end of the year Dawn's situation had become more stable (see Chapter 4) and her relationship with Cheryl had begun to change:

> At the beginning we met like once a week, twice a week and then through the bad times it's been a lot more contact. But recently it's just sort of died off again. She phoned me sort of like said, 'thanks for everything but I don't really need to see you as much now and me life's moved on.'

The young people spoke very positively about the project workers. Mentoring Plus was often described in terms of providing a 'relaxed' environment and the project workers were considered to have a key role in this regard. Their non-judgemental approach was contrasted favourably with the reactions of other adults, particularly those, such as teachers, who occupy the role of authority figures. According to one of the young people the project workers 'treat you like normal people' while another explained:

> When you think of a project like this, you would think that it was all people who put their nose up about you because you are all common … these don't look at you like that, and they think of ways to get you out of trouble. They don't just look at you and think 'oh there's no hope for that person'; like, if you've been arrested or anything like that, they still tell you that you've still got a chance, like they still help you out with trying to get a job and that, but a lot of people would just be like, 'well you've been arrested, you ain't getting the job', so they really help you (young person).

As well as providing practical help, the project workers were considered to have had a therapeutic role as they listened to the young people and talked through problems with them:

> It's the best place to go where people listen and do care and they help you get through whatever your troubles are … and greet you with open arms (young person).

> I love the sort of atmosphere, it is like a little unit. I like units, and I like family feeling … and they have given so much to me (young person).

Although the projects were generally described by the young people as providing a supportive environment much of what they did involved an underlying sense of instability and unpredictability. In private moments some of the workers expressed serious misgivings about the 'violent', 'intolerant', 'misogynistic' and 'disrespectful' nature of some of the young people's attitudes and behaviour. At the projects the young people often goaded one another and low-level verbal conflict was commonplace and, although much of this took the form of 'playful' banter, there was a clear potential for escalation. On most occasions this potential was avoided as the staff maintained a reasonable degree of control. However, on some occasions this control broke down and instances of violence and anti-social behaviour were observed by the research team. These incidents occurred most often during the residential.

The residential provides a key early element of the Mentoring Plus programme. Taking the young people away, out of their usual surroundings, is intended to 'build self-awareness and respect, trust in others, cooperation and communication skills' (Benioff 1997: 40). While some of the young people and mentors spoke positively about the residential and described such outcomes there were clear problems with this element of the programme. Indeed, the extent of the problems we observed suggests that there is something inherently unpredictable about the residential experience. Residentials were characterized by an underlying sense of chaos and tension between the young people and adults (both as project workers and mentors). The young people routinely refused to go to bed at the set time and often kept workers and mentors (and researchers!) up until three or four o'clock in the morning. Among the other challenges that the young people presented were drinking, drug use (mainly cannabis), violence and sexualized behaviour:

> I would go again. It was just mad though, chaos, a weekend where there was just no sleep, and they [the project workers] say they are the sex police, and the women patrol the girls' landing and the men patrol the boys' landing … there is no sex, but it is just jumping out of each others' bedroom, you know, and keeping each other apart. But some people want to sleep, so they put the mentors in the bedrooms with us, because the lads crept in, but we weren't doing nothing. We were just sat on the beds talking and then my mate nearly had a fight with one of the lads over something – a packet of crisps or something – so the lads just kept bursting into our room and they broke the door … [The mentors] didn't like it. The first ones got out and got another bedroom ; the second ones come in and they was all right, they was funny (young person).

On one residential a young person attacked another with a pool cue; at a second, a group of three young people covered another with toothpaste while he slept and then urinated on him; on a third, one of the young people from Mentoring Plus assaulted a young person from another group bursting his ear-drum; and, at a fourth, one of the young people became drunk, fell over and had to be taken to hospital. In addition, a Mentoring Plus sports day in London ended with a street fight between young people from different projects and the police had to be called.

While residentials and related activities are designed to provide an intense experience which breaks down barriers and builds relationships, the potential for some very negative unintended consequences is ever present. Placing a group of young people who are likely to be highly impulsive (Smith and McVie 2003) in unfamiliar situations with people they do not know appears to constitute a flash point for problematic behaviour. In order to protect the valuable contribution that such events make, the notions of risk and risk assessment should be central to their planning and implementation.

Conclusion

There are a number of important conclusions that can be drawn from this discussion of mentoring in practice. First, it is hugely important to recognize that despite difficulties in implementation, Mentoring Plus achieved relatively high levels of engagement with extremely 'hard to engage' young people. This achievement should not be underestimated. As we outlined in the first two chapters of the book, one of the core characteristics of disaffection is an unwillingness or inability to 'engage'. That the programmes should have successfully involved such a high proportion of these young people is, in itself, an important indicator of success. Particular concerns have been voiced about the difficulties of engaging black and minority ethnic young people. However, they too were generally well represented on the mentoring programmes, although the low level of south-Asian representation is notable.

Secondly, as we have demonstrated in some detail, mentoring cannot be reduced to a simple model. Mentoring contains many elements, phases and stages. Although much talk of mentoring appears to assume that the term is clear, unproblematic and subject to general consensus, in practice mentoring is a fairly capacious term that can very easily encompass a variety of activities. Mentoring Plus, the particular variety of mentoring under analysis here, included both the establishment of some form of relationship between the young person and a 'mentor' – what is generally considered to be the essence of 'mentoring' – but, at least as importantly, placed great emphasis on the educational 'plus' element as well. Thus, when hearing 'mentoring' discussed it is generally wise to ask what is meant and what the particular activity or activities include. The young people's accounts of their experiences in this research suggest that the 'Plus' element of Mentoring Plus was at least as important as the 'mentoring' element.

Perhaps predictably, this research suggests that the mentoring relationship is difficult to establish and difficult to sustain. Not surprisingly, given what we have had to say about the young people accepted on to these programmes, and arguably given the difficulty of establishing new relationships even under the most propitious circumstances, creating a positive relationship between mentor and mentee was often far from straightforward. Once mentor and mentee had been brought together, and even when they had established some rapport, there were considerable barriers to be overcome in maintaining that relationship. It is relatively easy for misunderstanding to occur, for one or other party to become disappointed or disenchanted with the other. Mentoring relationships are best thought of, therefore, as being inherently fragile. It is important, in particular, that mentors understand this, that they are supported in their attempts to establish relationships with young people, and that they are helped to be realistic about what can be achieved and how quickly.

Although the 'ideal type' model of mentoring contains an assumption of action towards particular goals (that is to say towards substantive work), in practice mentoring is significantly more complex than this. Substantive work is something which, ideally, mentors and mentees should be working towards but, in reality, will often occur, if at all, after quite some time has passed and then only for a short period of time. In practice, far from involving substantive work, much mentoring is mundane and reactive. That much 'mentoring' is mundane should be made clear to mentors at the outset. By contrast, and as is often the case currently, the existence of assumptions about the likelihood of a linear development in relationships towards substantive work places significant burdens, and often unrealistic expectations, on mentors. It is easy for mentors to become frustrated, and to lose confidence, in the face of what may feel like a lack of progress. Progress – inasmuch as it is defined as moving towards substantive work – should not necessarily be an expectation within mentoring. At the very least, a shift towards substantive working is not something that should be expected early on in a mentoring relationship nor, if established at all, should it be assumed that it will form a long-term or continuous element in such work.

Notes

1 The degree of programme integrity achieved by each project was assessed formally through a mixture of quantitative and qualitative measures. Staff turnover was a key measure and was considered to be low if no more than two members of staff left the project during the course of the evaluation, as moderate if three or four members of staff left and as high if five or more members of staff left. The extent to which staff turnover was routine (staff were replaced within three months) or problematic (staff were not replaced within three months) was also taken into account. Qualitative judgements were also made about the extent to which each project adhered to the Mentoring Plus model and the extent to which the programme was implemented as planned.

2 Project workers were asked to rate how often each of the young people recruited to the programme had engaged with the project and his or her mentor. Information was provided for 86 per cent of the young people although some of the projects were unable to provide it: under these circumstances, individuals were classified on the basis of their responses to the first follow-up survey. Using both sources of data, levels of engagement were classified for 93 per cent of the young people recruited to the programme.

3 Active engagement refers to that which took place on a monthly basis or more often, while rare engagement refers to that which only occurred once or twice.

4 Young people were considered to have engaged actively with the programme if they engaged with the project and/or the mentors on a monthly basis or more often. The rates of engagement given here are based on all the young people who took part in the recruitment process (those young people who were not recruited to the programme were combined with those who were recruited but did not engage).

5 Although the number of cases was small (only 19 south-Asian young people took part in the recruitment process) the difference is sufficiently marked to be considered meaningful.

6 Cramer's v = 0.12 (level of engagement by sex); 0.12 (level of engagement by ethnicity) and Kendall's tau-c = 0.01 (level of engagement by age).

7 Cramer's v = 0.10 (level of engagement by current activity); Kendall's tau-c = 0.04 (level of engagement by frequency of offending); and Cramer's v = 0.66 (level of engagement by offended persistently); 0.12 (level of engagement by committed serious offence) and 0.11 (level of engagement by family structure).

8 The latter is the name of a laser tag game. Details at:
http://www.laserquest.co.uk/

Chapter 8

Impact of the programme

Until recently, interventions aiming to reduce youth disaffection have been surrounded by a considerable degree of pessimism. For many years, the conventional wisdom within criminology, penology, psychology and social work was that 'nothing works'. Over the last fifteen years or so, however, there has been a significant shift in thinking. Mair (1991: 7) expressed early dissatisfaction with the received view when he declared that 'For an emperor which has been scantily clad, "Nothing Works" has had a long reign.' Over the next few years the evidence which had given rise to the idea that nothing works was called into question and a substantial amount of counter-evidence was produced. By the mid-1990s, the focus had moved on to 'What Works?' and commentators were able to argue, with some confidence, that 'Across the range of evidence now bearing on this point, a number of features emerge with sufficient consistency for it now to be possible to identify ingredients of effective intervention programmes' (McGuire and Priestley 1995: 4).

While there is a large body of research on 'delinquency treatment' which shows 'positive average treatment effects of modest but not trivial magnitude', positive outcomes have not been evident uniformly across all interventions, young people and circumstances (Lipsey 1995: 77). There is, in addition, strong evidence that simply providing opportunities for change is unlikely to be sufficient. Multi-modal interventions which recognize the variety of problems that individuals face have been found to be particularly effective, while some specific types of approach have been more strongly endorsed than others. Cognitive-behavioural approaches currently appear to have most evidence of impact, while the value of skills-oriented approaches, which focus on problem-solving, social inter-action and coping skills, has also been established (Lipsey 1995; McGuire and Priestley 1995; Audit Commission 1996; though see also Falshaw *et al.* 2003). By contrast, considerable doubt has been cast over the value of classic psychotherapeutic models and approaches which use general counselling, casework, family counselling and psychodynamic therapy based on gaining insight (Audit Commission 1996: 109). There is, however, an element of ambiguity here as counselling and psychotherapy may employ structured cognitive-behavioural approaches and the literature suggests that such approaches have a positive impact (Gendrau and Ross 1980; Thornton 1987).

As we noted earlier programme integrity has been identified as an im-portant influence on effectiveness. This notion covers a range of distinct, but related, issues including programme design, management and staff-ing. For a programme to have a high level of integrity, it must employ skilled practitioners, the stated aims should be clearly linked to the methods being used and management should be sound (Hollin 1995; McGuire and Priestley 1995). As we outlined earlier, programme integrity is concerned with the process by which a programme is implemented, delivered and managed and 'simply means that the programme is conducted in practice as intended in theory and design' (Hollin 1995: 196).

Assessing the impact of the programme

Programme evaluations often employ apparently 'objective' outcome measures with little, if any, consideration of participants' 'subjective' experiences. This, it seems to us, is an important omission. Participants' attitudes towards a programme are likely to be highly suggestive of impact and may act as an important intermediary between implementa-tion and outcome. We saw in the previous chapter that the young people involved in Mentoring Plus were reasonably positive about the programme and we now consider whether this extended to a feeling that the programme had been helpful to them. As part of the follow-up surveys the young people recruited on to programme were asked to assess how helpful Mentoring Plus and their mentor had been, both generally and in relation to specific areas such as education, employment and offending. We begin by considering the young people's responses to these questions and then go on to consider whether any discernible changes were apparent in their objective circumstances.

Perceived helpfulness of the programme

By the time their involvement in the programme was coming to an end, most of the young people felt that both the Plus element and the mentors had been of some help (see Figure 8.1). Overall, the Plus element of the programme tended to be rated more favourably than the mentors. The proportion of participants who rated the Plus element 'very helpful' was slightly greater than the proportion who rated the mentors in this way. In addition, although levels of non-engagement were very similar for both components, the mentors were rated as 'not at all helpful' at almost twice the rate of the Plus element.

These judgements proved to be fairly robust and generally still applied some six months after the end of the programme. Two in three (66 per cent) young people gave the Plus element precisely the same rating in response to both follow-up surveys and a similar degree of consistency was evident in relation to the mentors (63 per cent).[1] Where opinions changed, they tended to become less favourable, although this trend was very modest. By the time of the second follow-up survey one in five (22 per cent) young people felt that their mentor had been 'not at all helpful' and one in ten (9 per cent) felt this way about the Plus element.

The perceived helpfulness of the programme varied markedly across the projects. At the end of the programme, the proportion of young people

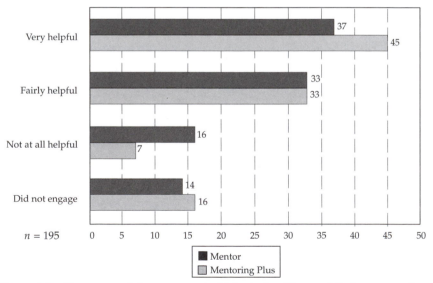

Figure 8.1 Young people's assessment of Mentoring Plus and their mentors (per cent of the cohort)
Source: Mentoring Plus cohort (first follow-up survey).

who rated the Plus element as 'very helpful' varied from approximately two in three (63 per cent) to one in four (25 per cent). And a similar degree of variation was evident in relation to the mentors (58–27 per cent). The ratings given to the different elements of the programme were highly consistent, so that projects that were rated most highly in relation to the Plus element also tended to be rated most highly in relation to the mentors.[2]

Overall judgements about the helpfulness of the programme[3] were linked to the integrity with which they were implemented. The key distinction was between projects that achieved a high or moderate level of integrity and those that achieved a low level of integrity. Participants in projects which were highly or moderately well implemented were one and a half times as likely as those in poorly implemented projects to rate the programme as 'very helpful' (62 per cent, 60 per cent and 40 per cent respectively).[4]

As well as providing general assessments of how helpful the programme had been, the young people who responded to the follow-up surveys were asked to indicate how, or in which areas, the programme had helped them. The most frequently identified areas of help were those connected to general functioning such as goal-setting, self-confidence and decision-making (see Figure 8.2). In terms of social exclusion, the

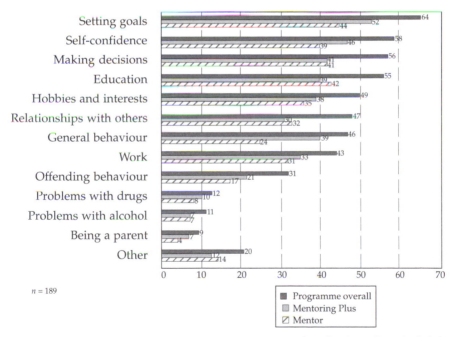

n = 189

Programme overall
Mentoring Plus
Mentor

Figure 8.2 Areas in which the programme was considered to have been helpful (per cent of the cohort)
Source: Mentoring Plus cohort (first follow-up survey).

programme was thought to have been most helpful in relation to education and somewhat less so in relation to work and offending:

> When we first met up we had to write my CV and sort out my hostel and we did that and then I got a job for the summer, she sorted out all my school 'cause I weren't going to school and didn't go in for all my exams, and so she sorted that out for me … She's just helped me feel more organized, basically, I've told her what I want to do, and she just helped me to do it, and she's been there to push me the few steps I've needed to be pushed … If she weren't there I wouldn't be going back to school. I used to go and hang around the streets and do crime and stuff but now I can't be bothered to do that because I want to get a job, just want to go to college (young person).

> In my last school I was really, really bad and I got excluded four times … [for] hitting a teacher with a chair, punching a teacher in the head, fighting and throwing a chair through the window … I had a bad temper problem and I couldn't control it … I normally meet Janine [mentor] every Tuesday or Wednesday or Monday to talk to see what I have done at school, I show her the work, what I done and then we talk … [Mentors] help you control your temper and they take you out places and it helps you in school because they give you targets and that helps you get merits and smiles – so it gives you targets to do (young person).

While the Plus element of the programme was, once again, generally rated as more helpful than the mentors, there were a few exceptions to this trend. Most notably, the number of young people who indicated that their mentor had helped them in the areas of education and work was almost the same as the number who indicated that they had been helped by the Plus element in these areas. In part, this reflected the way in which the two elements of the programme in relation to education and work tended to complement one another. The proportion of young people who indicated that they had been helped by either element of the programme was not very much greater than the proportion who indicated that they had been helped by either the mentors or the Plus element. It follows from this that, in most cases, the young people had been helped by both elements, rather than by one of them in isolation:

> My young mentee, it's helped here a lot and I think it's the education programme that's made her realize that 'yeah I can do things', you know it's got her confidence as well. Every now and again we like sit

down on a one-to-one and do the work together … She's gained entry level one in maths and English and we talked about level two and it was 'no, I'm not doing that, that's too hard'. Like at the presentation the other evening she picked up four certificates and I said to her 'I'm really proud, are you glad you did it now?' and she went 'yeah I'm glad'. And I said to her jokingly, 'well, we'll start that level two soon' and she went 'no', but the next day she was on the phone, 'I want to start level two, will you come and help me?' (mentor).

Changing circumstances?

As a substantial proportion of the young people recruited to Mentoring Plus felt that the programme had helped them in some way, it is crucial to consider whether these subjective assessments were matched by changes in their objective circumstances. The potential impact of the programme was assessed in relation to engagement with education, training and work; family relationships; offending; substance use; and self-esteem. For each of these areas, we begin by considering whether any changes were evident among the young people in the cohort during the course of the programme and in the six months which followed. We then compare programme participants and non-participants[5].

We noted earlier that levels of engagement in Mentoring Plus varied according to the young people's demographic characteristics (see Chapter 7) and it is important to assess the implications that this may have in relation to impact. If the profiles of the two groups vary markedly from one another then it may be that it is these variations, rather than participation in the programme, which explain any differences in outcome. A breakdown of the key demographic characteristics for programme participants and non-participants is shown in Table 8.1.

Crucially, the age profiles of the two groups are very similar. This is particularly important as our key outcome indicators – such as engagement in education, training and work, offending and substance use – vary markedly with age. Although the sex and ethnicity profiles of participants and non-participants differ this arguably has less serious implications for measuring impact. At the start of the programme the key outcome indicators tended to vary more markedly with age than with either ethnicity or sex.

Education, training and work

Important changes were evident in the current status of the young people who joined Mentoring Plus during the year of the programme and, in

Table 8.1   Demographic characteristics of programme participants and non-participants (per cent of participants and non-participants)[6]

	Participants	Non-participants
Age		
12–14	17	15
15	48	47
16	21	23
17–19	14	16
	100	100
Sex		
Male	65	72
Female	35	28
	100	100
Ethnicity		
White	39	53
Black Caribbean	37	24
Black African	9	6
Asian	2	10
Mixed-race/dual heritage	13	7
	100	100

Note:
n = 164 (participants), 70 (non-participants).
Source: Mentoring Plus cohort (first survey).

many ways, these changes reflected the transition through adolescence and into early adulthood (see Figure 8.3).[7] The biggest shift appeared to be from school to college/university as the proportion of young people in the cohort who were, or should have been, in school almost halved while the proportion in college/university more than tripled. Large relative increases were also evident in relation to training schemes and paid work, although the numbers involved in these activities remained fairly small.

The proportion of young people who appeared to be completely disengaged from education, training and work remained largely the same. If this category is combined with those who were truanting regularly or were excluded from school, however, there was, arguably, some overall improvement in the position of the young people who joined the programme (the proportion in these categories fell from 46 to 35 per cent).

Further changes were evident by the time of the second, 18-month follow-up, primarily in relation to school and paid work. The proportion

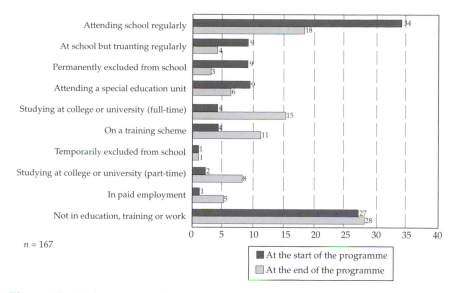

Figure 8.3 Main activity at the beginning and end of the programme (per cent of the cohort)
Note: The figures given here are based on members of the cohort who responded to both the original questionnaire and the first follow-up.
Source: Mentoring Plus cohort (original survey and first follow-up).

of the cohort in paid work more than doubled to one in eight (13 per cent); while the proportion who were, or should have been, attending school fell to below one in four (17 per cent were at school, less than 1 per cent were temporarily excluded from school and 3 per cent were attending a special education unit).[8] In contrast, the numbers of young people who were studying at college or university (18 per cent full time and 8 per cent part time) or were on a training scheme (9 per cent) remained largely unchanged, as did the proportion who were disengaged from education, training and work (32 per cent).

As they moved from school to college, training and work a reasonably large number of the young people who joined Mentoring Plus secured formal qualifications. During the year they were involved in the programme one in four (27 per cent) gained GCSEs, one in twelve (8 per cent) gained an NVQ and one in twenty (5 per cent) gained a BTEC or City and Guilds qualification. In addition, during the six months that followed the end of the programme, one in seven (15 per cent) gained GCSEs, one in ten (9 per cent) gained an NVQ and one in thirty-three (3 per cent) gained a BTEC or City and Guilds qualification.

Table 8.2 Main activity at the beginning and end of the programme by participation (per cent of participants and non-participants).

	Beginning of programme	End of programme	Change
Participants			
Attending school/special education unit	38	21	−17
Studying at college or university	6	25	+19
On a training scheme or in paid employment	6	17	+11
At school but truanting regularly	10 ⎫	5 ⎫	−5 ⎫
Excluded from school	11 ⎬ 51	5 ⎬ 38	−6 ⎬ −13
Not in education, employment or training	30 ⎭	28 ⎭	−2 ⎭
	100	100	
Non-participants			
Attending school/special education unit	47	38	−9
Studying at college or university	15	18	+3
On a training scheme or in paid employment	7	12	+5
At school but truanting regularly	7 ⎫	1 ⎫	−6 ⎫
Excluded from school	4 ⎬ 31	0 ⎬ 33	−4 ⎬ +2
Not in education, employment or training	20 ⎭	32 ⎭	+12 ⎭
	100	100	

Notes:
n = 152 (participants), 67 (non-participants).
The figures given here are based on individuals who responded to both the original questionnaire and the first follow-up.
Source: Mentoring Plus cohort (original survey and first follow-up).

To assess whether any of these changes might reasonably be attributed to Mentoring Plus, the young people who had participated in the programme were compared with those who had not. Given that education and work were two of the areas in which the mentors and the Plus element of the programme appeared to be most helpful to the young people we may expect to see some evidence of impact here. In terms of their main activity, programme participants and non-participants shared a broadly similar profile at the time of the first survey, although the former appeared

Case study: Dawn's story

Dawn was 16 years old when she joined Mentoring Plus and had been living in care for two years. Prior to this she had lived with her mum but they argued all the time and, following a fight, they both decided that it 'was best if I went away. It was only meant to be for one night to sort my head out, but then it was a month and then a year and it just went on'. Dawn spent a lot of time on her own and described her life as 'boring'.

Dawn had been referred to Mentoring Plus by an education welfare Officer who was concerned that she was not attending school. Dawn was told that Mentoring Plus was 'not like mainstream school' and that, while she could not do her GCSEs there, she could do some maths, english and computer work. Dawn didn't mind about the GCSEs as she said she had not wanted to do them anyway.

Although she was a little nervous about going to Mentoring Plus, Dawn went to see what it was like. She felt that the young people at the project were in the same situation as her and described Mentoring Plus as being better than school: 'It's better than school because they treat you like an adult whereas at school they treat you like kids, so it's good like that.' She attended the project three times a week and participated in the education workshops, the girls' group and social events. She also met regularly with her mentor.

Dawn met Cheryl, her mentor, on the residential. She had chosen two mentors and said she wasn't bothered whom she was matched with. Although she knew that she was going to get a mentor, Dawn didn't know what to expect as 'it was all new'. Dawn and Cheryl met 'all the time'; they would meet at McDonald's or Burger King to chat and eat. Dawn liked meeting with her mentor and appreciated the way that Cheryl did not 'push her into things' she did not want to do. When they first met, Dawn wanted to be a hairdresser and Cheryl helped her enrol on a hairdressing course. Dawn did not like it, however, and left, saying she was glad that Cheryl had not judged her. Dawn felt Cheryl was there for her 'at any time' and would call her 'dead late in the night' when she needed help. Although Dawn felt her mother 'would probably be there for her' she felt more comfortable calling Cheryl.

Dawn felt that the main benefit she had gained from being involved with Mentoring Plus was that it had helped increase her confidence: 'it has helped me with my self-confidence and that because before I came I didn't have no confidence about myself and it has helped my with my confidence.' Dawn gained certificates for maths and English through Mentoring Plus. At the time of the interview she was studying a health and social care course at college and was enjoying it.

to be somewhat more disaffected than the latter (see Table 8.2). While there was very little difference in the proportion of these groups who were in paid work or on a training scheme, non-participants were more likely to be attending school or a special education unit or to be studying at college or university. As many as one in two (51 per cent) participants were either excluded from school, regularly truanting or completely disengaged from education, employment and training and this compared with less than one in three (31 per cent) non-participants.

By the end of the programme this gap had all but closed (38 per cent of participants and 33 per cent of non-participants were in such a position). The proportion of both participants and non participants attending school or a special education unit fell and this trend was particularly marked in relation to participants (the percentage of participants in this category fell by 17 points compared with 9 points among non-participants). Differences in relation to school, however, were more than offset by differences in relation to college/university, training schemes and paid work and it was through these activities that participants in the programme reduced their rate of disengagement relative to non-participants. Crucially, while the proportion of participants who were not in education, employment or training fell slightly during the course of the programme this coincided with a quite marked increase in the proportion of non-participants who were in this position.

The increased levels of engagement that were evident among programme participants were matched by an improved qualifications profile. At the start of the programme, participants were markedly less well qualified than non-participants but by the end of the programme this difference had all but disappeared. Among those who were due to have reached the school-leaving age by the end of the programme, the pro-portion of participants who had passed (at least) one GCSE increased almost fourfold (from 11 to 40 per cent), which was more than twice the rate of increase that was evident among non-participants (from 28 to 41 per cent).[9]

Changes in the young people's main activity may be thought of as movements between positions of social inclusion and exclusion. For the purposes of this analysis, attending school or a special education unit, studying at college/university, training and paid work were defined as states of social inclusion while truanting regularly, school exclusion and disengagement from employment, education and training were con-sidered to be states of social exclusion. A smaller proportion of participants than non-participants maintained a position of social inclusion during the course of the programme and a larger proportion maintained a position of social exclusion (see Figure 8.4). To some extent this simply reflected the

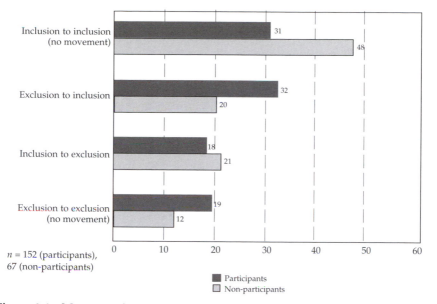

Figure 8.4 Movement between inclusion and exclusion (per cent of participants and non-participants)
Note: The figures given here are based on individuals who responded to both the original questionnaire and the first follow-up.
Source: Mentoring Plus cohort and comparison group (original survey and first follow-up).

situation at the start of the programme, as participants were less likely to have been in a position of social inclusion and were more likely to have been in a position of social exclusion at this point.

Among non-participants there was considerable continuity in the balance between inclusion and exclusion during the period covered by the programme, as movements between these categories cancelled each other out (the proportion of non-participants who were in a position of inclusion fell slightly from 69 to 67 per cent). Among programme participants, by contrast, there was a marked increase in social inclusion. Almost twice as many participants moved from positions of exclusion to inclusion as moved from positions of inclusion to exclusion and, between the start and end of the programme, the proportion that were in positions of inclusion increased by more than a quarter (from 49 to 63 per cent).[11] Three fifths (59 per cent) of the participants who were disengaged from education, employment and training at the start of the programme were either attending college or university, or were on a training scheme or were in paid work by the end of the programme and this constituted the key movement within this group.

These differences between participants and non-participants suggest that the programme had a positive effect on rates of social inclusion. There were, moreover, further indications that Mentoring Plus played an important role in bringing about the positive changes that were evident among programme participants. Nearly three in four (73 per cent) participants who moved from a position of exclusion into a position of inclusion noted that their mentor or the Plus component had helped them in relation to education and/or work: two in three (66 per cent) indicated that they had been helped by their mentor, three in five (60 per cent) indicated that they had been helped by the Plus component and one in two (50 per cent) indicated that they had been helped by both elements of the programme. A strong degree of overlap was evident here as the vast majority of those who felt they had been helped by their mentor also felt they had been helped by the Plus element and vice versa (76 per cent and 83 per cent respectively).

In addition, the apparent impact of the programme varied across the projects and was greatest among those with the highest level of programme integrity. In one of the projects fewer participants were in a position of inclusion at the end of the programme than at the start (38 per cent compared with 63 per cent), while, among the remaining projects, rates of inclusion increased by between one tenth to more than two thirds (9 per cent to 70 per cent). These differences were clearly linked to the integrity with which the programme was implemented (see Table 8.3). For projects with a low level of programme integrity the balance between

Table 8.3 Changing rates of inclusion among participants by programme integrity (per cent within each level of programme integrity)

| | Proportion of participants in positions of inclusion ... | | | |
	At the beginning of the programme	At the end of the programme	Change	n
Level of programme integrity				
High	46	65	+19	81
Moderate	53	71	+18	41
Low	52	52	0	30

Note: The figures given here are based on individuals who responded to both the original questionnaire and the first follow-up.
Source: Mentoring Plus cohort (original survey and first follow-up).

Case study: Gary's story

Gary was 18 years old when he joined Mentoring Plus and was living in a hostel around the corner from the project. It was the fifth hostel he had lived in since being 'kicked out' by his step-father some months earlier. He said he was 'happy' with this hostel as it was not like the 'disgusting, nasty hostels' he had lived in previously.

Before joining Mentoring Plus, Gary had been involved in 'all sorts of crime': stealing cars, stealing mobile phones and 'craziness like that'. Thinking back to that time he described himself as a 'street rat'. Gary said he had got involved in crime because everybody he knew was doing robberies and because he wanted to fit in with the people he was hanging around with. Unlike his friends, Gary had grown up in 'a posh area' and described himself as a 'posh bloke' but felt he had had to change in order to fit in.

Gary joined Mentoring Plus when his cousin told him he was going on to the programme. At that time Gary was in 'a bit of trouble' and felt 'any help would have been appreciated at that time so I just took it up'. Over the course of the year he was in regular contact with his mentor and the project workers, whom he saw as being more like mentors. He got involved with the music workshop, helped teach the other young people mixing, etc., and completed a community work course.

By the time we interviewed Gary he had got a 'well paid job' as a sports community worker and had another one 'lined up'. He felt that everything was going smoothly for him and, even though he was financially less well off than before, he said he would not go back to his old lifestyle: 'there's nothing there for me anymore. It's not fun any more, it's just boring and I've grown out of it now.' Gary said that Mentoring Plus had played an important role in bringing about this change:

> It was because I was bored that I was doing the crimes or whatever I was doing, so whenever I was bored I would just come here and talk to the people in the project or talk to my mentor and they would just show me different ways to get a job, go out and study, I mean they put me on different courses that I've done ... There's things that you can talk to your mentor about that sometimes you can't talk to your friends about and knowing that they are your mentor and they have got that adult responsibility whereas my friends would probably have just laughed at the things I would have told them.

Without the project, Gary felt he would not have got his job 'because I've got no experience, I would have never have even thought about doing anything like that before, but doing it showed me a lot of things that I can do now'.

inclusion and exclusion remained unchanged, while for those with a moderate or high level of integrity rates of inclusion increased by a third (34 per cent) and two-fifths (41 per cent) respectively.[11]

Family

The family contexts within which the young people were living remained largely unchanged during the period covered by the programme. The vast majority (74 per cent) of the cohort were living in the same family structure at the end of the programme as at the beginning and, although a fairly large proportion indicated that the programme had helped to improve their relationships with others, there was little evidence of increased family attachment. The proportion showing strong family attachment remained largely unchanged (16 and 19 per cent respectively) as did the proportion showing moderate (69 and 65 per cent respectively) and weak attachment (16 and 17 per cent respectively). There was, however, some evidence of moderately improved relationships during the aftermath of the programme as three-quarters (77 per cent) of those who showed weak family attachment at the end of the programme showed moderate attachment six months later. By this stage, the proportion of the cohort showing weak family attachment had fallen to below one in ten (9 per cent).

There was little suggestion that these modest improvements in family relationships were directly due to participation in Mentoring Plus. During the lifetime of the programme the balance between strong and weak family attachment remained largely unchanged among both participants and non-participants.

Offending

At the start of the programme most of the young people who were recruited to Mentoring Plus had yet to reach the age at which we might expect to see substantial reductions in their offending and there was little, if any, suggestion that they were 'growing out' of crime. The vast majority had offended during the 12 months leading up to the start of the programme and many had done so persistently (see Chapter 6). Nevertheless, a sizeable proportion of these young people indicated that Mentoring Plus had helped to tackle their offending. And further analyses confirmed that fairly substantial reductions in offending were evident during the lifetime of the programme. In assessing the following evidence it is important to remember that participation in the programme was voluntary and that referrals tended to focus on young people for whom it was thought to be appropriate. Thus, those who were referred to, and/or participated in, the programme may have differed from the wider offending population in important ways. Certainly, a large proportion of them indicated that they had joined the programme because they wanted to stop getting into trouble.

On average, members of the cohort reported having committed only one of the listed offences during the 12 months covered by the programme which was two less than in the previous 12 months. By the end of the programme more than one in four (29 per cent) indicated that they had not offended in the previous 12 months, and this represented an increase of almost two thirds compared with the start of the programme (18 per cent). The vast majority of those who had offended in the 12 months leading up to the programme either stopped doing so or continued at a reduced rate (30 and 43 per cent respectively; 8 per cent reported no change while 19 per cent reported an increased rate of offending). The general downturn in offending was particularly marked among members of the cohort who had offended persistently in the year before the programme as, on average, they went on to commit four fewer offence types during the following year. As a result the number of persistent offenders fell by more than a third (from 58 to 37 per cent).

Based on patterns of offending in the general population, we may expect to see the greatest reduction in criminal damage as young people are most likely to 'grow out' of this type of crime. With the exception of

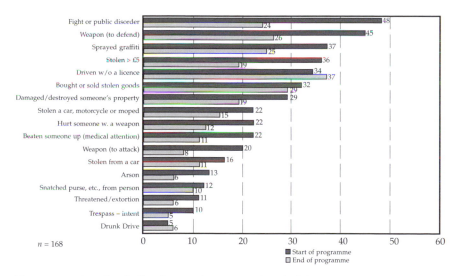

Figure 8.5 Levels of offending at the start and end of the programme (per cent of the cohort)

Note: The figures given here are based on individuals who responded to both the original questionnaire and the first follow-up.

Source: Mentoring Plus cohort (original survey and first follow-up).

traffic violations, however, fairly substantial reductions were evident across the range of offence categories. The greatest proportionate decrease was evident in relation to violence, with the number of young people committing such offences during the previous 12 months falling by almost two fifths (from 62 to 35 per cent). Fairly substantial reductions were also evident in relation to criminal damage (from 53 to 34 per cent) and property crimes (from 55 to 43 per cent). The number committing traffic violations, by contrast, remained stable (35 compared with 37 per cent).

These general patterns were confirmed by analysis of more specific offences (see Figure 8.5). The greatest proportionate reduction was evident in relation to carrying a weapon to attack somebody (the numbers committing such an offence in the previous 12 months fell by three fifths or 60 per cent),[12] while other violent offences such as beating somebody up, fighting in a public place and hurting somebody with a weapon were also subject to fairly substantial decreases. More moderate reductions tended to be apparent in relation to acts of criminal damage and property offences, while the rate at which traffic violations were committed remained largely unchanged.

The reduced levels of offending that were evident during the lifetime of the programme were more than maintained in the following six months.[13] The vast majority (83 per cent) of young people who had not offended while the programme was in place continued not to do so once it had come to an end. Added to this, one in three (34 per cent) of those who had committed an offence while the programme was running refrained from doing so in the following period. Furthermore, those who continued to offend did so at a relatively moderate rate, committing an average of two of the listed offences which was one less than in the previous 12 months and three less than in the 12 months before that. Consequently, while the proportion of non-offenders increased to almost one in two (45 per cent), following the end of the programme the proportion of persistent offenders fell to one in four (26 per cent).

Although these reductions in offending were consistent with the aims of Mentoring Plus they cannot be attributed directly to the programme. Participants and non-participants showed similar levels of offending at the outset of the programme and, while fairly substantial subsequent reductions were evident among programme participants, similar – and in some cases – more marked reductions were reported by non-participants (see Table 8.4).

This general pattern was replicated in relation to specific offences, as the largest proportionate reductions tended to be evident among non-participants. Closer scrutiny of the changes that were apparent among programme participants reinforced the conclusion that reductions in

Table 8.4 Offending by participation in Mentoring Plus – general measures.

Participated in Mentoring Plus?	Offended (%)		Offended persistently (%)		Mean no. of offences[1]		*n*
	Year one	Year two	Year one	Year two	Year one	Year two	
Yes	82	71	58	39	4.0	2.8	155
No	84	62	53	37	4.1	2.5	68

Notes:
1 The mean has been used here, rather than the median, on the basis that it provides a more sensitive measure of change. Figures have been given to one decimal place as this further increases the sensitivity of the analysis. Programme participants committed a median of three offences in year one and two offences in year two, while non-participants committed a median of three offences and one offence respectively.
2 The figures given here are based on individuals who responded to both the original questionnaire and the first follow-up; year one = 12 months prior to programme; year two = 12 months covered by programme.
Source: Mentoring Plus cohort and comparison group (original survey and first follow-up).

offending could not be attributed to the programme with any confidence. Inconsistencies were evident across the projects which could not be readily explained either by the content of the programme or by the integrity of the implementation: reductions in offending were evident regardless of how well the programme had been implemented.[14] Moreover, while the design of Mentoring Plus might lead us to expect the most marked reductions in offending among participants who moved from positions of social exclusion to inclusion, no such pattern was evident. Indeed, during the course of the programme and the six months that followed, the greatest reductions were evident among those who continued to be socially excluded.[15] It remains possible, however, that the increased rates of inclusion associated with participation in the programme will have a positive impact on levels of offending over a longer period of time.

Finally, those participants who indicated that the programme had helped to tackle their offending behaviour did not show particularly marked reductions in actual offending. The proportion of these participants who reported having offended in the previous 12 months did not change between the start and end of the programme; and the proportion who offended persistently fell by a very modest amount (from 68 to 58 per cent). A much more marked reduction in persistent offending was evident among those who did not indicate that the programme had helped to tackle their offending behaviour (the proportion of persistent offenders in this group fell from 53 to 26 per cent). In the six months that followed, however, the proportion of persistent offenders within these groups converged (19 per cent of both groups offended persistently). Over this extended period the proportion of persistent offenders fell by approximately two thirds regardless of whether or not they indicated that the programme had helped to tackle their offending behaviour.[16]

Drinking, smoking and drug use

The young people's smoking and drinking habits developed in markedly different ways during the period covered by the study. Smoking patterns within the cohort were highly stable, at both the aggregate and individual level. The proportion of young people who were smoking on a daily basis remained largely unchanged from the beginning to the end and to six months after the programme (45, 50 and 44 per cent respectively), as did the proportion of non-smokers (42, 38 and 42 per cent). This general pattern reflected the persistent nature of individuals' smoking habits. Most of those who were smoking regularly at the start of the programme were still doing so 12 months and 18 months later, and most non-smokers continued not to smoke throughout this period. The changes that were evident during the lifetime of the programme, moreover, were similar among participants and non-participants and thus it appeared that the programme had little, if any, impact on smoking.[17]

Drinking and drunkenness, by contrast, increased markedly within the cohort during the course of the study (see Figure 8.6). The proportion of young people who drank alcohol on a weekly basis increased from one in seven (at the start of the programme), to one in five (at the end of the programme) and then to one in four (six months later). During the same period, the proportion who did not drink at all almost halved. Of those who started out as non-drinkers, slightly more than half (55 per cent) had started to drink by the end of the programme and more than two in three (68 per cent) had done so six months later. In terms of drunkenness, there was a clear trend towards polarization, as the proportion getting drunk frequently and the proportion who did not get drunk at all increased simultaneously. Infrequent drunkenness became markedly less common as the young people in this category either stopped getting drunk or became drunk more often. A quarter (28 per cent) of those who were getting drunk less than once a week at the start of the programme were doing so more often by the end of the programme, while one in three (36 per cent) were no longer getting drunk at all.

Given the age of the young people involved in Mentoring Plus the changes that were evident in their consumption of alcohol are

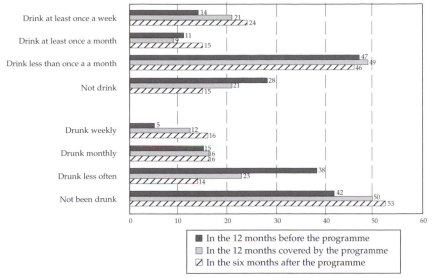

Figure 8.6   Drinking and drunkenness in the cohort (per cent of the cohort)
Notes
n = 170 (12 months before the programme and 12 months covered by the programme).
n = 108 (six months following the programme).
Figures given here for the 12 months before the programme and the 12 months covered by the programme are based on individuals who responded to both the original questionnaire and the first follow-up.
Source: Mentoring Plus cohort (first survey; first and second follow-up).

unsurprising. The mid-to-late teens constitute a key phase in drinking transitions as young people learn to drink like adults (Newburn and Shiner 2001). Comparisons with non-participants on the programme indicated that there was nothing remarkable in the way drinking patterns changed among participants, many of whom continued to drink moderately. Between the start and end of the programme the proportion of participants and non-participants who did not drink fell by approximately a quarter (from 25 to 18 per cent and 32 to 24 per cent respectively) and the proportion that got drunk on a weekly basis doubled (from 6 per cent to 11 per cent and 6 to 13 per cent respectively). At the same time, however, approximately half of the young people in both groups did not get drunk during the 12 months covered by the programme (46 and 56 per cent respectively).[18]

The mid-to-late teens also constitute a key period of change in relation to illicit drugs, as levels of use tend to increase sharply. To some extent this was reflected in the cohort as one in three (33 per cent) of the young people

159

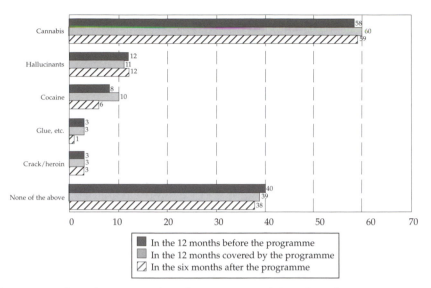

Figure 8.7 Illicit drug use in the cohort (per cent of the cohort)[20]
Notes:
n = 162 (12 months before the programme and 12 months covered by the programme).
n = 101 (six months following the programme).
Figures given here for the 12 months before the programme and the 12 months covered by the programme are based on individuals who responded to both the original questionnaire and the first follow-up.
Source: Mentoring Plus cohort (first survey; first and second follow-up).

who had not used drugs during the 12 months prior to the programme did so in the following year. This apparent movement into drug use was offset, however, by movements the other way: while one in eight of the young people in the cohort started to use drugs during the period covered by the programme an almost identical number stopped doing so (13 and 12 per cent respectively). Alongside these changes, there was a considerable degree of stability. Most of the young people who had used drugs in the year before the programme continued to do so and most of those who had not done so continued not to (81 and 67 per cent respectively).[19] This pattern carried over into the six months following the programme (83 per cent of those who used drugs during the 12 months prior to the programme continued to do so and 76 per cent of those who had not done so continued not to). As movements into, and out of, illicit drug use tended to cancel each other out, there was very little change in overall levels of use (see Figure 8.7).

The high degree of consistency that was evident in the young people's use of illicit drugs suggests that the programme had little, if any, impact in this regard. Comparisons between participants and non-participants pointed to a similar conclusion. At the start of the programme drug use was more widespread among participants than non-participants. Almost two in five (39 per cent) participants had used cannabis on a weekly basis during the previous 12 months, for example, compared with one in four (26 per cent) non-participants; and slightly more than one in ten (11 per cent) had used cocaine in this period compared with none of the non-participants. These differences continued to be evident throughout the period covered by programme, as overall levels of use remained very stable among both participants and non-participants.[21]

Self-esteem and locus of control

Notions of self-esteem and empowerment are central to the way in which people talk about mentoring and the young people's assessments of the programme might lead us to expect greatest impact in these areas. There was some evidence of improved self-esteem scores during the course of the programme but it was limited to a discrete sub-group and did not amount to a general trend. While overall levels of self-esteem within the cohort remained largely unchanged throughout the study – average scores only varied by one point – some potentially important differences were evident according to how the young people felt about themselves at the outset. Those members of the cohort who had had the poorest self-image

Table 8.5 Self-esteem (average score within the cohort)[23]

Self-esteem	Start of progamme	End of programme	Six months later
Very high	16	16	17
Moderately high	20	19	20
Moderately low	23	21	20
Very low	27	23	22

Notes:

$n = 156$ (first survey and first follow-up).

$n = 96$ (second follow-up).

The figures given here are based on individuals who responded to both the original questionnaire and the first follow-up; scores on this scale could vary between 10 and 40, low scores indicated high self-esteem and high scores indicated low self-esteem.

Source: Mentoring Plus cohort (first survey; first and second follow-up).

Case study: Karen's story

At the time of her first interview, Karen was living with her 'auntie'. She did not get on with her father and was missing her mother who was living abroad with her brother and sister:

> It is horrible, I miss my mum ... Sometimes I just cry and I think I wish I had my mum because I am at that age now where I want to talk to my mum ... and I haven't got that and it is really like horrible ... I used to wake up in the morning and every morning 'morning, mum, good night, mum', and now it is just like I don't use the word mum no more, and it is horrible.

Karen was unhappy living with her auntie, who she felt was favouring her own children. Karen spent most of her time at home by herself, as she had been excluded from school. At night, she used to 'hang out' with a group of older boys, and felt it was fun until people started to 'call me names and call me a slag':

> It made me feel upset, depressed, had like low self-confidence and every time I used to go out and I used to just look at people and think 'why are they looking at me?', and I used to get paranoid, 'do they think I am a whore?' and I used to get paranoid.

Karen felt that Mentoring Plus, in particular the girls' nights, had helped her to think more positively about herself and her relationship with her mother. She also felt that the project helped her be more confident when dealing with other people, especially young men. By the time of her second interview, Karen was no longer 'hanging out' with older boys and was mixing more with young people her own age:

> Girls' night – it's really just a couple of girls and some workers and we go upstairs and we talk about self-esteem, self-respect, and them kind of things, and it's good because it helps you to understand certain things about yourself and how to deal with certain things, like if you're walking down the road and a boy comes up to you – he looks threatening and he asks you for your number – don't say yes just because he looks threatening; just say no, speak your mind.

With regard to her mother, Karen said that:

> I never used to cope with it very well – I used to run away from home and do bodily harm and try and just get away from it all, but now I just think about it, but I try not to think about it the way I used to and

Continued

> think that it is all bad – maybe it isn't all bad and maybe something
> good can come out of it – so I just try and push past it and move on.
>
> Overall, she felt that Mentoring Plus had been very helpful, especially in
> terms of raising her self-esteem:
>
> > Before I came to Mentoring Plus, I had very low self-esteem and I
> > didn't have no confidence. Mentoring Plus helped me – by the time I
> > had finished my self-esteem had gone up. I wouldn't say I have
> > untold self-esteem, but my self-esteem had gone up and I felt more
> > certain … sure about myself.

at the start were the most likely to say that the programme had helped improve their self-confidence and this pattern was replicated in relation to self-esteem.[22] For those whose self-esteem was very or moderately high at the outset there was very little evidence of change, but for those whose self-esteem was very or moderately low there was clear improvement over the course of the programme, which was maintained during the six months that followed (see Table 8.5).

It is unclear whether or not these changes can be attributed to Mentoring Plus. On the one hand, those young people who indicated that the programme had helped to improve their confidence did record improved self-esteem scores: their scores improved, on average, by two points during the course of the programme and this compared with a slight worsening of half a point for those who indicated that they had received no such help. On the other hand, improvements in self-esteem were not limited to those young people who participated in the programme. Indeed, the self-esteem profiles of participants and non-participants were very similar and those young people who had relatively low self-esteem at the outset recorded very similar rates of improvement regardless of whether or not they had participated in the programme. Among those who started out with very low self-esteem, the average score improved by four points for both participants and non-participants (from 27 to 23 and from 26 to 22 respectively). On balance, it seems likely that Mentoring Plus helped to enhance the self-esteem of those participants who had a poor self-image, while non-participants with a poor self-image found similar help/support elsewhere.

Given the emphasis that is often placed on self-esteem it is worth considering how changes in this dimension related to changes in other areas.[24] To a limited extent, self-esteem appeared to rise and fall with changes in current status. The young people who moved from positions of social exclusion to inclusion during the course of the programme recorded a slightly improved self-esteem score (the average score for this group fell from 22 to 20) although a similar degree of improvement was evident among those who continued to be socially excluded (their average score fell from 21 to 20). There was, by contrast, a slight drop in the self-esteem of those young people who moved from positions of inclusion to exclusion (the average score for this group increased from 19 to 20), while scores for those who maintained a position of social inclusion remained unchanged (their average score stayed at 20). Improvements in self-esteem were not associated with any particular reduction in offending. On average, those young people who recorded an improved self-esteem score committed one of the listed offences in the 12 months covered by the programme, compared with three during the previous 12 months. Similar reductions were evident among those whose self-esteem appeared to have worsened as, on average, they committed two of the specific offences in the 12 months covered by the programme, compared with four during the previous 12 months.

Although many of the young people recruited to Mentoring Plus indicated that the programme had helped them to set goals and make decisions this did not translate into any clear changes in their locus of control. Their average scores on this indicator remained very stable throughout the period covered by the study, varying from seven at the start of the programme to six at both the end of the programme and six months later. The profile for participants and non-participants remained almost identical, with participants scoring an average of seven at the start of the programme and six at the end while non-participants scored an average of seven at both points. Among those recruited to the programme, the extent of change did not vary markedly according to their initial position: their locus of control score fell by an average of one point regardless of whether they had a moderately internal, moderately external or highly external locus of control at the start of the programme; and by 1.6 points if they had a highly internal score. Nor were there particularly marked changes among those who indicated that the programme had helped them to make decisions and set goals. The young people who felt they had been helped in either of these ways scored an average of seven points at the start of the programme and six points at the end. This was identical to the profile that was evident for those who did not feel they had been helped to set goals and was very similar to the profile that was evident for those who did not feel they had been helped to make decisions (they scored an average of six points at both the start and end of the programme).

Conclusion

The analysis presented in this chapter supports much of the recent literature on working with disaffection. In particular, it challenges the old orthodoxy that 'nothing works'. Fairly substantial changes were evident among the young people referred to Mentoring Plus during the lifetime of the programme, particularly in relation to rates of social inclusion and levels of offending. While these are notable findings, it should be remembered that participation in the programme was voluntary and that referrals focused on young people for whom the programme was thought to be appropriate. Many of those who were referred to Mentoring Plus identified areas of their life that they wished to change and it may be that, in this regard, they differed from the wider population of disaffected young people.

It is also important to note that not all the changes that were evident within the cohort can be attributed to participation in the Mentoring Plus programme. Evidence of impact was strongest in relation to engagement with education, training and work. This evidence is particularly noteworthy as it highlights the role of programme integrity. Previous research has indicated that effective programmes are those where the stated aims are directly linked to the methods being used and, within Mentoring Plus, such symmetry was most apparent in relation to social inclusion. Key elements of the programme, including the literacy and numeracy classes, were specifically tailored to the aim of increasing participation in education, training and work and positive changes were associated with participation in the programme. The proportion of participants who were engaged in such activities increased substantially during the course of the programme, while no such changes were evident among non-participants. There are, moreover, good reasons for thinking that the programme played an important part in bringing about these changes. The vast majority of participants who moved from a position of exclusion to inclusion indicated that the programme had helped them in relation to education and/or work (most of them indicated that both the mentors and the Plus component had helped them in this way). Movement into positions of inclusion was most marked in projects that achieved a moderate or high level of programme integrity. In projects which ran into difficulty, the overall balance between inclusion and exclusion remained unchanged.

While there was no clear evidence of impact in any of the other areas we considered, this is, perhaps, unsurprising given the design of the programme. In these other areas the methods employed by Mentoring Plus were less directly linked to its apparent aims. Tackling offending may, for instance, have been a stated aim of the programme but there was very little structured work with an explicit focus on challenging offending behaviour. In so far as Mentoring Plus sought to reduce offending, it did so indirectly by reducing the barriers to social inclusion. The gains that were evident in relation to social inclusion, however, did not translate directly into reduced offending. Substantial reductions in offending were evident among programme participants but similar, and in some cases more marked, reductions were evident among non-participants. In addition, these changes did not mirror movements between positions of social inclusion and exclusion and the greatest reductions in offending were evident among those who remained in positions of exclusion.

One of the central messages to emerge from this study is that simply providing opportunities for change is unlikely to be enough to bring about change. Much greater thought needs to be given to how change is achieved and not just to whether it is achieved. The notion of programme integrity is clearly useful in this context as it helps to specify the ways in which interventions may be expected to achieve certain outcomes, but consideration must also be given to the way in which individuals change. To the limited extent that individual processes of change were explicitly considered within the programme, improved self-esteem and empowerment were suggested to be key mechanisms of change. Such hypotheses appear to be unconvincing in the light of this study. The programme did not have any clear impact on the young people's self-esteem or locus of control and yet this did not prevent substantial improvements being made in their rates of inclusion. In addition, at the individual level, positive changes in rates of inclusion and reduced offending were not associated with changes in self-esteem and locus of control. The question remains, then, how is the process of change to be understood?

Notes

1 Kendall's tau-b = 0.59 (rating of the mentors at the end of the programme by rating 6 months later) and 0.61 (rating of the Plus component at the end of the programme by 6 months later).
2 This was assessed through rankings based on the percentage of young people who rated the Plus element and the mentors to be 'very helpful'. Four projects were given the same ranking in relation to the mentors and the Plus element; while three projects were ranked one place apart and the remainder were ranked two places apart.
3 Ratings of Mentoring Plus and the mentors (whichever was highest) were used as a proxy measure for the overall helpfulness of the programme.

4 Cramer's $V = 0.29$ (helpfulness of the programme by project); Kendall's tau-c = 0.13 (helpfulness of the programme by integrity of the programme).

5 Programme participants were defined as all members of the cohort group who engaged with the mentors and/or the project, regardless of the term of their engagement. Non-participants included the comparison group and members of the cohort group who had not engaged with the programme at all.

6 The figures given here are based on the young people who responded to both the initial survey and the first follow-up.

7 Throughout this chapter figures for the 12 months before the programme are based on individuals who responded to both the initial survey and the first follow-up as this provides the basis for the most accurate assessment of change over time. It does mean, however, that there may be some discrepancies when compared with figures quoted in previous chapters as they were based on the entire cohort regardless of whether individuals responded to the follow-up survey.

8 By this time none of the young people in the cohort were permanently excluded from school. Note also that the figure given here for school attendance included those who were truanting regularly: as most of the young people in the cohort had passed the age at which they could legally leave school questions about truancy were omitted from the second follow-up survey.

9 This analysis was limited to those who were aged 15 years or above at the time of the first survey.

10 At the start of the programme 49 per cent of participants were in positions of inclusion and this increased to 63 per cent by the end of the programme: an increase of 14 percentage points which represented a proportionate increase of 29 per cent (i.e. $14/49*100$). At the start of the programme Cramer's $V = 0.20$ (inclusion/exclusion by participation/non-participation) but by the end of the programme Cramer's $V = 0.04$ (i.e. the difference had all but disappeared).

11 In high-integrity programmes the percentage of participants in positions of social inclusion increased by 19 points from 46 to 65 per cent, which represented a proportionate increase of 41 per cent (i.e. $19/46*100$); while in moderate integrity programmes it increased by 18 points which represented a proportionate increase of 34 per cent ($18/53*100$).

12 In the 12 months before the programme 20 per cent of the young people in the cohort carried a weapon to attack somebody and this fell to 8 per cent in the following 12 months: a decrease of 12 percentage points which represents a proportionate decrease of 60 per cent (i.e. $12/20$).

13 Some care is required here as the figures relate to different time frames. In the initial survey and the first follow-up, questions were asked about a 12-month period while in the second survey questions were asked about a six-month period.

14 Among participants in projects with a high degree of integrity, the proportion of persistent offenders fell from 66 per cent in the 12 months prior to the programme, to 42 per cent during the 12 months covered by the programme and to 22 per cent during the six months after the end of the programme. A

very similar profile was evident among participants in projects with a low degree of integrity: within this group the rate of persistent offending fell from 62 to 41 per cent and to 22 per cent. A less marked fall was evident among participants in projects with a moderate degree of integrity (40 to 33 to 20 per cent).

15 Among those who moved from a position of exclusion to inclusion between the start and end of the programme, the proportion of persistent offenders fell from 65 per cent in the 12 months prior to the programme, to 51 per cent during the 12 months covered by the programme and to 28 per cent during the six months after the end of the programme. Among those who were in a position of social exclusion at the beginning and end of the programme the rate of persistent offending fell from 77 to 27 and to 22 per cent.

16 Among those who indicated that the programme had helped to tackle their offending behaviour, the proportion of persistent offenders fell by 72 per cent (68–19/68). Among those who did not indicate that the programme had helped them in this way, the proportion of persistent offenders fell by 64 per cent (53–19/53).

17 Participants were more likely to smoke than non-participants and this difference became slightly more marked during the period covered by the programme. The proportion of participants who were daily smokers increased (from 45 to 56 per cent) while the proportion of non-participants who were daily smokers fell (from 39 to 35 per cent). These changes were due mainly to irregular smokers becoming regular smokers: the proportion of participants who smoked but did not do so every day fell (from 15 to 8 per cent) while the proportion of non-participants in this category increased slightly (from 7 per cent to 9 per cent). The proportion of non-smokers in each group remained fairly consistent (40 and 36 per cent for participants and 54 and 56 per cent for non-participants). At the start and end of the programme Cramer's $V = 0.16$ and 0.21 respectively (smoking by participation in the programme).

18 At the start and end of the programme Cramer's $V = 0.14$ and 0.08 respectively (drinking by participation) and 0.14 and 0.12 respectively (drunkenness by participation).

19 Cramer's $V = 0.48$ (used drugs in 12 months prior to the programme by used drugs in the 12 months covered by the programme) and 0.59 (used drugs in 12 months prior to the programme by used drugs in the six months after the programme).

20 The proportion using cannabis weekly remained largely unchanged (37, 41 and 36 per cent respectively).

21 The proportion of participants who used each of the substances (or group of substances) shown in Figure 8.7 during the year of the programme was within one or two percentage points of the proportion who had done so during the 12 months prior to the programme. Similarly the proportion of non-participants who used each of these substances during the year of the programme was within three percentage points of the proportion who had done so during the 12 months previously. Finally, the differences between the proportion of participants and non-participants who used these substances during these

two periods changed by no more than three percentage points. Thus for example while 60 per cent of participants and 46 per cent of non-participants used cannabis in the year before the programme (a difference of 14 per cent), 62 and 47 per cent did so respectively in the following year (a difference of 15 per cent).

22 Self-esteem at the start of the programme was classified according to the percentile values so that four groups of approximately equal size were produced. The categories do not have any external validity outside the cohort and simply indicate how individuals' scores compared with those of other members of the cohort. Of those whose self-esteem had been very low at the outset, 75 per cent indicated that the programme had helped improve their self-confidence and this compared with 47 per cent of those whose self-esteem had been very high (Cramer's $V = 0.20$).

23 We used Rosenberg's (1965) scale to measure self-esteem. For information on this scale please refer to Appendix II.

24 The analysis described in this paragraph included both participants and non-participants in the programme.

Chapter 9

Understanding change

Mentoring, as we have seen, can have an impact on the lives of highly disaffected young people. But, how do individuals change? This is an important, yet deceptively simple, question, with no obviously satisfactory answer. While interventions targeting *disaffected* young people invariably aim to bring about some changes in their circumstances or behaviour, the mechanisms by which such changes are expected to occur often remain obscure. In this sense, work with disaffected young people may be considered to be under-theorized. That is to say, there is often little explicit discussion of the aims of the particular programme, beyond the most banal identification of 'reductions in offending' or something similarly general and this lack of clarity is then compounded by the absence of any explicit model of change. Why is it that a particular intervention might be thought to work? And, by what means might it be expected to change participants' behaviour? These are fundamental questions which often remain unanswered and are, indeed, often unasked.

The lack of attention that is typically given to processes of individual change has been highlighted recently by McNeil and Batchelor (2002) in relation to work with persistent young offenders. Youth justice agencies, they argued, have developed a 'bureaucratic' rather than 'therapeutic' stance which prioritises containment over behavioural change. In this context, creating change out of 'what is often the chaos of the personal and social circumstances of society's most troubled and troubling young people' has remained 'the youth justice equivalent of the alchemist's quest' (2002: 34). While this bureaucratic orientation may be linked to a shortage of resources, it also reflects a lack of clear guidance. According to Maruna (2000), the existing literature offers little assistance to practitioners in terms of how they should encourage processes of desistance. By concentrating on the question of what works, he suggests, offender rehabilitation research 'has largely ignored questions about *how* rehabilitation works, why it works with some and why it fails with others' (Maruna 2000: 12, emphasis added). Even in areas which are, perhaps, more explicitly concerned with behavioural change there is often a lack of clarity about how this is to be achieved. The ways in which people intentionally change addictive behaviours, for example, are poorly understood (Prochaska *et al.* 1992).

Similar difficulties were evident in relation to Mentoring Plus. Although a discernible mechanism for change was evident within the design of the programme, it had not been made explicit and little attention was given to processes of individual change. In essence, the programme rests on a social deficit model which views offending and other negative outcomes as being driven by disadvantage and exclusion. Structured activities within the programme concentrate on helping young people back into education, training and work, while much less immediate attention is given to tackling offending, etc. It is implicit within such a design that if *disaffected* young people can be reconnected to education, training and work then other positive outcomes, including reduced offending, will flow naturally from this. While the social deficit model provides a reasonably clear sociological basis for change, psychological dimensions were less well defined. Traces of psychological theory and practice were evident in some elements of the programme. Workshops were conducted with a focus on smoking cessation and violence/weapons which included significant cognitive-behavioural elements and the role of the mentors was defined in terms which reflected social learning theory (Bandura 1977). For all the talk of 'role models' and 'empowerment', however, there was no clear sense of how the young people were expected to change. Mentoring Plus does not work to any clear model of individual change and has no template of the stages that young people might be expected to go through. Moreover, in some senses the programme endorses a one-size-fits-all approach. Although the emphasis on each component may have varied according to individual need, the basic structure of the programme was the same for all young people: thus, for example, all participants were expected to have a mentor, regardless of whether they wanted one.

In this chapter we consider processes of individual change in some detail. We begin by considering whether the social deficit model provides a convincing basis for understanding change. We then examine the concept of 'role models' by exploring the extent to which the apparent impact of the programme varied according to the sociodemographic characteristics of the mentors and the mentees. Our focus then shifts on to the notion of stages of change. We consider whether this notion may be meaningfully applied to the *disaffected* young people included in this study and, if so, whether it helps to explain the changes that were evident in their circumstances and behaviour.

The social deficit model

In its reliance upon the social deficit model, the Mentoring Plus programme is part of a broader trend within social policy. Under New Labour, the promotion of social inclusion has come to be seen as both an end in itself and a means to an end. If, as is often claimed, social exclusion gives rise to many social ills then it follows that increasing rates of inclusion will help to alleviate these associated ills. Because crime has come to be seen as the product of social exclusion, for example, it follows that it must be tackled, in part at least, by policies of inclusion which will, in time, bring down crime rates. A key feature of this inclusionary policy is provided by back-to-work programmes which are presented as a way of tackling the 'causes' of crime (Young 2002).

The social deficit model has a certain logical appeal. There is, after all, a well established link between youth offending and social exclusion (Farrington 1997; Flood-page *et al.* 2000), which was demonstrated by the young people on the Mentoring Plus programme (see Chapter 6). In view of this link, it may be argued that promoting social inclusion serves to counter specific risk factors associated with offending and enhances known protective factors. While promoting social inclusion may form part of a sensible crime reduction strategy, it does not necessarily follow that it provides an effective way of encouraging desistance among young people whose offending is already fairly entrenched. The findings presented in the previous chapter highlight both the value and the limitations of the social deficit model. On the one hand, the efforts of Mentoring Plus to promote participation in education, training and work appeared to yield positive results. On the other hand, this increase in the rate of social inclusion did not appear to have any knock-on effect in terms of reduced offending. Moreover, while the social deficit model would lead us to expect the most marked reductions in offending among participants who moved from positions of social exclusion to inclusion, no such pattern was evident. Indeed, the greatest reductions were evident among those who continued to be socially excluded (see Chapter 8). It is, of course, possible that the increased rates of inclusion associated with participation in the programme will have a positive impact on levels of offending over a longer period of time. None the less, it remains the case that the findings from this study indicate that the social deficit model does not appear to offer a sufficient basis for reductions in offending among *disaffected* young people in the short term.

In view of the emphasis that is often placed on self-esteem and empowerment, it is also worth noting that these notions did not provide a convincing explanation for change. At the start of the programme there was little evidence that the young people's self-esteem and locus of control were linked to offending and truancy (see Chapter 6). In addition, the positive changes that were evident in relation to offending and engagement in education, training and work over the course of the pro-gramme were independent of any changes in self-esteem and locus of control. While overall levels of self-esteem and self-control remained largely unchanged during the course of the programme, the changes that were evident were not clearly associated with reduced offending or increased rates of engagement in education, training and work (see Chapter 8).

Role models?

Role modelling, we have already suggested, describes a complex set of processes (see Chapter 5). While assuming an element of difference – the role model provides an example to which the other person can aspire – it also requires a degree of affiliation. The discourse surrounding mentoring often implies that affiliation depends upon shared characteristics and this is most evident in claims about the need for (black) male role models. Detailed analysis presented some important challenges to this discourse. Levels of engagement between mentors and mentees did not vary greatly according to the sociodemographic profiles of those involved; the young people tended to emphasize the importance of mentors' qualities rather than their characteristics; and the young people's attitudes towards their mentors did not appear to depend on shared sociodemographic characteristics. It is clear, however, that in some respects mentoring relationships were influenced by the sociodemographic characteristics of those involved. Female mentees were matched exclusively with female mentors and a considerable degree of broad ethnic matching was evident. In addition, some of the young people emphasised the importance of shared characteristics and it remains possible that similar sociodemographic profiles may create points of contact between mentor and mentee which create opportunities for particularly powerful forms of role modelling.

In assessing this possibility we focused on the young people's judgements about the helpfulness of their mentor and the young people's levels of engagement in education, training and work. Judgements about helpfulness were considered on the grounds that they offered some insight into the general impact that the mentors may have had, while rates of engagement in education, training and work were considered because they provided the greatest objective evidence of impact by the pro-gramme. Although the perceived helpfulness of the mentors varied according to a number of characteristics the differences that were evident tended to be fairly modest and often did not reveal any clear patterns. In general, female mentees tended to rate their mentor as having been more helpful than did male mentees, although the differences were very small (41 per cent compared with 36 per cent indicated that their mentor had been 'very helpful'). More marked differences were apparent according to the sex of the mentor, with female mentors having generally been rated more positively than male mentors (49 per cent compared with 32 per cent were rated as 'very helpful'). The ratings that female mentors were given by male and female mentees were almost identical and, while male mentors who been matched with male mentees tended to be rated less positively, the vast majority of them were rated as having been of some help (31 per cent were rated 'very helpful' and 46 per cent as 'fairly helpful').[1]

While judgements about the helpfulness of the mentors varied according to ethnic dimensions, they did so in ways which challenged the assumptions that are often implied in much of the discourse about role models. In general terms, black African/Caribbean and mixed-race young people tended to rate their mentor more positively than did white young people (43 per cent, 42 per cent and 31 per cent indicated that their mentor had been very helpful respectively). By contrast, there were no discernible differences according to the ethnicity of the mentors. More detailed analysis of the pairings indicated that the most 'helpful' matches appeared to have been those that cut across ethnic groups. White young people tended to rate black and minority ethnic mentors more highly than white mentors (55 per cent compared with 36 per cent were rated as 'very helpful'); and black African/Caribbean young people tended to rate white mentors more positively than black African/Caribbean mentors (64 per cent compared with 36 per cent were rated as 'very helpful'). Once again, the differences that were evident were differences of degree, as the proportion of mentors that were rated 'not at all helpful' was very similar across all ethnic-matches. This analysis should be treated with caution as there were very few cases in some of the analytical categories.[2]

Other variations in the perceived helpfulness of the mentors were either very small, unclear or were based on too few cases to be treated with any degree of confidence. It is, however, worth noting that mentors who were employed in professional occupations tended to be rated more positively than those who were employed in non-professional occupations (61 per cent compared with 34 per cent were rated as 'very helpful'). This difference was related mainly to the degree of helpfulness, as mentors in non-professional occupations were more likely to be rated 'fairly helpful' than were those in professional occupations (45 per cent compared with 21 per cent). Unemployed mentors tended to be rated positively (64 per cent were judged to have been 'very helpful') although the number of cases was very small. In a similar vein, mentors with a (disclosed) criminal record tended to be rated less positively than those with no (disclosed) criminal record, although this difference was, once again, driven by the degree to which mentors were considered to have been helpful (of the mentors with a criminal record, 39 per cent were rated 'very helpful' and 46 per cent were rated 'fairly helpful', compared with 47 and 31 per cent of mentors with no criminal record respectively). Finally, very modest variations in the perceived helpfulness of the mentors were evident according to the age of the mentors and the age of the mentees and in both instances no clear or consistent patterns were evident.[3]

The extent to which the young people reengaged with education, training and work varied according to a range of characteristics. Striking differences were evident according to the sex of the young people and the mentors (see Table 9.1). The overall increase in social inclusion was most marked among male mentees: at the start of the programme fewer male than female mentees were in a position of inclusion, but by the end of the programme this difference had been eliminated. A similar, but more marked, pattern was evident in relation to the sex of the mentors: the increased rate of inclusion was greater among young people who had had a male mentor than among those had had a female mentor. Male mentors were more likely to have been matched with young people who were in positions of social exclusion at the start of the programme but, once again, this gap had closed by the end of the programme. When we consider the sex of the young people and the mentors together the pattern becomes even more striking. The most modest increase in inclusion was evident among male mentees who had been matched with female mentors, while the most marked increase was evident among male mentees who had been matched with male mentors: female mentees who had been matched with female mentors were in an intermediate position.

Table 9.1   Rates of social inclusion by sex[4] (per cent of each category)

	Proportion of participants in positions of inclusion			
	At the beginning of the programme (%)	At the end of the programme (%)	Proportionate change	n
Young person				
Male	47	63	+0.34	82
Female	52	62	+0.19	45
Mentor				
Male	39	64	+0.64	33
Female	54	65	+0.20	83
Young person–mentor				
Male–male	36	65	+0.81	31
Male–female	59	66	+0.11	41
Female–female	51	64	+0.25	42

Source: Mentoring Plus cohort (original survey and first follow-up).

How might we interpret these results, particularly given that the young people tended to view the male mentors as having been less helpful than female mentors? Considerable care is required here because the study was not specifically designed to examine the role of gender within mentoring relationships. Nevertheless, the results are highly suggestive of important gender effects. Thus, we may speculate that the female mentors tended to adopt a supportive and tolerant role in their relationships with the mentees, through which they provided considerable practical support and this led their mentees to perceive them as 'helpful'. Male mentors, by contrast, may have taken a more challenging, and possibly confrontational, stance which was perceived to have been less straightforwardly 'helpful' but which had more substantive impact. Alternatively, without being perceived to have offered as much practical help as female mentors, male mentors may have been able to challenge some of the young people's prevailing views about what it means to be male in ways that were simply not available to female mentors. In so doing, male mentors may have played a particularly important role in encouraging male mentees to reconsider their options and (re)engage with education, training and work. It is likely, given their domestic circumstances, that many of the young people on the programme had little immediate contact with positive male role models and it is, arguably, precisely these circumstances in which male mentors may be especially influential.

Other demographic variations were evident although they tended to be less striking than those relating to sex. While increased rates of social inclusion were evident across all age groups, they were most marked among the youngest mentees. The proportion of 12–14-year-olds who were in a position of social inclusion increased by almost a half, compared with increases of approximately a fifth to a quarter for the remaining age groups. There was some variation according to the age of the mentor, but there was no clear or consistent pattern.[5] By contrast, notable ethnic differences were evident in relation to both the young people and the mentors. The proportion of white young people who were in a position of social inclusion increased by slightly more than a half, compared with an increase of approximately a quarter among black African/Caribbean and mixed-race young people. A similar, albeit slightly less marked, pattern was evident in relation to the ethnicity of the mentors although more detailed analysis, based on pairings, pointed to a more complex situation. Among white young people, the greatest increase in social inclusion was evident among those who had been matched with a black African/ Caribbean mentor, while, among black African/ Caribbean young people, the increased rate of social inclusion did not vary according to the ethnicity of the mentor.[6]

Changes in the rate of social inclusion showed little systematic variation according to the mentors' occupational class. The rate of inclusion among the young people increased by approximately two fifths, regardless of whether their mentor was employed in a professional or non-professional occupation. More marked variations were evident according to whether the mentor was a student or was unemployed, but the small number of cases in these categories means that the analysis must be treated with a great deal of caution. Where the mentor was a student, the rate of inclusion doubled and where the mentor was unemployed the rate of inclusion remained unchanged. It is also worth noting that the rate of inclusion among the young people remained unchanged where the mentor had a criminal record.[7]

Stages of change

The idea that change must come from within has become something of a truism within the counselling and self-help literature (Palin and Beatty 2000). It has, by contrast, traditionally made little impression on interventions aimed at reducing youth disaffection, reflecting the 'bureau-cratic' orientation of much of the work that is carried out in this area. Where a more 'therapeutic' orientation has been considered, emphasis has been placed on the importance of young people's motivation to change. In their discussion of youth crime, for example, McNeil and Batchelor (2002: 41) describe desistance as a protracted 'back and forth' or 'zigzag' process and argue that fleeting but important opportunities to support desistance could be exploited more effectively if interventions were more consciously attuned to the interplay between 'shifting' mindsets and vacillating motivations:

> The qualities and skills of workers remain vital in developing the relationships within which such magic processes occur. But it may be that these relationships are better understood as a catalyst than a cause of change which requires both the provision of personal, social and economic opportunities and the development of motivation and capacity to exploit the few chances that come the way of socially excluded young people.

In order to explore the importance of motivation, we drew on the transtheoretical approach developed by Prochaska and DiClemente (1992). This approach rests on a model of behavioural change which is built around a number of motivational stages. While originally formulated on the basis of psychotherapeutic work with people who wanted to quit smoking, the transtheoretical approach has been extended to cover a range of behaviours including alcohol consumption, drug use, eating disorders, safer sex and adolescent delinquent behaviour (McConnaughy et al. 1983; Prochaska and Di-Clemente 1983; Prochaska et al. 1994). It has also been used in a variety of settings by a range of practitioners, including non-psychotherapists (Neesham 1993).

According to the transtheoretical approach change is an evolutionary process which can be conceptualized as a series of distinct stages, each of which represents a period of time and a set of tasks: precontemplation (not seriously thinking about changing), contemplation (thinking about changing but taking no action), preparation (getting ready to change), action (making an attempt to change) and maintenance (upholding the new behaviour pattern).[8] This approach is rooted in a wide range of psychotherapeutic theories and has been subject to an extensive process of hypothesis testing. According to Prochaska et al. (1994: 45): 'To date, we have found that processes of change that have their theoretical origins in such variable and supposedly incompatible approaches as behavioural, cognitive, experiential, and psychoanalytical therapies can be integrated empirically within the stage of change.' The stages of change described above have been validated through research, although there is some doubt as to whether preparation and maintenance constitutes distinct stages

(Heather *et al.* 1993). There is also some evidence to suggest that processes of change occur in a similar way across a diverse range of groups and problem behaviours (McConnaughy *et al.* 1983; Prochaska and DiClemente 1983; Prochaska *et al.* 1992; Rollnick *et al.* 1992). In addition, stage of change has been found to be a useful predictor of outcomes and drop-out from treatment for smoking cessation and heavy drinking (Prochaska and DiClemente 1992; Heather *et al.* 1993; Spencer *et al.* 2002; but see also Riemsma *et al.* 2003). Alongside the stages of change, ten distinct processes of change have been identified and it has been noted that different processes are used at different stages (Prochaska and DiClemente 1983, 1992).

The transtheoretical approach has important implications for practice as it suggests that interventions will be most successful where processes of change are tailored to individuals' stage of change (McConnaughy *et al.* 1983; Prochaska and DiClemente 1992). Put bluntly, giving people skills to change behaviour is likely to be a waste of time if most of them are not ready to change and it may be more effective to employ motivational interviewing techniques under such circumstances (Rollnick *et al.* 1992). It has also been noted that individuals in the contemplation stage are most open to information and reflection about their behaviour and that getting to this stage, and moving through it, involves increased use of cognitive, affective and evaluative processes. Preparation for action, on the other hand, requires changes in the ways that individuals think and feel about their problem behaviours. Social reinforcement and helping relations have been identified as an important influence on the translation of thought into action (Prochaska and DiClemente 1983). It follows that resistance to change may occur if significant others are involved in a different stage of change (McConnaughy *et al.* 1983). Movement into, and through, action does not simply depend on affective and cognitive processes, however, but also requires that individuals are able to use behavioural processes (such as counter-conditioning and stimulus control) in order to cope with external influences that may encourage a return to old forms of behaviour (Prochaska and DiClemente 1983, 1992).

Assessing the young people's stage of change

In drawing on the transtheoretical approach, our initial concern was to assess whether the stages of change model could be meaningfully applied to the young people who were referred to Mentoring Plus.[9] Previous attempts to apply the stages of change model have sought to do so in relation to fairly specific forms of behaviour, such as drinking and drug use, although some attempts have been made to apply it more generically

(McConnaughty *et al.* 1983). We attempted to apply the stages of change model in a general way which was not tied to any specific type of behaviour. As part of the first survey, the young people who were referred to Mentoring Plus were asked to respond to the following statements on the basis of a five-point scale – strongly agree, agree, neither agree nor disagree, disagree or strongly disagree:[10]

- *Precontemplation*
  I don't think there is anything in my life that needs changing.
  I'm not the problem one, it doesn't make much sense for me to be here.
  For me, trying to change my life would be pointless.

- *Contemplation*
  Sometimes I worry about where I'll end up if I don't change.
  I have a problem and I really think I should work on it.
  I'm hoping this place will help me to make some improvements to my life.

- *Action*
  I am doing something about the problems that had been bothering me.
  Anyone can talk about changing, but I'm actually doing something about it.
  I am actually changing my life right now.

- *Maintenance*
  It worries me that I might go back to a problem I have already sorted out, so I am here to seek help.
  I'm happy with the way my life is, but I'm worried I might pick up some of the bad habits that I used to have.
  I've made some positive changes in my life, but I feel I need some support to keep going.

'Preparation' statements were omitted from the questionnaire because previous research has suggested that it is unclear whether or not there is a distinct preparation stage. Moreover, while preliminary analysis pointed to the need for such a stage in this instance, the young people were allocated to it on the basis of their responses to the contemplation and action items (see below). A range of preliminary analyses were conducted in order to establish the appropriateness of stages of change model to the young people included in the study. Factor analysis has been widely used to assess whether items designed to measure stages of change may be understood meaningfully in terms of the theoretically defined stages

(McConnaughy *et al.* 1983; Rollnick *et al.* 1992). In replicating this analysis, we considered the cohort and comparison groups separately as some of the items did not apply to the comparison group.[11] The results for the two groups were highly consistent and indicated that there were distinct and identifiable precontemplation, contemplation and action stages. Initial analyses indicated that there was no identifiable maintenance stage, but once the items for this stage were omitted, a clear three-factor solution emerged which accorded to the remaining stages (see Table 9.2).

Once the theoretical stages of change had been validated, the young

Table 9.2 Stages of change – principal components (item loadings, Varimax rotation)

	Components		
	1	2	3
Precontemplation			
I don't think there is anything in my life that needs changing	**6.4**	−.45	.15
I'm not the problem one, it doesn't make much sense for me to be here	**.78**	.02	.07
For me, trying to change my life would be pointless	**.80**	.11	.25
Contemplation			
Sometimes I worry about where I'll end up if I don't change	.03	**.51**	.21
I have a problem and I really think I should work on it	.10	**.82**	.11
I'm hoping this place will help me to make some improvements to my life	.15	**.68**	.22
Action			
I am doing something about the problems that had been bothering me	.09	.03	**.81**
Anyone can talk about changing, but I'm actually doing something about it	.07	.28	.77
I am actually changing my life right now	−.09	.31	**.60**

Note:
Item loadings show the correlation between an item and a factor.
Loadings > 0.6 = high, > 0.3 = moderate, and < 0.3 = low (Kline 1994).
Source: Mentoring Plus cohort (original survey).

people were then allocated to a particular stage (Rollnick *et al.* 1992). As part of this process, their responses were converted into a series of scores, with each item being scored on the following basis: +2 = strongly agree; +1 agree; 0 = neither agree nor disagree; –1 = disagree; and –2 = strongly disagree. For each stage, the scores on the relevant items were added together to give a total stage score:[12] as there were three items on each stage, possible scores ranged from –6 to +6 for each stage. On average, the young people scored –2 on precontemplation, indicating a tendency to dizagree with these items; +2 on contemplation, indicating a tendency to agree with these items; +3 on action, indicating a slightly more marked tendency to agree with these items; and +1.5 for maintenance, indicating a slightly less marked tendency to agree with these items. Analysis of the relationships between the young people's scale scores broadly confirmed the results of the principal component analysis (see Table 9.3). The precontemplation stage was clearly distinct as scores on this scale were inversely related to scores on all the other scales. As such, the young people who scored highly on precontemplation tended to score low on contemplation, action and, to a lesser degree, maintenance and vice versa. The maintenance stage was not distinct as scores on this scale correlated quite strongly with scores on the contemplation and action scales. There was, in addition, a moderately strong correlation between contemplation and action scores, which suggested that some of the young people may have been caught in between these two stages: pointed towards the need for a further, 'preparation', stage (see below).

Analysts have used two main methods to allocate individuals to a stage of change (Rollnick *et al.* 1992; Heather *et al.* 1993). According to the simplest approach individuals are classified according to their highest scale score and, in cases where two scale scores are tied, they are assigned to the furthest stage of change. The second, and more sophisticated,

Table 9.3 Correlations between readiness for change scale scores (Spearman's rho)

	P	C	A	M
Precontemplation (P)	–	–.24	–.18	–.07
Contemplation (C)		–	.33	.42
Action (A)			–	.41
Maintenance (M)				–

Note: $n = 520$.
Source: Mentoring Plus cohort and comparison group (first survey).

Table 9.4 Allocation to stage of change

Profile	Precontemplation score	Contemplation score	Action score	Allocated stage
A	+	+	+	Unclear
B	+	+	–	Unclear
C	+	–	–	Unclear
D	+	–	–	Precontemplation
E	–	+	+	Preparation
F	–	+	–	Contemplation
G	–	–	+	Action
H	–	–	–	Unclear

Source: Rollnick *et al.* (1992).

method of allocation takes account of whether individuals showed a positive or negative/zero score on each of the scales (see Table 9.4).

Where individuals scored positively on one scale and negatively/zero on all others, this indicated that they were located within a single stage of change. Taken together, however, these profiles only accounted for approximately one in four (27 per cent) of the young people referred to Mentoring Plus. By far the most common profile among these young people was that where individuals scored negatively/zero on precontemplation and positively for both contemplation and action (this profile accounted for 50 per cent of the young people). In previous studies, this profile (i.e. profile E) has been taken to indicate a 'decision-making' or 'preparation' stage (Heather *et al.* 1993). This stage 'reflects an involvement in thinking and taking action on the identified problem' (McConnaughy *et al.* 1983: 498). While preparation may constitute a distinct stage, it is plausible for individuals who are engaged in action still to be concerned about the behaviour in question. It is, consequently, important to distinguish between those who are preparing to take action and those who are actively engaged in action but are still concerned about the behaviour (Heather *et al.* 1993). Thus, the young people who had a '– + +' profile were allocated to the preparation or action stage on the basis of their highest score; those whose contemplation score was greater than their action score were considered to be in preparation; and those whose action score was greater, or equal, to their contemplation score were considered to be in the action stage. In addition, those with a '+ – –' profile were allocated to the precontemplation stage, while those with a '– + –' profile were allocated to the contemplation stage. Almost four in five (77 per cent) of the young people referred to Mentoring Plus were assigned to stage of change on this basis. The remainder did not meet any of the profiles described above and were classified according to their highest scale score.

The vast majority of the young people referred to Mentoring Plus had, at the very least, begun to contemplate change by the time the programme started (see Figure 9.1). This is, perhaps, unsurprising. Involvement in the programme was largely voluntary and many of the referrers indicated that they only referred those young people who indicated an interest in attending. The desire to attend something like Mentoring Plus may indicate a readiness to change, while joining the programme may be thought of as action (i.e. it may result from a decision to change).

While the quantitative analysis supported the stages of change model, it is also worth noting that the basic idea underlying this model was endorsed by the young people during the depth interviews. Those who felt they had made positive changes during the course of the programme attributed this to a variety of influences, including Mentoring Plus, the project workers, their mentor and 'growing up'. But most agreed that the programme would not have made any difference to them had they not *wanted* to change. For changes to occur, they argued, young people must be prepared to change and must be open to the help that is available:

> If you're getting in trouble but there's part of you that thinks, 'oh, I like want to fix up', then it will work. But, I reckon, if you knows that there's no part of you that wants to do it, then it ain't going to work (young person).

> If they [Mentoring Plus] were to grow around the country, they make a lot of young people – whether they are good, bad or normal – better as they are and will get them further in life. Let people help you and

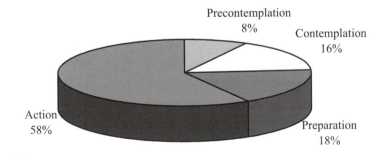

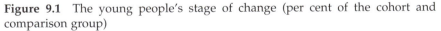

$n = 515$

Figure 9.1 The young people's stage of change (per cent of the cohort and comparison group)
Source: Mentoring Plus cohort and comparison group.

they will help you, and you can help yourself, and everything will go all right for you (young person).

As an extension of this idea, some of the young people were critical of others whom they felt attended the programme for the 'wrong' reasons and were taking advantage of the project:

Mentoring Plus is good … but that is if you are willing to look at it in that light. There are some people that might … come in and get some free food, some free drink or just some free films, go to the cinema for free; they don't see the other side of it which is the trying to like lighten up a little bit or help you with certain stuff (young person).

Stage of change, engagement in the programme and evidence of change

In order to assess further the potential value of the transtheoretical approach, we considered whether the young people's stage of change at the start of the programme was linked to their subsequent participation in it and to any actual changes in their offending and inclusion/exclusion. Before reviewing the findings from this analysis, it is worth emphasizing that our data only allowed us to assess the potential value of the transtheoretical approach in a rather general way. Mentoring Plus did not use the stages of change model and, had it done so, there might have been greater evidence of change, particularly among young people in certain stages. In addition, we assessed the young people's stage of change in a general rather than specific sense. We did not assess their stage of change specifically in relation to engagement with education, training and work or offending and it may be that the young people were contemplating change (or making changes) in other aspects of their lives. Taken together, this may mean that the potential of the stages of change model has been diluted or masked by our data. Nevertheless, by considering the relationship between stages of change, however crudely measured, and actual change we are able to gain a general sense of whether this model is likely to be of value in working with disaffected young people.

Levels of engagement in the programme varied quite sharply according to the young people's stage of change. The key distinction lay between those who were, at the very least, contemplating change at the start of the programme and those who were not doing so. The young people who had moved beyond precontemplation by this point were more than three times as likely as those who had not done so to engage actively with the programme. One in eight (13 per cent) of those in precontemplation engaged actively with the programme, compared with at least one in three (between 35 and 42 per cent) of those in the subsequent stages. Conversely, those who were in precontemplation were twice as likely as those in subsequent stages not to have engaged at all (80 per cent had not done so compared with 37 to 41 per cent of those who had moved into contemplation and beyond).[13]

The changes that were evident in relation to the key outcome measures also appeared to be linked to the young people's stage of change at the start of the programme. Increases in the rate of inclusion were only apparent among those young people who had already moved into the later stages of change. Among those who were in precontemplation or contemplation, there was very little evidence of change, as their rates of inclusion remained (almost) identical (see Table 9.5). For those who were in precontemplation this may, to some extent, be explained by their starting position. A relatively large proportion of these young people started out in positions of inclusion and there was, perhaps, less need for them to change in this regard. This explanation is less convincing for those who were in the contemplation stage, however, as a fairly large proportion of these young people started out in positions of social exclusion. The greatest increase in inclusion was evident among those young people who were preparing to change at the start of the programme: the rate of inclusion within this group increased by slightly more than a third. While a more moderate increase was evident among those who were in the action stage this may well reflect changes that occurred prior to the start of the programme, as a relatively large proportion of the young people in this group started out in a position of social inclusion.

Changes in offending also varied according to the young people's stage of change, although the evidence for this was a little ambiguous. No systematic variations were evident in relation to the general measures

Table 9.5 Rate of social inclusion by stage of change (per cent of those in each stage)[14]

	Rate of social inclusion		Proportionate change	n
	Start of programme (%)	End of programme (%)		
Precontemplation	72	72	0.00	14
Contemplation	55	54	−0.02	37
Preparation	47	63	+0.34	36
Action	60	67	+0.11	124

Source: Mentoring Plus cohort (first survey, first and second follow-up).

Table 9.6 Offending by stage of change (average number of offences among those in each stage)[15]

	Ever	Year one	Year two	Change (year 1–2)	n
Precontempation	7.3	5.0	4.3	−0.7	13
Contemplation	5.7	4.0	2.0	−1.9	39
Preparation	6.7	5.0	3.5	−1.5	37
Action	5.2	3.9	2.4	−1.5	125

Notes
The mean has been used here, rather than the median, on the basis that it provides a more sensitive measure of change. Figures have been given to one decimal place as this further increases the sensitivity of the analysis. Programme participants committed a median of three offences in year one and two offences in year two, while non-participants committed a median of three offences and one offence respectively.
Ever = ever committed (by the time of the first survey).
Year one = 12 months prior to the first survey; year two = 12 months between the first and second survey.
Source: Mentoring Plus cohort and comparison group (original survey and first follow-up).

which indicated whether the young person had offended during the last 12 months and whether he or she had done so persistently. However, the precise number of offence-types committed during this period did reveal a clear pattern (see Table 9.6). Reductions in offending were least marked among the young people who had not moved beyond the pre-contemplation stage at the start of the programme. On average, those who had moved into, or beyond, the contemplation stage went on to desist from twice as many offence types as those who were in precontemplation. Moreover, the relatively low rate of desistance associated with pre-contemplation could not be explained in terms of lower rates of overall offending: the young people in the precontemplation stage had relatively extensive offending repertoires and, in this sense, there was considerable room for reduction.

This study was not ideally suited to assessing the stages of change model and the evidence we have presented is in no way conclusive. It is, however, highly suggestive and indicates that the stages of change model may be usefully employed in work with *disaffected* young people. Not only were the key stages of this model evident among the young people referred to Mentoring Plus, but they also helped to explain levels of engagement and apparent incidence of change. The young people who had, at the very least, started to contemplate change when they were referred to the programme were the most likely to engage actively with it and were most likely to report actual changes in offending behaviour and engagement in education, training and work. These findings are particularly noteworthy given the way in which processes of individual change have largely been neglected in the context of such work. On the basis of this evidence we suggest that greater attention should be given to the particular needs of *disaffected* young people who are located in the various stages of change.

The stages of change model does not prescribe a particular intervention for each stage. It may, rather, be used as a map of the stages people might be expected to go through when changing their behaviour and as a broad guide to the type of intervention that may be most appropriate at any given time (Neesham 1993). The model is not prescriptive, in part at least, because it is largely descriptive. It does not explain why, for example, some people who appear ready to change do so successfully, while others fail to do so. In thinking about these processes, we might identify various types of barrier to change. These might be cognitive, where people lack information; behavioural, where people are unable to translate intentions into behaviour; structural, where they lack the means or opportunities to change; and/or emotional, where they continue to act out in anger (Miller 1998; Gilligan 1999). Once an individual has begun to contemplate change, we may suppose that a repertoire of responses is required which helps to minimise the various barriers to realising such change. This flexibility is important because it means that the individual focus of the stages of change model may be integrated with approaches that include a focus on social structure and exclusion (McNeil and Batchelor 2002). Thus, for example, interventions aimed at reducing offending may encourage offenders who are in the action phase to take part in education, employment and training on the basis that unemployment and boredom are triggers to offending.

Conclusion

In this chapter we have moved beyond the question of what works to consider how things might be expected to work. That is, we have attempted to understand how it is that individuals change. Like many social welfare interventions, the Mentoring Plus programme was predicated upon the idea that participants would change without working to an explicit model of how they might be expected to do so. Although it lacked a clear model of change, the design of the programme implied a number of possible mechanisms for change. In essence, it rested on a social deficit model, which views offending and other negative outcomes as being driven by disadvantage and exclusion. Engagement in education, training and work was identified as the key to positive change and many of the structured activities within the programme focused on this outcome. Other possible outcomes, including reduced offending, were dealt with only tangentially. In addition, while the social deficit model provided a reasonable sociological basis for change, psychological dimensions were less well developed. Mentors were frequently described as 'role models' and there was talk of 'empowering' the young people and raising their self-esteem, but these notions were used fairly loosely and were not built into the fabric of the programme.

Some of these ideas about change have been challenged during the course of this chapter. Although participation in the Mentoring Plus programme was associated with an increased rate of social inclusion, this did not appear to have a positive knock-on effect in terms of reduced offending. Consequently the general efficacy of the social deficit model remains open to question. In addition the emphasis that was placed on empowerment and self-esteem did not provide a convincing explanation for change. The Mentoring Plus programme had no discernible impact on the young people's locus of control and while there was some suggestion that it may have helped to improve the self-image of those who had low self-esteem at the outset this did not bring additional gains in terms of reduced offending or increasing levels of social inclusion.

How then might we explain change? Our analysis provides some support for the emphasis that the programme placed on the need for male role models. Most of the young people on the programme were male and many of them had little contact with their fathers or felt that their relationship with their father was poor. Moreover, while most of the mentors were female, the impact of the programme (measured in terms of increased rates of social inclusion) was most marked where male mentees had been matched with male mentors. We are unable to offer much insight into why this was so and suggest that future research consider the gender dynamics surrounding mentoring and work with *disaffected* young people more generally. The particular emphasis that was placed on the need for black male role models remains a more open question. While black young people tended to be matched with black mentors there was no evidence that ethnic matching was associated with increased impact.

Our analysis indicates that the stages of change model provides a useful basis for understanding change among *disaffected* young people. The key stages of this model were evident among the young people referred to the programme and those who had already started to contemplate change were the most likely to engage actively and were most likely to report actual changes in offending behaviour and rates of social inclusion. Most of the young people referred to Mentoring Plus had already started to think about change, presumably reflecting the voluntary nature of the programme. The stages of change model may be even more important in the context of compulsory programmes, such as those run within the youth justice system, as it is likely that these programmes will come into contact with many young people who are yet to consider change. Regardless of whether programmes are voluntary or compulsory, there are three key messages from this Chapter. First, it is essential that programmes have an explicit model or theory of change. Secondly, this model should draw on and seek to integrate sociological and psychological factors. And finally, activities should take account of participants' stage of change.

Notes

1 Cramer's V = 0.11 (helpfulness of mentor by sex of young person); 0.16 (helpfulness of mentor by sex of mentor); 0.14 (helpfulness of mentor by sex of young person and mentor).

2 Cramer's V = 0.12 (helpfulness of mentor by ethnicity of young person); 0.07 (helpfulness of mentor by ethnicity of mentor); and 0.18 (helpfulness of mentor by ethnicity of young person and mentor). It should be noted that the analysis only included 13 white young people who had a black or minority ethnic mentor and 16 black African/Caribbean young people who had a white mentor.

3 Cramer's V = 0.18 (helpfulness of mentor by occupational status of mentor); 0.12 (helpfulness of mentor by whether mentor has a criminal record); Kendall's tau-c = 0.05 (helpfulness of mentor by age of mentor); 0.05 (helpfulness of mentor by age of young person). Note the analysis only included 13 unemployed mentors and 15 mentors who had a criminal record.

4 Cramer's V = 0.05 (young people's movements between inclusion and exclusion from the start to the end of the programme by their sex); 0.17 (young people's movement between inclusion and exclusion by sex of their mentor); and 0.15 (young people's movement between inclusion and exclusion by sex of pairings).

5 Among 12–14-year-olds, the proportion of young people in a position of social inclusion increased from 52 to 76 per cent; among 15 year olds it increased from 46 to 59 per cent; among 16-year-olds it increased from 54 to 63 per cent and among 17–19 year olds it increased from 46 per cent to 59 per cent. Cramer's V = 0.11 (young people's movement between inclusion and exclusion by their age); 0.13 (young people's movement between inclusion and exclusion by age of mentor).

6 The proportion of white young people who were in a position of social inclusion increased from 40 to 62 per cent, compared with an increase from 56

to 71 per cent among black African/Caribbean young people and from 38 to 47 per cent among mixed-race young people. Cramer's $V = 0.18$ (young people's movement between inclusion and exclusion by their ethnicity). Among young people who had a white mentor, the rate of inclusion increased proportionately by 28% (from 43 to 55 per cent) compared with proportionate increase of 16% among those with a black African/Caribbean mentor (62 to 72 per cent). Cramer's $V = 0.19$ (young people's movement between inclusion and exclusion by ethnicity of mentor). Among white young people who had been matched with a black African/Caribbean mentor, the proportion who were in a position of social inclusion increased proportionately by 97 per cent (from 38 to 75 per cent), compared with a proportionate increase of 33 per cent among those who had been matched with a white mentor (from 42 per cent to 56 per cent). Cramer's $V = 0.26$ (young people's movement between inclusion and exclusion by ethnicity of pairing). Note the analysis only included 12 white young people who had been matched with a black African/Caribbean mentor and 14 black African/Caribbean young people who had been matched with a white mentor.

7 Where the mentor was employed in a professional occupation, the young people's rate of inclusion increased proportionately by 38 per cent (from 42 to 58 per cent); where the mentor was employed in a non-professional occupation, the young people's rate of inclusion increased proportionately by 35 per cent (from 51 to 69 per cent); and where the mentor was a student, the young people's rate of inclusion doubled (from 38 to 78 per cent). Note, in only 11 cases was the mentor a student, in only 12 cases was the mentor unemployed and in only 15 cases did the mentor have a criminal record. Cramer's $V = 0.13$ (young people's movement between inclusion and exclusion by mentor's occupational status); 0.14 (young people's movement between inclusion and exclusion by whether mentor had a criminal record).

8 For a conceptual critique of this model, see Herzog *et al.* (1999) and Sutton (2001).

9 The analysis described in this section was based on the young people in both the cohort and comparison groups as the focus was no longer specifically on assessing the impact of Mentoring Plus. Including the comparison group in this way boosted the number of cases and increased the power of the analysis. The initial analyses, focusing on the extent to which the stages of change model could meaningfully be applied to the young people, were conducted separately for the cohort and comparison groups. Thereafter, the two groups were combined.

10 These statements were based on Rollnick *et al.*'s (1992) short readiness to change questionnaire, the University of Rhodes Island Change Assessment Scale (McConnaughy *et al.* 1983) and the Stages of Change Readiness and Treatment Eagerness Scale or SOCRATES (http://www.niaaa.nih.gov). Items from these scales were adapted and tailored to our population.

11 Unforeseen changes to the recruitment process meant that some of the young people in the comparison group had never been to Mentoring Plus and thus statements which referred to 'this place' or 'being here' were invalidated. A

relatively large number of the young people in the comparison group did not respond to these items and those who did respond tended to concentrate in the neither/nor category, suggesting that these items were confusing to these young people. Consequently, while these items were included in the analysis of the cohort group they were excluded from analysis of the comparison group. Note, the analysis was based on an approach known as principal component analysis and was repeated using both Varimax and Oblique rotations. The results were almost identical, regardless of which type of rotation was employed, and thus the Varimax rotation was preferred (for discussion see Kline 1994).

12 For the comparison group, invalid items were replaced with individual's average (mean) score for the remaining items on the given scale.

13 Kendall's tau = 0.11 (level of engagement by stage of change).

14 Cramer's V = 0.13 (change in status by stage of change).

15 The change variable shown in this table compared the number of offences committed in the two time periods for each young person. The number of offences committed in year one was subtracted from the number committed in year two: a negative number indicates desistance – fewer of the listed offences were committed in year two than year one; and a positive number indicates escalation – more offences were committed in year two than year one. The figures given in this table are based on the mean, rather than the median, as the former provided the most sensitive measure of change. Median values for the change variable indicated that the young people in *each* stage of change had committed one less offence type during the 12 months covered by the programme than in the 12 months that preceded it. This obscured important differences between stages which were reflected in the mean values. In contrast to those provided elsewhere, the figures in this table have been given to one decimal place as rounding would have obscured the extent of the differences that were evident. Eta = 0.09 (change in offending by stage of change).

Chapter 10

Conclusion: youth disaffection, mentoring and social inclusion

Interventions aimed at disaffected young people abound. All too often, however, they get caught up in a negative cycle. Every so often a 'new' approach is identified which captures the imagination of politicians, policy-makers and practitioners alike. Grandiose claims are made, new funding opportunities arise and initial 'evaluations' appear to indicate promising outcomes. Before long, however, confidence turns to disillusionment as the reality fails to match the initial claims. As a result, promising interventions are undermined by unrealistic expectations (advocates of particular approaches may unwittingly collude in this process as they seek to maintain their programmes and sustain their funding base). This pattern has a number of other negative consequences: considerable amounts of public money may be spent on interventions whose impact is not fully understood, potentially positive interventions may be abandoned before they are properly evaluated, and the possibility that interventions are actually harmful remains unaddressed. As social scientists, one of our major concerns is the lack of commitment shown by politicians and practitioners to rigorous evaluation of interventions aimed at young people. If, for no other reason, evaluation is crucial given the potential for the development of interventions which are actually harmful to those they seek to help. It seems to us that there is a limited potential for harm associated with mentoring, but the possibility of negative outcomes means it is incumbent on those involved to ensure that the impact of such interventions is evaluated formally.

The rise of mentoring

There is a very real risk that the cycle described above is currently being repeated in relation to mentoring. Although mentoring-type relationships can no doubt be found in all societies at any point in history, their use as a formal response to youthful disaffection is a relatively recent development, particularly in the UK. Since the late 1990s mentoring programmes have been heavily sponsored by the Labour government and have spread rapidly in a broad array of contexts, though mainly in connection with young people. While the rise of mentoring undoubtedly reflects the intuitive appeal of this approach, it has also been based upon its compatibility with New Labour thinking, particularly the emphasis that has been placed on community mobilisation. What is absolutely clear is that the popularity of mentoring has little to do with the weight of evidence. As we indicated in Chapter 4, there is very little research evidence which either provides general support for mentoring as an intervention, or which helps in the design of such programmes.

It was against this backdrop of considerable political support, but very little evidence that the research reported in this book was designed. Our aims were to describe, in some detail, the nuts and bolts of one approach to mentoring and to measure the impact that it had on a group of disaffected young people. Although we feel we were largely successful in meeting these objectives, it remains difficult to distil straightforward messages from the study. Nevertheless our analysis has clear implications for the future of mentoring and for work with disaffected young people more generally.

Does mentoring work?

The reality of mentoring, it seems to us, cannot be conveyed adequately through a 'mentoring works' or 'mentoring does not work' formula. Our study indicates that mentoring has real potential as a means of working with disaffected young people, but not necessarily in the ways that some might expect. The main achievements of the Mentoring Plus programme that we have documented are as follows. The programme recruited and actively engaged a large number of young people who were at con-siderable risk of social exclusion (including a large proportion from black African/Caribbean communities). Family breakdown was common, often resulting in poor or non-existent relationships with parents; school attendance was often disrupted and school-leavers showed very low levels of qualification; many of the young people were completely disengaged from education, training and work; their levels of offending were high; and many had already had considerable contact with the criminal justice system. One way or another, the young people recruited on to the programme were in trouble and they faced a very real prospect of becoming 'permanently lost' (Newburn 2002).

The programme demonstrated that fairly substantial changes can be achieved in the lives of even the most highly disaffected young people. There was a marked improvement in the rate of social inclusion among programme participants, which can be attributed to the programme with a reasonable degree of confidence. It is also worth noting that increased rates of social inclusion may bring additional benefits in the long term, including reductions in offending, even though there was no evidence of such changes resulting from mentoring during the course of the study (marked reductions in offending were evident among participants and non-participants).

The achievements of the Mentoring Plus programme should not be underestimated and are all the more impressive when set in context. Interventions with disaffected young people are inherently difficult to implement and these difficulties are exacerbated by a climate of insecure funding, fixed short-term employment and high staff turnover. Delivering a consistent and coherent service under such circumstances is far from straightforward and this study adds to the significant body of research which shows that implementation failure (or at least inadequate implementation) often lies at the heart of the inability to deliver better outcomes. While many of the Mentoring Plus projects ran into operational difficulties, those that achieved the highest level of programme integrity also had the greatest impact in terms of encouraging young people (back) into education and work. It follows that in a more secure environment the overall impact of the programme would have been greater and it therefore behoves policy-makers and funders to think carefully about how they support such programmes in the future. All too often, it appears, potentially positive work with young people is undermined by circumstances that serve to undermine, or at least limit, programme integrity.

The need for a more fully theorised approach

In terms of future development, mentoring requires more than secure and longer-term funding. There is also a need to think through the process more fully. The impact that Mentoring Plus had on the young people who took part in the programme was not necessarily of the order that some advocates might expect and nor was it solely or straightforwardly related to the 'mentoring' element of the programme. The extent to which the success of the programme rested on the mentoring or the Plus element must remain something of an open question as participants tended to engage actively with both components. Nevertheless, the Plus element appears to have been at least as important as the mentoring relationship and, on balance, it seems likely that these two components tended to reinforce one another. It is possible that mentoring, in isolation, does not provide an effective way of working with disaffected young people and the approach may be best applied as part of a professionally led structured programme. In addition, as mentoring encountered a greater degree of ambivalence than the Plus component, it may best be used as an *optional* source of support within the context of such programmes.

The impact of Mentoring Plus appeared to be greatest in relation to those areas where the structured activities related directly to the aims of the programme. Thus, seeking to increase young people's involvement in education, training and work was a clearly specified goal both of the programme in general and, more specifically, of the Plus element. By contrast, although reducing offending was a general aim, it was not a specific goal of any of the structured elements of the Plus programme. When set out in these terms such findings may seem unsurprising and yet their implications for practice typically remain unrealised. It is all too often the case that work with young people is under-theorised. That is to say, there is often little explicit discussion of the aims of particular programmes, other than the most banal identification of 'reductions in offending' or something similarly general, and this lack of clarity is then compounded by the absence of any explicit model of change. Why is it that a particular intervention might be thought to work? And by what means will it change the behaviour of programme participants?

In large part, the Mentoring Plus programme rested on an under-specified model of change. Although it had a reasonably well developed social deficit model, the way in which individuals might achieve change was less well thought through. The result was something of a 'one size fits all' approach: the programme is designed and established, young people and mentors are recruited and, allowing for a small amount of variation, the model is applied to all those participating. Unsurprisingly, perhaps, this programme, like all others, appears to have greater impact on some young people than others. While there are many reasons why this might be the case, one possibility is that the method of delivery is appropriate to some, but not all, participants. A more sophisticated understanding of individual change may lead eventually to a more nuanced model of programme delivery and to greater impact. This, in part, is what we mean by a more fully *theorised* approach. Simply providing opportunities for change may be a *necessary* condition for achieving change but it is rarely a *sufficient* condition. Programmes need to develop explicit theories or hypotheses about what they believe 'works' with young people, under what circumstances particular interventions work and, most particularly in this regard, with which young people such interventions are most likely to succeed. This can then be tested and, where appropriate, refined.

In thinking about what works with whom we would argue that careful attention should be paid both to individual or psychological factors as well as to broader structural features. As we described earlier, to the extent that Mentoring Plus had a theory of change, it tended to rest on a social deficit model: that is, manifestations of 'disaffection' were generally considered to be the result of social exclusion or disadvantage. Seeking to remedy such disadvantage, or to facilitate inclusion, was therefore viewed as the fundamental basis for dealing with disaffection. Now, on a general sociological level, we have little difficulty with such a theory, although we think it should be made more explicit and articulated in greater detail. What was conspicuously lacking in Mentoring Plus (and in this it is little different from most other interventions with disaffected youth) was any explicit consideration of the individual, or psychological, dimensions of change.

The lack of attention that has been given to individual dimensions of change is, we think, highly problematic at both a practical and theoretical level. According to Elias (1978: 128, emphasis in the original), 'the conventional divorce of the scientific study of *the person* from the scientific study of *people* is questionable – but only the divorce, let it be noted, not the distinction between them'. The implications for interventions with disaffected young people are clear. A sociological theory must present, in Elias' terms, not only a clear conception of people as societies, but also as individuals. In this regard, we draw attention to the potential importance of individual motivation to change. For all the evidence of disaffection and disruption in the lives of the young people recruited on to the Mentoring Plus programme, they displayed highly conventional attitudes and aspirations. Their sense of alienation from the process of schooling, for example, rarely extended to the cultural goals of education and work. The apparent dissonance between their current situations and future aspirations was reflected in their attitudes to change. At the time of their recruitment, the vast majority of the young people on the programme had already started to think about making changes and most were actively doing so. While possibly reflecting the voluntary nature of participation, this positive orientation to change was almost certainly crucial to the success of the programme. Understanding the influence that orientation to change plays is, it seems to us, vital to improving the delivery of interventions.

Identifying impact

This leads us to two final points. First, not only do programmes need a clear model of practice underpinned by an explicit theory of change, but they also need to be implemented as precisely as possible. This study has clearly demonstrated the link between degree of impact and 'programme integrity'. Assuming the theory of change has some veracity, then the closer the programme comes to matching the design, the greater the chances are that it will have some positive effect. If relatively little attention is paid to ensuring that service delivery is faithful to the model, or if the circumstances in which services operate undermine the ability of practitioners to deliver the programme in the intended manner, then it follows that impact will be limited or non-existent.

Mentoring has undoubtedly benefited in the past from being the latest fashionable idea. There is, however, a danger, as with all fashions, that they will become unfashionable just as quickly (and irrationally) as they became fashionable. Unless positive outcomes can be demonstrated relatively quickly it is likely that policy-makers and other funders will quickly move on to the next 'silver bullet'. Under these circumstances, we must try to ensure that interventions operate in an environment of greater security in which the likelihood is that programme integrity is maximized. We must also pay greater attention to understanding and measuring outcomes. This leads us back to the quotation from Sherman and colleagues (1999) that we used in the Introduction. Their plea to government was that rather than ploughing money into yet more unevaluated and unproven programmes, they should seek to ensure an increase in carefully controlled evaluations of existing practices. This is something with which we wholeheartedly concur. It is a sorry state of affairs that almost none of the work carried out with disaffected young people, and there is a considerable array of work being undertaken, is subject to rigorous assessment and evaluation. In large part this is because there is very little commitment to scientific evaluative research among politicians, policy-makers and practitioners, although it also reflects the willingness of the contemporary social scientific community to accept, indeed embrace, research that pays scant regard to the need for methodological rigour.

It seems to us that with something like mentoring there is a very clear case for the use of experimental research designs. This is not to suggest that we think quantitative methods should take priority over qualitative methods, merely that in attempting to assess outcomes there is much to be gained from random allocation. Such an approach seeks to assess the impact of an intervention by comparing the experiences (using quantitative and qualitative methods) of 'treatment' and 'non-treatment' groups. In this study we adopted as robust a design as was possible under the prevailing circumstances; using a comparison group and measuring impact over time. Nevertheless, so far as future work in this area is concerned, it is our view that random allocation would help to identify the relative contributions of different elements of a programme; would help to improve our understanding of the impact that the personal attributes of mentors and mentees have in the process of change; and would help to clarify the nature of any links between, for example, increasing involvement in education, training and work, and reductions in offending. Most importantly, random allocation would provide the basis upon which we could reorient practice so as to maximize the impact of intervening in the lives of disaffected young people.

Conclusion

While often overstated, youth disaffection is undoubtedly a considerable problem. Large amounts of public money are spent attempting to intervene in the lives of disaffected youth and even larger amounts responding to the consequences of disaffection. However, it continues to be the case that very little is known about what works with these young people and, more particularly, how it works. Though mentoring is not a panacea the signs are that it has considerable promise. Realising its potential requires four steps: mentoring needs to be discussed *realistically*, planned *carefully*, implemented *faithfully* and evaluated *rigorously*. Only then will we be able to judge the value of this approach and make decisions about its role in dealing with disaffection.

Appendix I

Table I.1 Current status, orientation to school and qualifications (per cent)

	Mentoring Plus cohort	General youthful population	
		Estimate	Range
Current status			
Attending school	46	74	71–77
Studying at college/university	8	13	11–15
On a training scheme	5	2	1–3
Working	1	7	6–9
Disengaged	40	4	3–5
	100	100	
Truanting from school			
Every week	34	5	4–7
Two or three days a month	18	1	1–2
Less often	17	14	12–16
Not at all	31	79	77–82
	100	100	
Qualifications (17–19-year-olds only)			
GCSE	47	82	77–86
NVQ Foundation/Intermediate	17	3	1–4
BTEC Certificate	2	4	1–6
City and Guilds	13	6	3–8
No qualifications	45	9	6–12

Note: The 1998/9 *YLS* was adjusted to reflect the age and sex structure of the Mentoring Plus cohort.
Source: Mentoring Plus cohort (first survey) and *YLS* (1998/9).

Table I.2 Comparative rates of offending (per cent)

	Mentoring Plus cohort	General youthful population	
		Estimate	Range
Committed an offence			
No, never	7	42	39–45
Yes – but not in last 12 months	8	20	17–23
Yes – in last 12 months	85	38	35–41
	100	100	
Criminal damage			
No, never	31	67	64–70
Yes – but not in last 12 months	16	18	15–21
Yes – in last 12 months	54	15	13–18
	100	100	
Property offences			
No, never	27	71	68–74
Yes – but not in last 12 months	14	13	11–15
Yes – in last 12 months	60	16	14–19
	100	100	
Violent offences			
No, never	22	76	73–78
Yes – but not in last 12 months	14	10	8–2
Yes – in last 12 months	64	14	12–17
	100	100	
Traffic violations			
No, never	50	78	75–81
Yes – but not in last 12 months	8	10	7–12
Yes – in last 12 months	42	13	10–15
	100	100	
Persistent offender			
No	38	89	87–91
Yes	62	11	9–3
	100	100	
Serious offence			
No, never	30	85	82–87
Yes – but not in last 12 months	13	7	5–9
Yes – in last 12 months	57	8	6–0
	100	100	

Note: The 1998/9 *YLS* was adjusted to reflect the age and sex structure of the Mentoring Plus cohort.
Source: Mentoring Plus cohort (first survey) and *YLS* (1998/9).
Some of the percentages shown in this Table do not add up to exactly 100 because of rounding.

Table I.3 Comparative rates of illicit drug use (per cent)

	Mentoring Plus cohort	General youthful population	
		Estimate	Range
Cannabis			
Used in the last 12 months	60	24	21–27
Used but not in last 12 months	10	6	4–7
Never used	30	70	67–73
	100	100	
Hallucinants			
Used in the last 12 months	10	9	7–10
Used but not in last 12 months	5	5	4–7
Never used	85	86	84–89
	100	100	
Solvents			
Used in the last 12 months	4	4	3–5
Used but not in last 12 months	3	4	3–6
Never used	93	92	90–94
	100	100	
Cocaine			
Used in the last 12 months	7	1	0–2
Used but not in last 12 months	3	1	0–2
Never used	90	98	9–99
	100	100	
Crack and/or heroin			
Used in the last 12 months	4	0.3	0–1
Used but not in last 12 months	3	0.5	0–1
Never used	94	99	98–100
	100	100	

Source: Mentoring Plus cohort (first survey) and *YLS* (1998/9).
Some of the percentages shown in this Table do not add up to exactly 100 because of rounding.

Rosenberg's measure of self-esteem

Rosenberg (1965) viewed self-esteem as an evaluative *attitude* – that is, a generally positive or negative feeling about oneself. High self-esteem would mean that the individual respects him or herself for what he or she is, considers him or herself worthy (but does not necessarily consider him or herself better than others); while a low self-esteem was seen to imply 'self-rejection, self-dissatisfaction, self-contempt' (Rosenberg 1965: 31). Rosenberg's scale was one of the first attempts to measure self-esteem and continues to be widely used. It has a low level of error and is known to produce very similar results on successive occasions; it was originally devised to study adolescents and seemed appropriate for our study; and is fairly short and was thus considered to be well suited to our purpose, given that we also wanted to focus on many other questions.

Rosenberg's scale is based on the following statements:

1. On the whole, I am satisfied with myself.
2. At times I think I am no good at all.
3. I feel that I have a number of good qualities.
4. I am able to do things as well as most other people.
5. I feel I do not have much to be proud of.
6. I certainly feel useless at times.
7. I feel that I'm a person of worth, at least on an equal plane with others.
8. I wish I could have more respect for myself.

9. All in all, I am inclined to feel that I am a failure.
10. I take a positive attitude towards myself.

Responses to these statements were sought using a four-point scale of agreement, from strongly agree to strongly disagree. For negatively worded items (i.e. 2, 5, 6, 8, and 9) the scoring system was reversed and responses were converted into a scores ranging from 10 to 40, where low scores indicated high self-esteem and high scores indicated low self-esteem. Although widely used, there are no established norms regarding which scores and/or cut-off points can be seen as reflecting high or low self-esteem.

References

Advisory Council on the Misuse of Drugs (1998) *Drug Misuse and the Environment*. London: HMSO.

Ainley, P. (1991) *Young People Leaving Home*. London: Cassell.

Armstrong, D. (1997) 'Is there a problem? Quantitative estimates of the nature and extent of Status 0', in D. Armstrong *et al.* (eds) *Status 0: A Socio-economic Study of Young People on the Margin*. Belfast: Training and Employment Agency.

Armstrong, D., Loudon, R., McCready, S., Wilson, D., Istance, D. and Rees, G. (1997) *Status 0: A Socio-economic Study of Young People on the Margin*. Belfast: Training and Employment Agency.

Aspire Consultants (1996) *Disaffection and Non-participation in Education, Training and Employment by Individuals Aged 18–20*. Sheffield: Aspire Consultants.

Audit Commission (1996) *Misspent Youth*. London: Audit Commission.

Baldwin, D., Coles, B. and Mitchell, W. (1997) 'The formation of an underclass or disparate processes of social exclusion? Evidence from two groupings of "vulnerable youth"', in R. McDonald (ed.) *Youth, the 'Underclass' and Social Exclusion*. London: Routledge.

Bandura, A. (1977) *Social Learning Theory*. Englewood Cliffs, NJ: Prentice-Hall.

BBBSA (www.bbbsa.org/about/about_faqs.asp).

Bebbington, A. and Miles, J. (1989) 'The background of children who enter local authority care', *British Journal of Social Work*, 19: 349–68.

Benioff, S. (1997) *A Second Chance: Developing Mentoring and Education Projects for Young People*. London: Dalston Youth Project/Crime Concern.

Bentley, T. and Gurumurthy, R. (1999) *Destination Unknown: Engaging with the Problems of Marginalised Youth*. London: Demos.

Bhasin, S. (1997) *My Time, My Community, Myself: Experiences of Volunteering Within the Black Community*. London: National Centre for Volunteering.

Biehal, N., Clayden, J., Stein, M. and Wade, J. (1994) 'Leaving care in England: a research perspective', *Children and Youth Services Review*, 16: 231–54.

Biehal, N., Clayden, J., Stein, M. and Wade, J. (1995) *Moving On: Young People and Leaving Care Schemes*. London: HMSO.

BMRB (1999) *Mapping Troubled Lives: Young People not in Employment, Education or Training*. Draft report for the Social Exclusion Unit and the Department for Education and Employment.

Bottoms, A.E. and Wiles, P. (1997) 'Environmental criminology', in M. Maguire *et al.* (eds) *The Oxford Handbook of Criminology* (2nd edn). Oxford: Oxford University Press, 305–49.

Brain, K., Parker, H. and Carnwarth, T. (2000) 'Drinking with design: young drinkers as psychoactive consumers', *Drugs: Education, Prevention and Policy*, 7 (1): 5–20.

Brewer, D.D., Hawkins, J.D., Catalano, R.F. and Neckerman, H.J. (1995) 'Preventing serious, violent and chronic juvenile offending: A review of evaluations of selected strategies in childhood, adolescence and the community', in J.C. Howell *et al.* (eds) *Serious, Violent and Chronic Juvenile Offenders: A Sourcebook*. Thousand Oaks, CA: Sage.

Brown, L. and Gilligan, C. (1992) *Meeting at the Crossroads: Women's Psychology and Girls' Development*. Cambridge, MA: Harvard University Press.

Bullock, R., Little, M. and Millham, S. (1998) *Secure Treatment Outcomes: The care Careers of Very Difficult Adolescents*. Aldershot: Ashgate.

Byrne, D. (1999) *Social Exclusion*. Buckingham: Open University Press.

Carlen, P. (1996) *Jigsaw: A political Criminology of Youth Homelessness*. Buckingham: Open University Press.

Casey, B. and Smith, D.J. (1995) *Truancy and Youth Transitions. Youth Cohort Report* 34. London: Department for Education and Employment.

Centre for Economic and Social Inclusion (2003) *Welcome to the Inclusion Website – Home Page* (www.cesi.org.uk).

Centrepoint (1996) *The New Picture of Youth Homelessness in Britain*. London: Centrepoint.

Charlton, A. and Blair, B. (1989) 'Absence from school related to children's and parental smoking patterns', *British Medical Journal*, 298: 90–2.

Clutterbuck, D.R.R.B. (2002). *Mentoring and Diversity: An International Perspective*. Oxford: Butterworth-Heinmann.

Coffield, F., Borrill, C. and Marshall, S. (1986) *Growing up at the Margins*. Buckingham: Open University Press.

Coles, B. (1995) *Youth and Social Policy*. London: UCL Press.

Condon, J. and Smith, N. (2003) *Prevalence of Drug Use: Findings from the 2002/2003 British Crime Survey*, London: Home Office.

Courtenay, G. and McAleese, I. (1993) *Cohort 5: Aged 16–17 in 1991. Report on Sweep 1. Employment Department Research Series Youth Cohort Report 22*. London: Department of Employment.

Crime Concern (undated a) *Mentoring Plus*. London: Crime Concern.

Crime Concern (undated b) *Mentoring Work with Minority Ethnic Young People*. London: Crime Concern.

Darling, N.E.A. (2002) 'Naturally occurring mentoring in Japan and the United States: social roles and correlates', *American Journal of Community Psychology*, 30 (2): 245–70.

Davis Smith, J. (1997) *The 1997 National Survey of Volunteering*. Berkhamsted: National Centre for Volunteering.

Department for Education and Skills (2000) *Youth Cohort Study: Education, Training and Employment of 16–18 Year Olds in England and the Factors Associated with Non-participation. Statistical Bulletin 02/2000*. London: DfES.

Department for Education and Skills (2001) *Youth Cohort Study: The Activities and Experiences of 16 Year Olds: England and Wales 2000*. London: DfES.

Department for Education and Skills (2002) *Youth Cohort Study: The Activities and Experiences of 16 Year Olds: England and Wales 2002*. London: DfES.

Department for Education and Skills (2003) *Permanent Exclusions from Schools and Exclusion Appeals, England 2001/02* (provisional). London: DfES.

Department of Health (1998a) *Children Looked after in England 1997/8. Statistical Bulletin 1998/33*. London: Department of Health.

Department of Health (1998b) *Patterns and Outcomes in Child Placement*. London: HMSO.

Department of Health (2000) *Educational Qualifications of Care Leavers, Year Ending 31st March 2000: England. Bulletin 2000/25*. London: Department of Health.

Department of Health (2002) *Statistical Bulletins: Children Adopted from Care, Year Ending 31 March 2002 and Children Looked after in England by Local Authorities, at 31 March 2002, England*. London: Department of Health.

Department of Health and Social Security (1985) *Social Work Decisions in Child Care*. London: HMSO.

DfEE (1997) *Compendium of reports on truancy and disaffected pupils projects 1995–96* (Volumes 1–3). London: Department for Education and Employment.

Dicken, C., Bryson, R. and Kass, N. (1977) 'Companionship therapy: a replication in experimental community psychology', *Journal of Consulting and Clinical Psychology*, 45: 637–46.

Drugs Strategy Directorate (2002) *Updated Drugs Strategy*. London: Home Office.

DuBois, D.L., Holloway, B.E., Valentine, J.C. and Cooper, H. (2002) 'Effectiveness of mentoring programmes for youth: a meta-analytic review', *American Journal of Community Psychology*, 30 (2): 157–97.

Education and Employment Select Committee (1998) *Disaffected Children*. London: HMSO.

Ekblom, P. and Pease, K. (1995) 'Evaluating crime prevention', in M. Tonry and D.P. Farrington (eds) *Building a Safer Society*. Chicago, IL: University of Chicago Press.

Elias, N. (1978) *What is Sociology?*. London: Hutchinson.

Falshaw, L., Friendship, C., Travers, R. and Nugent, F. (2003) *Searching for 'What Works': An Evaluation of Cognitive Skills Programmes. Home Office Findings* 206, London: Home Office.

Farrington, D.P. (1980) 'Truancy, delinquency, the home and the school', in L. Hershov and I. Berg (eds) *Out of School: Modern Perspectives in Truancy and Refusal.* Chichester: Wiley.

Farrington, D.P. (1995) 'The development of offending and antisocial behaviour from childhood: key findings from the Cambridge study in delinquent development', *Journal of Child Psychology and Psychiatry*, 36: 929–64.

Farrington, D. (1996) *Understanding and Preventing Youth Crime.* York: Joseph Rowntree Foundation.

Farrington, D.P. (1997) 'Human development and criminal careers', in M. Maguire *et al.* (eds) *The Oxford Handbook of Criminology* (2nd edn). Oxford: Oxford University Press, 361–408.

Flood-Page, C., Campbell, S., Harrington, V. and Miller, J. (2000) *Youth Crime: Findings from the 1998/1999 Youth Lifestyles Survey.* London: Home Office.

Fo, W.S.O. and O'Donnell, C.R. (1974) 'The Buddy System: relationship and contingency conditioning in a community intervention program for youth with nonprofessionals as behavior change agents', *Journal of Consulting and Clinical Psychology*, 42: 163–9.

Fo, W.S.O. and O'Donnell, C.R. (1975) 'The Buddy System: effect of community intervention on delinquent offenses', *Behavior Therapy*, 6: 522–4.

Freedman, M. (1993) *The Kindness of Strangers: Adult Mentors, Urban Youth and the New Voluntarism.* San Francisco, CA: Jossey-Bass.

Furlong, A. and Cartmel, F. (1997) *Young People and Social Change: Individualization and Risk in Late Modernity.* Buckingham: Open University Press.

Furlong, A. and Cooney, G. (1990) 'Getting on their bikes. Early home leaving among Scottish youth', *Journal of Social Policy*, 19: 535–51.

Gillborn, D. and Gipps, C. (1996) *Recent Research on the Achievements of Ethnic Minority Pupils.* London: HMSO.

Gilligan, J. (1999) *Violence: Reflections on our Deadliest Epidemic.* London: Jessica Kingsley.

Gilligan, R. (1999) 'Enhancing the resilience of children and young people in public care by mentoring their talents and interests', *Child and Family Social Work*, 4: 187–96.

Gilroy, P. (1990) 'The myth of black criminality', in P. Scraton (ed.) *Law, Order, and the Authoritarian State: Readings in Critical Criminology.* Buckingham: Open University Press.

Glennerster, H. (1998) 'Tackling poverty at its roots? Education', in C. Oppenheim (ed.) *An Inclusive Society: Strategies for Tackling Poverty.* London: IPPR.

Godfrey, R. and Parsons, C. (1998) *Follow-up Survey of Permanent Exclusions.* London: DfEE.

Goodman, G. (1972) *Companionship Therapy: Studies in Structured Intimacy.* San Francisco, CA: Jossey-Bass.

Graham, J. and Bowling, B. (1995) *Young People and Crime.* London: Home Office.

Green, B.C. (1980) 'An evaluation of a Big Brothers program for father-absent boys: an eco-behavioral analysis'. PhD dissertation, New York University.

Hagell, A. and Newburn, T. (1994) *Persistent Young Offenders*. London: Policy Studies Institute.

Hagell, A. and Shaw, C. (1996) *Opportunity and Disadvantage at Age 16*. London: Policy Studies Institute.

Hammersley, R., Marsland, L. and Reid, M. (2003) *Substance Use by Young Offenders: The Impact of the Normalisation of Drug Use in the Early years of the 21st Century*. London: Home Office.

Hayden, C. (1997) *Children Excluded from Primary School: Debates, Evidence, Responses*. Buckingham: Open University Press.

Heath, A., Colton, M. and Aldgate, J. (1994) 'Failure to escape: a longitudinal study of foster children's educational attainment', *British Journal of Social Work*, 19: 447–60.

Heather, N., Rollnick, S. and Bell, A. (1993) 'Predictive validity of the Readiness to Change Questionnaire', *Addiction*, 88: 1667–77.

Herzog, T.A., Abrams, D.B., Emmons, K.M., Linnan, L.A. and Shadel, W.G. (1999) 'Do processes of change predict smoking stage movements? A prospective analysis of the transtheoretical model', *Health Psychology*, 18 (4): 369–75.

Hibbett, A. and Fogelman, K. (1990) 'Future lives of truants: family formation and health-related behaviour', *British Journal of Educational Psychology*, 60: 171–9.

Hibbett, A., Fogelman, K. and Manor, O. (1990) 'Occupational outcomes of truancy', *British Journal of Educational Psychology*, 60: 23–36.

Hills, J., Le Grand, J. and Piachaud, D. (2002) *Understanding Social Exclusion*. Oxford: Oxford University Press.

Hobcroft, J. (2002) 'Social exclusion and the generations', in J. Hills *et al.* (eds) *Understanding Social Exclusion*. Oxford: Oxford University Press.

Hollin, C.R. (1995) 'The meaning and implications of programme integrity', in J. McGuire (ed.) *What Works: Reducing Reoffending*. Chichester: Wiley.

Hope, T. (1996) 'Communities, crime and inequality in England and Wales', in T. Bennett (ed.) *Preventing Crime and Disorder*. Cambridge: Institute of Criminology.

Howell, J.C. (ed.) (1995) *Guide for Implementing the Comprehensive Strategy for Serious, Violent, and Chronic Juvenile Offenders*. Washington, DC: OJJDP.

Hutton, W. (1996) *The State We're In*. London: Verso.

ISDD (1994) *Drug Misuse in Britain*. London: ISDD.

ISDD (1997) *Drug Misuse in Britain*. London: ISDD.

Istance, D., Rees, G. and Williamson, H. (1994) *Young People Not in Education, Training or Employment in South Glamorgan*. Cardiff: South Glamorgan TEC/ University of Wales Cardiff.

Istance, D. and Williamson, H. (1996) *16 and 17 Year Olds in Mid-Glamorgan not in Education, Training or Employment (Status 0)*. Pontypridd: Mid-Glamorgan TEC.

Jackson, S. (1988) 'Residential care and education', *Children and Society*, 4: 335–50.

Jones, G. (1995) *Leaving Home*. Buckingham: Open University Press.

Joseph Rowntree Foundation (1995) *Income and Wealth: Report of the JRF Inquiry Group, Summary*. York: Joseph Rowntree Foundation.

Kinder, K., Wilkin, A. and Wakefield, A. (1997) *Exclusion: Who Needs It!*. Slough: National Foundation for Educational Research.

Kline, P. (1994) *An Easy Guide to Factor Analysis*. London: Routledge.

Labour Party (1996) *Tackling Youth Crime: Reforming Youth Justice*. London: Labour Party.

Leat, D. (1983) 'Explaining volunteering: a sociological perspective', S. Hatch (ed.) *Volunteering: Patterns, Meanings and Motives*. Berkhamsted: Volunteer Centre.

Le Grand, J. (1998) 'Social exclusion in Britain today.' Paper presented at ESRC conference, 'Counting me in: pathways to an inclusive society', 3 December.

Leitner, M., Shapland, J. and Wiles, P. (1993) *Drug Usage and Drugs Prevention: The Views and Habits of the General Public*. London: HMSO.

Levitas, R. (1998) *The Inclusive Society: Social Exclusion and New Labour*. Basingstoke: Macmillan.

Liddle, M. (1998) *Wasted Lives: Counting the Cost of Juvenile Offending*. London: NACRO.

Lloyd, C. (1998) 'Risk factors for problem drug use: identifying vulnerable groups', *Drugs: Education, Prevention and Policy*, 5 (3): 217–32.

Loudon, R., McCready, S. and Wilson, D. (1997) 'The experience of Status 0: some reflections from young people and professionals', in D. Armstrong *et al.* (eds) *Status 0: A Socio-economic Study of Young People on the Margin*. Belfast: Training and Employment Agency.

Mair, G. (1991) 'What works – nothing or everything?', *Home Office Research Bulletin*, 30: 3–8.

Maruna, S. (2000) 'Desistence from crime and offender rehabilitation: a tale of two research literatures', *Offender Programs Report*, 4(1): 1–13.

Marx, G. (1995) 'The engineering of social control: the search for the silver bullet', in J. Hagan and R. Peterson (eds) *Crime and Inequality*. Stanford, CA: Stanford University Press.

Mather, M., Humphrey, J. and Robson, J. (1997) 'The statutory medical and health needs of looked after children: time for a radical review?', *Adoption and Fostering*, 21 (2): 36–40.

McCann, J.B., James, A., Wilson, S. and Dunn, G. (1996) 'Prevalence of psychiatric disorders in young people in the care system', *British Medical Journal*, 313: 1529–30.

McCartney, C.A., Styles, M.B. and Morrow, K.V. (1994) *Mentoring in the Juvenile Justice System: Findings from Two Pilot Programs*. Philadelphia, PA: Public/Private Ventures.

McConnaughy, E.A., Prochaska, J.O. and Velicer, W.F. (1983) 'Stages of change in psychotherapy: measurment and sample profiles', *Psychotherapy*, 20: 368–75.

McCord, J. (1978) 'A thirty-year followup of treatment effects', *The American Psychologist*, 33: 284–389.

McCord, J. (1990) 'Understanding motivations: considering altruism and aggression', in J. McCord (ed.) *Facts, Frameworks, Forecasts: Advances in Criminological Theory*. New Brunswick, NJ: Transaction.

McGuire, J. and Priestly, P. (1995) 'Reviewing what works: past, present and future', in J. McGuire (ed.) *What Works: Reducing Re-offending – Guidelines from Research and Practice*. Chichester: Wiley, 3–34.

McNeil, F. and Batchelor, S. (2002) 'Chaos, containment and change: responding to persistent offending by young people', *Youth Justice*, 2 (1): 27–41.

Millham, S., Bullock, R., Hosie, K. and Haak, M. (1986) *Lost in Care*. Aldershot: Gower.

Mott, J. and Mirrlees-Black, C. (1993) *Self-reported Drug Misuse in England and Wales: Main Findings from the 1992 British Crime Survey. Research and Statistics Department Research Findings* 7. London: Home Office.

Murray, C. (1990) *The Emerging British Underclass*. London: Institute of Economic Affairs.

National Children's Bureau (1992) *Child Facts: Young People Leaving Care*. London: NCB.

Neesham, C. (1993) 'A model for change', *Healthlines*, September: 15–17.

Newburn, T. (1997) 'Youth, crime and justice', in M. Maguire *et al.* (eds) *The Oxford Handbook of Criminology* (2nd edn). Oxford: Oxford University Press.

Newburn, T. (1998) 'Young offenders, drugs and prevention', *Drugs: Education, Prevention and Policy*, 5 (3): 233–44.

Newburn, T. (2001) 'Community safety and policing: some implications of the Crime and Disorder Act 1998', in G. Hughes *et al.* (eds) *Crime Prevention and Community Safety: New Directions*. London: Sage.

Newburn, T. (2002) 'Young people, crime, and youth justice', in M. Maguire *et al.* (eds) *The Oxford Handbook of Criminology* (3rd edn). Oxford: Clarendon Press.

Newburn, T. and Shiner, M. (2001) *Teenage Kicks? Young People and Alcohol: A Review of the Literature*. York: Joseph Rowntree Foundation.

Noguera, P.A. (1996) *Responding to the Crisis Confronting California's Black Male Youth: Providing Support without Furthering Marginalization* (http://www.sistahspace.com/nommo /mv28.html).

Office for Standards in Education and Social Services Inspectorate (1995) *The Education of Children who are Looked After by Local Authorities*. London: Ofsted/SSI.

OFSTED (1996) *Exclusions from Secondary Schools 1995/6*. London: HMSO.

O'Sullivan, J. (2000) 'Mentoring', *Criminal Justice Matters*, 41 (Autumn).

O'Keefe, D. (1994) *Truancy in English Secondary Schools*. London: HMSO.

Oppenheim, C. and Harker, L. (1996) *Poverty: The Facts*. London: Child Poverty Action Group.

Parker, H., Aldridge, J. and Measham, F. (1998) *Illegal Leisure: The Normalization of Adolescent Recreational Drug Use*. London: Routledge.

Parker, H., Bakx, K. and Newcombe, R. (1998). *Living with Heroin: The Impact of a Drugs 'Epidemic' on an English Community*. Buckingham: Open University Press.

Parker, H., Bury, C. and Eggington, R. (1998) *New Heroin Outbreaks amongst Young People in England and Wales. Crime Detection and Prevention Series Paper* 92. London: Home Office.

Parker, H., Measham, F. and Aldridge, J. (1995) *Drug Futures: Changing Patterns of Drug Use Among English Youth*. London: ISDD.

Parsons, C. (1999) *Education, Exclusion and Citizenship*. London: Routledge.

Parsons, C. (undated) *Report on Follow-up Survey of Permanent Exclusions from Schools in England 1997/8*. Canterbury: Christ Church College.

Parsons, C. and Castle, F. (1999) 'The economics of exclusion', in C. Parsons (ed.) *Education, Exclusion and Citizenship*. London: Routledge.

Parsons, C. and Godfrey, R. (1999) 'The correlates of school exclusion', in C. Parsons (ed.) *Education, Exclusion and Citizenship*. London: Routledge.

Pawson R. and Tilley, N. (1997) *Realistic Evaluation*. London and Thousand Oaks, CA: Sage.

Payne, J. (1995) *Truancy and Youth Transitions*. London: Youth Cohort Study.

Pearce, N. and Hillman, J. (1998) *Wasted Youth: Raising Achievement and Tackling Social Exclusion*. London: Institute for Public Policy Research.

Pearson, G. (1983) *Hooligan: A History of Respectable Fears*. Basingstoke: Macmillan.

Philip, K. (1999) *Young People and Mentoring: A Literature Review for the Joseph Rowntree Foundation*. York: JRF.

Philip, K. (2000) (http://www.infed.org/learningmentors/mentoring.htm).

Pitts, J. (2001) 'Korrectional karaoke: New Labour and the zombification of youth justice', *Youth Justice*, 1 (2): 3–16.

Plant, M. and Plant, M. (1992) *Risk Takers: Alcohol, Drugs, Sex and Youth*. London: Routledge.

Power, S., Whitty, G. Edwards, T. and Wigfall, V. (1998) 'Schools, families and academically able students', *British Journal of Sociology of Education*, 19 (2): 157–76.

Powers, E. and Witmer, H. (1972) *An Experiment in the Prevention of Delinquency: The Cambridge–Somerville Youth Study*. Montclair, NJ: Patterson Smith (Original publication 1951).

Powis, B., Griffiths, P., Gossop, M., Lloyd, C. and Strang, J. (1998) 'Drug use and offending behaviour among young people excluded from school', *Drugs: Education, Prevention and Policy*, 5 (3): 245–56.

Prochaska, J.O. and DiClemente, C.C (1983) 'Transtheoretical therapy: toward a more integrative model of change', *Psychotherapy: Theory, Research and Practice*, 20: 161–73.

Prochaska, J.O. and DiClemente, C.C. (1992) 'The transtheoretical approach', in J.C. Norcross and M.R. Goldfried (eds) *Handbook of Psychotherapy Integration*. New York, NY: Basic Books.

Prochaska, J.O., Di Clemente, C.C. and Norcross, J. (1992) 'In search of how people change: applications to addictive behaviours', *American Psychologist*, 47(9): 1102–14.

Prochaska, J.O, Velicer, W.F., Rossi, J.S., Goldstein, M.G., Marcus, B.H., Rakowski, W., Fiore, C., Harlow, L.L., Redding, C.A., Rosenbloom, D. and Rossi, S.R. (1994) 'Stages of change and decisional balance for 12 problem behaviors', *Health Psychology*, 13 (1): 39–46.

Ramsay, M. and Percy, A. (1996) *Drug Misuse Declared: Results of the 1994 British Crime Survey*. London: Home Office.

Reid, K. (1986) *Disaffection from School*. London: Metheun.

Rhodes, J. (1994) 'Older and wiser – mentoring relationships in childhood and Adolescence', *Journal of Primary Prevention*, 14 (3): 187–96.

Riemsma, R.S., Pattenden, J., Bridle, C., Sowden, A.J., Mather, L., Watt, I.S. and Walker, M. (2003) 'Systematic review of the effectiveness of stage based interventions to promote smoking cessation', *British Medical Journal*, 326: 1175–7.

Roaf, P.A., Tierney, J.P. and Hunte, D.E.I. (1994) *Big Brothers/Big Sisters of America: A Study of Volunteer Recruitment and Training*. Philadelphia, PA: Public/Private Ventures.

Roberts, K. (1995) *Youth and Employment in Modern Britain*. Oxford: Oxford University Press.

Robinson, J.P., Shaver, P.R. and Wrightman, L.S. (1991) *Measures of Personality and Social Psychological Attitudes*. San Diego, CA: Academic Press.

Rollnick, S., Heather, N., Gold, R. *et al.* (1992) 'The development of a short "Readiness to change" questionnaire for use in brief opportunistic interviews among excessive drinkers', *British Journal of Addiction*, 87: 743–54.

Rosenberg, M. (1965). *Society and the Adolescent Self-image*. Princeton, NJ: Princeton University Press.

Rutter, M., Giller, H. and Hagell, A. (1998) *Antisocial Behaviour by Young People*, Cambridge: Cambridge University Press.

Rutter, M., Maughan, B., Mortimore, P., Ouston, J. and Smith, A. (1979) *Fifteen Thousand Hours: Secondary Schools and their Effects on Children*. London: Open Books.

St. James-Roberts, I. and Sambal Singh, C. (2001) *Can Mentors Help Primary School Children with Behaviour Problems?*. London: Home Office.

Sanders, D. and Hendry, L.B. (1997) *New Perspectives on Disaffection*. London: Cassell.

Sangster, D., Shiner, M., Patel, K. and Sheikh, N. (2002) *Delivery of Drug Services to Black and Minority Ethnic Communities*. London: Home Office.

Shaw, C. (1998) *Remember My Messages: The Experiences and Views of 2000 Children in Public Care in the UK*. London: The Who Cares? Trust.

Sherman, L., Gottfredson, D., MacKenzie, J.E., Reuter, P. and Bushway, S. (1999) *Preventing Crime: What Works, What Doesn't, What's Promising – A Report to the United States Congress*. National Institute of Justice, Department of Criminology and Criminal Justice, University of Maryland.

Sheroff, M.R. (1983) 'Fifty volunteers', in S. Hatch (ed.) *Volunteers: Patterns, Meanings and Motives*. Berkhamsted: The Volunteer Centre.

Sinclair, I. and Gibbs, I. (1998) *Children's Homes: A Study in Diversity*. Chichester: Wiley.

Skinner, J. and Flemming, A. (1999) *Mentoring Socially Excluded Young People: Lessons in Practice*. Leicester: Centre for Social Action.

Smith, D. and McVie, S. (2003) 'Theory and method in the Edinburgh study of youth transitions and crime', *British Journal of Criminology*, 43: 169–95.

Smith, J., Gilford, S. and O'Sullivan, A. (1998) *The Family Background of Homeless Young People*. London: Family Policy Studies Centre.

Social Exclusion Unit (1998a) *Rough Sleeping*. London: Social Exclusion Unit.

Social Exclusion Unit (1998b) *Truancy and School Exclusion*. London: Social Exclusion Unit.

Social Exclusion Unit (2000) *A Report of Policy Action Team 12: Young People*. London: Social Exclusion Unit.

Social Exclusion Unit (2001) *A New Commitment to Neighbourhood Renewal*. London: Social Exclusion Unit.

Social Exclusion Unit (2002) *Reducing Re-offending by Ex-prisoners*. London: Social Exclusion Unit.

Social Services Inspectorate (1991) *Corporate Parents*. London: HMSO.

Sparkes, J. and Glennerster, H. (2002) 'Preventing social education: education's contribution', in J. Hills *et al.* (eds) *Understanding Social Exclusion*. Oxford: Oxford University Press.

Spencer, L., Pagell, F., Hallien, M.E. and Adams, T.B. (2002) 'Applying the transtheoretical model to tobacco cessation and prevention: A review of the literature', *American Journal of Health Promotion*, 17: 7–71.

Stein, M. (1986) *Living Out of Care*. Ilford: Barnardos.

Stein, M. (1994) 'Leaving care, education and career trajectories', *Oxford Review of Education*, 20 (3): 349–60.

Stein, M. and Carey, K. (1983) *Leaving Care*. Oxford: Blackwell.

Stone, M. (1989) *Young People Leaving Care*. London: Royal Philanthropic Society.

Stratford, N. and Roth, W. (1999) *The 1998 Youth Lifestyles Survey Technical Report*. London: National Centre for Social Research.

Sutton, S. (2001) 'Back to the drawing board? A review of applications of the transtheoretical model to substance use', *Addiction*, 96 (1): 175–86.

Swadi, H. (1989) 'Adolescent substance use and truancy: exploring the link', *European Journal of Psychiatry*, 3 (2): 108–15.

Tarling, R., Burrows, J. and Clarke, A. (2001) *Dalston Youth Project Part II (11–14): An Evaluation*. London: Home Office.

Tierney, J.P., Baldwin Grossman, J. and Resch, N.L. (1995) *Making a Difference: An Impact Study of Big Brothers/Big Sisters*. Philadelphia, PA: Public/Private Ventures.

Tierney, J.P. and Branch, A.Y. (1992) *College Students as Mentors for At-risk Youth: A Study of Six Campus Partners in Learning Programs*. Philadelphia, PA: Public/ Private Ventures.

Townsend, P. (1979) *Poverty in the United Kingdom*. London: Penguin.

Utting, D. (1996) *Reducing Criminality among Young People: A Sample of Relevant Programmes in the United Kingdom*. London: Home Office.

Utting, Sir W. (1997) *People Like Us*. London: HMSO).

Walker, R. (1997) 'Poverty and social exclusion in Europe', in A. Walker and C. Walker (eds) *Britain Divided*. London: Child Poverty Action Group.

West, A. and Pennell, H. (2003) *Underachievement in Schools*. London: Routledge.

West, D. and Farrington, D.P. (1973) *Who Becomes Delinquent*. London: Heinemann.

West, D. and Farrington, D.P. (1977) *The Delinquent Way of Life*. London: Heinemann.

Wilkinson, C. (1995) *The Drop Out Society: Young People on the Margin*. Leicester: Youth Work Press.

Williamson, H. (1997) 'Status Zero youth and the "underclass": some considerations', in R. McDonald (ed.) *Youth, the 'Underclass' and Social Exclusion*. London: Routledge.

Williamson, H. and Middlemiss, R. (1999) 'The emperor has no clothes: cycles of delusion in community initiatives with "disaffected" young men', *Youth and Policy*, Spring: 13–25.

Wright, L. (1999) *Young People and Alcohol: What 11 to 24 Year Olds Know, Think and Do*. London: Health Education Authority.

Young, J. (2002) 'Crime and social exclusion', in M. Maguire *et al.* (eds) *The Oxford Handbook of Criminology* (3rd edn). Oxford: Clarendon Press, 457–90.

Index